Care

D0533492

Care in Chaos

Frustration and Challenge in Community Care

Roger Hadley and Roger Clough
With a foreword by Helena Kennedy QC

CASSELL

Cassell
Wellington House   PO Box 605
125 Strand   Herndon
London WC2R 0BB   VA 20172

Reprinted 1997

British Library Cataloguing-in-Publication Data
A catalogue record for this book is available from the British Library.

ISBN 0–304–33524-X (hb)
      0–304–33525–8 (pb)

Typeset by Action Typesetting Limited, 104 Northgate Street, Gloucester
Printed and bound in Great Britain by Redwood Books, Trowbridge, Wiltshire

Contents

Foreword   ix
Acknowledgements   xi
Abbreviations   xiii
Introduction   1

Part 1   Context   5

**1   Community care: the evolution of policy
    and practice**   7

Part 2   Views from the field: the case studies   21

2   Managers and generalists   23

Case study 1:   Damage limitation: managing the community
                care changes in a metropolitan authority.   24
                An assistant director

Case study 2:   'We had done some excellent things': the
                undermining of specialist services in a
                social services department.   34
                A senior manager

Case study 3:   From moving spirit to managerial ethos:
                change in an independent child care charity.   42
                A middle manager

Case study 4:   Order from chaos? Change in an inner city
                general practice.   52
                A general practitioner

3   **Working with older people**   61

Case study 5:   The politics of disintegration: the demise
                of a department of geriatric medicine.   62
                A geriatrician

Case study 6:   Quicker and sicker: the impact of change
                on community nursing.   73
                A community nurse

Case study 7:   'Where else can I go?' The effects of
                the Community Care changes on the regime
                of a nursing home.   82
                A qualified carer

Case study 8:   The price of caring: from trust employee
                to private sector employer.   90
                A community psychiatric nurse

4   **Working with people with learning disabilities**   100

Case study 9:   Resettlement in the community: fighting
                for principle-driven change in hospital
                and social services.   102
                A nurse manager

Case study 10: Learning disabilities: a service in
                jeopardy.   111
                A learning disabilities team leader

Case study 11: 'We're being pushed into competing against
                each other': change in a voluntary organization
                for adults with learning disabilities.   122
                The director of a voluntary organization

Case study 12: 'A merciful release': the life and death of a gentle man. 132
                A guardian and a care assistant

5   **Working with people with mental illness**   140

Case study 13: Change without leadership: a mental health team
                in a failing organization.   141
                A senior social worker

Case study 14: The death of excellence: the demise of a
                multi-disciplinary mental health team.   151
                An occupational therapist

Part 3   Analysis and discussion   161

6 **The worlds they have lost: providing community care before
   the changes**   163

7 **Brave new world? Providing community care after the changes**   173

8 **Emergent issues**   184

9 **An extravagant experiment? Change strategies in theory
   and practice**   198

10 **Alternative futures**   206

References   212

Appendix 1   The questionnaire   216

Appendix 2   The background to community care: legislation and guidance 219

Index   223

Foreword

The importance of providing good community care services is widely endorsed in this country. The idea that people rendered dependent through frailty or disability should be able to live their lives as normally as possible in their own homes is a humane and moral aspiration for any civilized society.

For this reason many of us welcomed the aims behind the major reforms contained in the 1990 NHS and Community Health Act to improve the organization of these services. However, in the last few years it has become increasingly apparent that the implementation of the Act is not going smoothly and there are signs that the rationale on which the reforms are based may be deeply flawed. It would, of course, be naïve to expect the implementation of social welfare reforms, which deal with issues as complex and difficult as those of community care, to be without problems. But if there are problems to be confronted and surmounted, they must be fully understood by all those involved. As citizens we urgently need to know what is going wrong and to have the opportunity to enter into informed debate on what can be done to put it right.

Yet it is extremely difficult to penetrate beyond the defensive rhetoric of government and management to establish exactly what is happening. The practitioners who are responsible for implementing the changes are best placed to tell us about their progress and difficulties. However, in the new culture of managerialism, which places loyalty to the organization above responsibility to the user, practitioners are effectively prevented from speaking out publicly about their experiences. This 'gag' ethos has penetrated whole areas of our public life.

The evidence in this book helps us to understand what happens in health and social services when a culture of secrecy and conformity prevents open debate and when staff who are strongly committed to their work and to developing better services are forbidden to speak out and powerless to act. Those who are most frustrated and angry are reflecting not so much the difficulties of increasing caseloads or deteriorating conditions, as the consequences of no longer being able to work in ways which can be true to the interests of those for whom they care. They feel they are unable to keep faith with the wider public or, indeed, themselves.

In recent times we have seen a denigration of public service, an aspect of British life of which we rightly felt proud. Those who choose to work in the fields of education, health care, social work and probation are given little recognition in a climate which only seems to idealize the entrepreneur. Undervaluing of those crucial functions – the care of the sick and needy, the teaching of our young, the maintenance of our social fabric – engenders low morale, with the inevitable consequence that those activities become less effective.

This book is an important reminder to us all that the issue of civil liberties stretches well beyond the confines of the law and embraces the work process itself. The right of employees to speak out freely and without fear about their work when it affects the public interest is an essential ingredient in a free society, and, as this study shows, it is crucial in the development of effective and responsive social services. The testimony in this book confirms my belief in the need for a public right to know.

HELENA KENNEDY QC

Acknowledgements

This book owes its genesis to many people, principal amongst them our social work students at Lancaster University and colleagues in the health and social services across the country. Over the last two years they have told us with growing concern of their experiences of the effects of the implementation of the community care reforms enacted in 1990 and of the forces which prevent free discussion of what is happening. As we encouraged them to analyse their experiences we realised increasingly the difficulties of getting objective information about the changes. We are grateful to them for stirring us into action and hope this book will play a part in opening up the debate which they and we feel is essential.

A number of people have contributed to the practical task of preparing the book. In particular, we would like to thank Sandra Irving for her meticulous transcription of the interview tapes and Heather Wilkinson for her thorough literature search and her detailed comments on drafts of the manuscript. We are also grateful to Mary Toder for administrative and secretarial support throughout the project.

We are fortunate to work in a department in which colleagues take a lively interest in each others' work. We would like to thank in particular Dr Richard Hugman, Dr Sue Penna and Suzanne Thorpe for their ideas and encouragement.

We owe a special debt to Professor Clare Wenger of the University of Wales who shares our view of the urgent need for a more rigorous and independent evaluation of the implementation of the community care reforms. She has been unstinting with her advice and support from the initial planning of the work, and has read and commented on the draft manuscript.

Our final and greatest debt is to the fifteen people who contributed the case studies that constitute the heart of this book. They have been generous in their openness and their trust and we only hope that they will feel we have done justice to the experiences they have shared with us and the problems they feel so strongly should be subjected to public debate.

Finally, it is appropriate to explain our respective roles both in this research and as joint authors of the book. In September 1994 Roger Clough convened a small group of academics at Lancaster University to discuss their common concerns about the growing crisis in our welfare services. Roger Hadley's proposal for a study based on the views of staff working in community care was supported by the group, and Roger Hadley and Roger Clough agreed to collaborate on the project. Roger Hadley has played the larger role in both the research and writing. He undertook most of the interviews and the analyses, and drafted most of the chapters. Nevertheless, the work has been driven by a joint concern about its subject, has been a collaborative undertaking at every stage, and has benefited greatly we believe from our different academic and professional backgrounds and perspectives.

Roger Hadley
Roger Clough

Abbreviations

AD	Assistant Director
ARM	Assistant Regional Manager
ASW	Approved Social Worker
CIPFA	Chartered Institute of Public Finance and Accountancy
CN	Community Nurse
CSPRD	Centre for Social Policy Research and Development
DGH	District General Hospital
DHA	District Health Authority
DHSS	Department of Health and Social Security
EEC	European Economic Community
EMI	Elderly Mentally Infirm
FHSA	Family Health Service Authority
FPC	Family Practitioner Committee
GP	General Practitioner
HAS	Health Advisory Service
ILF	Independent Living Fund
IP	Individual Planning
LD	Learning Disability
MDT	Multi-disciplinary Team
MDMHT	Multi-disciplinary Mental Health Team
NHS	National Health Service
NHSCA	National Health Service Consultants Association
NHSCC Act	National Health Service and Community Care Act (1990)
NVQ	National Vocational Qualification
PSS	Personal Social Services
PSSRU	Personal Social Services Research Unit
RGN	Registered General Nurse
RHA	Regional Health Authority
RMN	Registered Mental Nurse
SEN	State Enrolled Nurse
SSD	Social Services Department
SSW	Senior Social Worker
STG	Special Transitional Grant
TL	Team Leader

Give me the liberty to know, to utter, and to argue
freely according to conscience, above all liberties.

John Milton *Areopagitica*

Introduction

We live at a time when the base for welfare has been undermined. There is no longer common ground on the reasons why welfare is needed, the tasks it should be undertaking, or the mechanisms by which it should be produced. In this climate the contribution to the debate of practitioners who provide the services has been stifled. As we will show, criticism of policy and practice, whether at national or local government level, in public, voluntary or private sectors, has been repressed. This book is written for all those with an interest in the welfare services who are concerned about this situation and who want to know the views of such practitioners (written with the freedom of anonymity) on the impact of the recent community care reforms.

The community care reforms,[1] taken with the related health service changes, were intended to revolutionize the way in which services were organized and managed. The widely endorsed aim was to make them respond more effectively to the needs of their users.[2] The controversial method designed to achieve this was to replace traditional systems run by planners, administrators and professionals with systems which combined managerialism with market forces. The changes, although wide-ranging and radical in scope, were introduced rapidly with little more than cursory consultation. Now, in the wake of their implementation, there is widespread confusion and concern about the state of community care in Britain today.

Official and unofficial truths

The official view of the community care changes, as of the reforms to the NHS which interlock with them, is that they are on course. The reports of the Audit Commission admit that progress is faster in some areas than others but claim that overall there is steady progress in getting the system in place (Audit Commission 1992, 1994). The message is that the completion of the process will be a long haul but we will get there in the end.

---

[1] *reforms*: we use this word throughout the book in the neutral sense of 'reshaping' or effecting change, and not in the sense of implying that the change is necessarily an improvement.
[2] *user*: we use this term in preference to 'client' with its connotations of dependence and to 'consumer' with its emphasis on narrow market relationships.

Views from front-line social and health services practitioners, which we hear almost every day in our work, are much less uniformly optimistic. Some describe examples of improved practice such as an imaginative package of care which is enabling a frail old person to go on living in her own home, or the improved speed of initial assessments of need which have been achieved in many local authorities. More often, however, we hear accounts of confusion and chaos as organizations try to cope with the avalanche of changes descending on them from Westminster and Whitehall: of good services lost; specialisms disbanded; managers who feel forced to lie to staff and staff who find themselves required to lie to users. We are told of low morale, increasing sickness and absenteeism, of once enthusiastic managers and professionals now counting the days until they can apply for early retirement. And underlying many of these views, the belief that the reforms themselves contain fatal defects.

The government and other supporters of the new legislation are likely to dismiss such views as the whingeing of previously privileged professionals who have necessarily lost influence and status through the reforms. Radical change involves major upheavals in organizations and some people are bound to get hurt in the process. That is part of the price of progress. When the changes are bedded down even today's critics will come to see that they were right.

So who do those of us outside the organizations and away from the battlefield believe? The confusion is compounded by the prevailing lack of trust in government pronouncements and the scarcity of independently funded research. It is made worse by the climate of fear which strongly discourages open debate and criticism within the public services and accounts for the reluctance of practitioners to speak out.

What would practitioners say if they could speak freely and fully? And what would be the significance of their views? These are the questions this book sets out to explore.

Views from the front line

To this end we selected a sample of practitioners who, given the protection of anonymity, welcomed the opportunity to talk openly about their experiences of the reforms. We made no attempt to select our sample on a random basis but used our personal contacts to identify possible participants, aiming to include people from a wide range of organizations concerned with community care, working at different levels and in different roles.

What weight can be given to the views of a small purposive sample of this kind? Obviously it cannot be said to be representative, in any statistical sense, of practitioners as a whole. Indeed, by focusing on those who in most cases feel they can only speak out fully under the cloak of anonymity, we are consciously constructing a sample that is weighted towards critical views. It is, as we have said, the very purpose of this book to give such people their say and in so doing to make a contribution to redressing the balance in assessments of the reforms. But what the sample does provide is a cross-section of intelligent, informed and committed people working in a range of organizations, whose views are worth considering seriously both as individual statements and for their likely wider applicability.

The particular importance of such evidence, it seems to us, relates to a combination of factors:

- *Anonymity*. The anonymity of the interviews means that the interviewees can give their accounts of the changes, without fear of repercussions.
- *The case study approach*. Interviewees' comments on specific issues can be set in the context of their broader attitudes, experiences and attachments to their work.
- *First hand experience*. Unlike commentators and analysts in government ministries and academic ivory towers, these people have direct experience of the changes and their impact.
- *Perspectives from both health and social services*. Most studies of community care focus on health *or* social services. This study highlights issues and experience common to *both*.
- *Commitment*. Our interviewees are people who have been drawn into work in health and social services by moral rather than instrumental motives. Whatever is said about professional self-interest, it was evident to us that with our interviewees, at least, the needs of users come first as the nature of their evaluations of services both before and after the reforms demonstrates.
- *Generalizability*. Given the vantage points from which interviewees observed the changes, the nature of their accounts and the extent of common patterns in them, as well as evidence from other studies, it seems likely that their experiences and views are shared by many others who work in the health and social services.

So at the *minimum* the sample stands as the witness of fifteen people, given through fourteen case studies which provide slices of experience across a wide range of jobs contributing to community care. The interviewees raise questions that would need answering even if their applicability was no wider than their own organizations.

However, as we have suggested, there are grounds for regarding the sample as having a much wider significance. For these reasons, after the section containing the case studies, we have added further chapters in which we explore common themes in their experiences, and examine the general nature of their criticisms of the changes and the challenges they imply for the whole project of reform.

The structure of the study

To set the case studies in context, our first chapter outlines the development of community care policies and practice over the last three decades up to and including the recent radical changes introduced by the 1990 NHSCC Act.

The case studies are presented in Chapters 2 to 5 (Part 2 of the book) covering in turn experience of general management, and managers and staff working with older people, people with learning disabilities, and mentally ill people. Each chapter has a brief introduction to set the case studies in the broader context of the field concerned.

Part 3 presents our analysis and interpretation of the case studies, and discusses their wider relevance. Chapter 6 examines interviewees' accounts of the world of community care before the implementation of the 1990 Act. Chapter 7 reviews the impact of the changes on that world. Chapter 8 identifies common problems in the new order emerging from the analysis and considers other recent studies and the evidence in them that suggests that at least some of these problems are experienced widely in the health and social services. Taken together this work implies that, in spite of some positive features, the reforms contain fundamental contradictions and are deeply flawed. In an attempt to throw more light on the processes that have created this situation and the legacy inherited by those who would reform the reforms, Chapter 9 considers the change strategy used by the government to introduce the 'community revolution'. Chapter 10 concludes the book by briefly outlining and exploring feasible alternatives to the present policy.

Social science and political debate

In the field of applied social science, where the academic is deliberately aiming to inform the policy process, there is typically a tension between publishing research quickly and giving the analysis of the data all the time ideally needed before writing one's report. This study is no exception. We believe that the evidence of our sample is highly relevant to the current debate on community care and for that reason have produced it as rapidly as we could. The interviews were recorded between December 1994 and April 1995 and the manuscript completed by the end of August 1995. With more time we would have discussed our analytical chapters and our conclusions more fully with a larger number of academic and practitioner colleagues. That we have not been able to do so is the price of relative immediacy.

This study is as much a product of our times as its subject and it is sad that only when they are heavily disguised can people with critical views working in public and independent sector services feel safe to speak their minds. We hope, however, that the accounts of our contributors will serve to underline the crucial importance of establishing and defending free criticism within these services and the value of listening to what people have to say, whether we like their messages or not. It is hard to see how public services in a free society can be built on anything less.

Part 1

Context

1

Community care: the evolution of policy and practice

This chapter establishes the context in which the community care reforms were planned and implemented. It is divided into three main sections. The first outlines the development of community care against the background of the wider development of welfare policies in the three decades following the Second World War. The second concentrates on the growing criticisms of the welfare state in the 1970s and on the specific criticisms levelled at the provision of community care. The final section describes the shaping of the Conservative government's alternative agenda for community care during the 1980s and the first stages in the implementation of the resulting legislation, the 1990 National Health Service and Community Care Act (NHSCC Act).

'Community care' covers diverse objectives and diverse systems. It is often used imprecisely and this accounts in part for the confusion about both what is happening in community care and its effectiveness. The term initially seems to have come into general use with the introduction of policies at the end of the 1950s and in the early 1960s to begin to move patients from long-stay hospitals. Community care has acquired renewed significance as it has been increasingly used to describe alternatives to the *admission* of very dependent people, especially frail old people, to residential care. This theme was central to the inquiries leading up to the 1990 Act.

The White Paper which preceded the 1990 Act, *Caring for People* (Secretaries of State, 1989b, p.9) offered its own definition.

> Community care means providing the right level of intervention and support to enable people to achieve maximum independence and control over their own lives. For this aim to become a reality, the development of a wide range of services provided in a variety of settings is essential. These services form part of a spectrum of care, ranging from domiciliary support provided to people in their own homes, strengthened by the availability of respite care and day care for those with more intensive care needs, through sheltered housing, group homes and hostels where increasing levels of care are available, to residential care and nursing homes and long-stay hospital care for those for whom other forms of care are no longer enough.

Conspicuous by its absence in this key definition is any reference to the informal care, chiefly from family members, mainly women, which provides by far the largest element of support for most dependent people living in their own homes.

It is also somewhat bizarre to use the term 'community care' to include both arrangements for domiciliary care and for permanent living in residential and nursing homes.

However, since our study focuses on *formal* services involved in community care and specifically on the impact of the 1990 Act, we generally follow the definition used in the White Paper to describe the range of services concerned and the underlying rationale which justifies their work. We should emphasise that while social services departments have become the lead authority responsible for the implementation of the 1990 Act, primary and secondary health services are also key parts of community care and are therefore included in our study.

Community care is not a single entity, nor is there a linear progression to today's policy: there are several strands in its provision, resourced in different ways, managed with different organizational systems and having different objectives. There are two aspects that are essential to an understanding of today's community care and the accounts of our interviewees. The first is the history of its development, which we summarize briefly below, aware as we are of the dangers of simplification in such accounts. The second is the current context in which local authorities and health authorities provide services. In these the parameters within which people work are set in part by what may be termed community care legislation and in part by other government initiatives, for example in putting out specific services to compulsory, competitive tendering or in a drive for what is perceived as 'efficiency, economy and effectiveness'.

Social welfare and Community Care

The post-war settlement

The initial development of community care policies can only be understood in the broader context of the post-war settlement in the period 1945–50 which established the welfare state and subsequent developments in welfare policy. The origins of the British welfare state can be traced both to the slow evolution of policies in the first four decades of the century and to the more dramatic impact of the Second World War. The former had produced by 1939 a somewhat ramshackle system of provision but one in which there was, at least, a commitment to 'the maintenance of all its citizens according to need as a matter of right' (Gilbert, 1970, p.308). But the war greatly accelerated the pace of change, involving the government far more closely with the well-being of the population and in planning social as well as economic reconstruction after the return of peace (Titmuss, 1950). In its programme of welfare legislation the Labour government elected in 1945 was in many senses consolidating and completing work already begun.

While the Conservative opposition was formally opposed to much of this programme, it came to accept the main elements of the post-war settlement of which it was a part and subsequent Conservative administrations in the 1950s and 1960s did more to develop than dismantle public services.

The emergence of broadly similar trends in the social policies of other Western democracies in the quarter century following the end of the Second World War have suggested that the growing role of the state in welfare could be related to international economic and political developments of what some analysts have come to call 'Fordism'. According to this view, this period was one of

> unprecedented economic growth, based upon the dominance of mass production and mass consumption (especially of consumer goods) and massified, semi-skilled labour. It saw an enhanced status for the collective bargaining of wages and conditions ... and a correspondingly increased role for both large-scale capital and organised labour. (Pierson, 1995, p.97)

The welfare state had a central role in this world: it helped deal with dysfunctions in the market economy and also sustained consumption.

In Britain, although all legislative and tax-raising power ultimately lay with Parliament, local authorities were given full responsibility for implementing many of the policies decided centrally. It was rare for central government to dictate how services should be organized and managed.

The organizations providing welfare services during this period, apart from the new social security and national assistance agencies, were for the most part the direct successors of the pre-war system. Services covered in the spectrum of community care defined above, as far as they existed, were highly fragmented being spread between a wide range of organizations. For example, home helps, district nurses, health visitors, and later psychiatric social workers, were deployed by the local authority health department. Children were the responsibility of newly created children's departments. Most of the other categories of user who would formerly have been covered by the Poor Law became the responsibility of another new local authority department, the welfare department. The health services consisted of three separate parts – the local authority services, the hospitals and the general practitioner services. The availability of services to support users living in their own homes would normally be tied to the specialist departments concerned and no general provisions existed to coordinate their work.

In the following twenty-five years, as the economy grew and the system of social services established after the war was strengthened and developed, a number of key factors contributed to the growth of interest in community care and to changing conceptions of its role. The context in which it was delivered was also affected by major reforms in the organization of the NHS, social services and local government.

Factors affecting the development of Community Care

Five general themes are particularly worth consideration in tracing the growing pressures for the development of community care and in understanding the professional context in which the services were provided: the growing resource base of public services, rising demands, professionalization, changing patterns of treatment, and, as the most significant example of the last theme, deinstitutionalization.

Growing resources

In common with other western countries, Britain devoted an increasing proportion of its public spending to social purposes. Between 1960 and 1981 social expenditure expanded from 13.9 per cent to 23.7 per cent, involving a real annual growth rate between 1960 and 1975 of 26.6 per cent (Pollitt, 1993, p.29). A climate was created in which there were general expectations of continuing growth and optimism that new problems could be tackled with the help of additional resources.

Rising demand

Both demographic trends and increasing expectations fuelled growing demands on health and social services in general and community care in particular. The most immediately significant of the demographic changes was the increase in the number of people over the age of 75. The proportion of people over 75 in Britain grew from 4.2 per cent in 1961 to 5.9 per cent in 1981 (Pollitt, 1993, p.33). Other changes began to affect the taken-for-granted support of informal carers, which formal social services relied on to provide the bulk of care in the community. These included the growing number of single parents, greater geographical mobility, the increasing participation of women in the labour market and changing attitudes amongst them to their stereotyped role as carers, and the beginnings of proactive user movements campaigning for better services.

The strengthening of professionalism

The growth of the public services was accompanied by a substantial increase in the numbers of professional workers employed in them and also in their influence in how the services were provided. Doctors, in particular, came to play a central role in shaping the health service and social workers were increasingly influential in the development of the personal social services (Perkin, 1989, pp.343–8).

Changing concepts of treatment and good practice

Developments in professional knowledge and ideology combined with political and economic influences to determine changes in predominant patterns of treatment for different groups of users. Five themes were particularly important.

1. *Advances in drug therapies.* During the 1950s these made it possible to treat many people with mental illness in the community.
2. *Normalization or social role valorization.* At the heart of the approach is a belief that access to services should be equal.
3. *Integration.* In this the dominant concern is that, whether or not people are designated as being faced with particular problems, they should be able to live their lives as far as possible in mainstream society.
4. *Choice.* There should be the maximum possible amount of choice for all service users and professionals should have less influence in determining what service is to be selected.
5. *Living in one's own home whenever possible and in homelike situations where it is not.* This affected not only older people but also children, people with disabilities and mentally ill people. The change of policy as it affected these last two categories of user had major implications for community health and social services and was probably the main factor in the creation of the concept of community care.

De-institutionalization

The shift away from the incarceration of people in asylums resulted early in the 1960s in plans to reduce the numbers living permanently in long-stay hospitals with the aim, eventually, of closing many of them. This could only be achieved successfully in the general shift to home living through the parallel strengthening of health and social services in the community.

Organizational changes and community care

Organizational rationalization

The fragmentary nature of both health and personal social services became the subject of increasing criticism as the services grew and struggled to find more efficient and effective ways of working with each other. Eventually, with a substantial degree of consensus both within the services and politically, proposals for reorganization to create more integrated services were agreed in both fields. In 1970 in Scotland and in 1971 in England and Wales most of the previously separate personal social services were combined in integrated departments in their local authorities, as social work departments in Scotland and social services departments (SSDs) in England and Wales. Three years later the NHS was reorganized to bring its separate parts together at district level. At the same time local government was reorganized throughout the country to create larger authorities.

Organizational environments and organizational structures

The emerging environment of public service organizations in this period can be described as institutionally elaborate rather than technically complex (Meyer and Scott, 1992). The distinction is an important one in explaining differences in structure and management of public service and private enterprise at the time. The factory, exemplifying the latter, operates with complex technologies to produce highly specific products which it must sell in the market place to people who can compare them with competing products. This environment creates pressures for organizational structures which focus on the technical tasks of production.

In contrast, public services have usually been created in 'institutionally elaborated environments' where programmes are defined through a number of different institutions such as government, the professions, media, public opinion, local community understandings and so on. Public service organizations have to conform to institutional expectations and 'rules' including, for instance, the categories and qualifications of staff employed, the definition of clients or users and priorities between them, appropriate facilities and procedures. As a result they have adapted their structures to relate to these demands rather than to focus on the 'product' of the organization which is itself often highly complex and difficult to measure (e.g. the treatment of a patient; casework with users with multiple problems). The process of production itself has been buffered from close external evaluation, and is often effectively in the hands of professional workers and their immediate managers.

Community care

The reorganization of the health service and social services departments introduced some limited rationalization of community care services. For example, home helps were moved into the SSDs where their work could be more readily coordinated with that of social work teams. There were increasing attempts to achieve closer collaboration between health and social services through joint care planning teams and other initiatives. However, overall, responsibilities remained fragmented and progress in strengthening community care services was slow.

Emerging critiques of the welfare state

The official recognition of the major inadequacies of the system of community care and the remedies proposed need to be seen in the context of the larger debate on the welfare state that took place in the 1970s and early 1980s and the emergent strategy of the Conservative administration to introduce far-reaching reforms in social policy.

Growing criticism of the welfare state in the 1970s was not confined to parties of the right but included voices from across the political spectrum. On the left there was disappointment at the limited effect of social policy especially in reducing poverty and tackling inequality. Some on the left argued that a more radical redistribution of resources was required. The weakness of the economy only made the responsibility of the government to take appropriate action the stronger. Others suggested that at least a part of the problem was the way in which services were organized, that organizations dominated by bureaucrats and professionals encouraged dependence and denied citizens the opportunities to participate actively in the development of services they really wanted and needed (Hadley and Hatch, 1981).

The background to the debate was the world recession of the early 1970s and the subsequent economic problems that beset the country. Right wing analysis of the Welfare State was intimately related to analysis of the underlying nature of this economic malaise. The think tanks of the new right which had found an enthusiastic convert in the new leader of the Conservative Party, Margaret Thatcher, traced the roots of the problem to the excessive scale of the public sector and what they saw as the inevitable inefficiencies of public bureaucracies. In particular, they attacked what they claimed were the tendencies of such organizations to maximize their own budgets and status, the powerful professions for promoting their own interests, the threats posed to individual freedom, and the undermining of enterprise and creation of dependence (Pollitt, 1993, p.43).

The remedy was to drive back the frontiers of the state as far as possible, returning services to the invigorating world of market forces, and, where that was not possible, to make the remaining public agencies more efficient, economic and effective by replacing the influence of bureaucracy and professionalism with that of scientific managerialism. Such managerialism, often named neo-Taylorist after F.W.Taylor, the father of scientific mangagement (Taylor, 1911), is distinctive in terms of its emphasis on productivity defined in economic terms; its belief in technology as the key to such productivity; in the necessity of a disciplined labour force; in the unique place of managers in planning, implementing and measuring production; and in their unchallenged right to manage (Pollitt, 1993, pp.2–3). This managerialism was to be a key tool in the control of the local state and of public services, and in limiting the power of professionals, in particular lawyers, teachers, doctors and social workers. It can be contrasted with the emergent alternative approach to management, often referred to as the 'New Human Resources Management', which seeks to achieve control by winning the commitment of workers by encouraging their growth and involvement (Flynn, 1994, pp.212–8).

It is illuminating to consider these perspectives on economic and social policy in terms of the Fordist analysis introduced at the beginning of this chapter. On the premises of that analysis, the conditions for the postwar settlement – or the Fordist order – had begun to crumble and the economic crisis was the result. It is argued that the very processes that had initially ensured capital accumulation, became too rigid and began to hamper it. Big business, big labour and big government became too fixed in their ways, wages were too high, the Welfare State cushioned people from the pressures that should have made them change and consumed resources that should have been invested in the economy. Globalization of economies greatly reduced the power of national governments to control events (Pierson, 1995, pp. 97–9). Renewed capital accumulation would require the abandonment of the old cosy consensus and its system of controls, and the introduction of aggressive entrepreneurship, flexible labour, reduced state spending and social policies guided by the needs of the economy rather than ideals of social justice.

The Conservatives in power

The new right policies taking shape in the Conservative Party under Mrs Thatcher might have been designed with such an analysis in mind. Starting cautiously, but with growing confidence as the electorate returned the party to power in four successive elections (albeit it with never more than 43% of the vote), the government has sold off the main public utilities, dismantled many of the controls on industry and commerce, substantially reduced the powers of local authorities, and introduced major reforms in almost all the remaining public services. It has injected market forces where it could and sponsored the development of a managerialist culture everywhere.

Part of the continued political success of the government can be attributed to the failure of the main opposition parties to come up with clear and convincing alternative policies. The problem was compounded for those on the left in that the defence of welfare services too often failed to recognize or confront their problems, such as rigidity in the services offered or the intimidation of users attempting to negotiate with people in large bureaucracies to get services. It was not, however, that there was a lack of potentially viable alternative ideas. In particular, there were interesting and promising developments in organizing and delivering public services, based on approaches including decentralization, locally integrated services, stronger management, and user, staff and citizen participation. In the 1980s, a number of local authorities had considerable initial success (e.g. Audit Commission, 1986, pp.65–72; Hoggett and Hambleton, 1987; Bayley *et al.*, 1989; Hadley and Young, 1990). Further, the promotion of what became called the Public Service Orientation to local authority management also reflected a more flexible, community-oriented view of local government (Stewart and Clarke, 1987). However, these ideas failed to appeal to Labour, the main opposition party, with its strong centrist tradition.

The problem of Community Care: shaping an agenda for change

The first social services to be the target of the Tory reformers were housing and education. The health service, where the entrenched professional interests were the strongest and which was very popular with the public, was left alone for the first decade of the administration. Personal social services also escaped attention for several years, probably because in expenditure terms they seemed relatively unimportant. The problems of community care became the subject of political debate in the mid-1980s. A series of reports were produced: the House of Commons Social Services Select Committee (1985), the report of the Audit Commission *Making a Reality of Community Care* in 1986 (Audit Commission, 1986), the Firth Report in 1987 (Firth, 1987), followed by the Griffiths Report in 1988 (Griffiths, 1988). The details of these are set out in Appendix 2.

There were two distinct issues. The first was slow and uneven development with insufficient resources being transferred from hospitals and residential homes to services 'in the community'; indeed, social services departments were able to do little more than maintain existing services for the increasing numbers of very old people. This was linked to fragmented organizational responsibility for community care services and to inadequate staffing.

Secondly, there was mounting government concern about the funding of residential care through social security payments which, unlike the funding of social services, were not cash-limited. Supplementary benefit payments for residential care were escalating out of control; they increased rapidly from £10 million in 1979 (for 12,000 claimants) and were to reach £1,872 million in 1991 (for 231,000 claimants) (Wistow, *et al.*, 1994, p.6).

The government asked Sir Roy Griffiths to propose solutions. His report recommended that to reduce the fragmentation of responsibilities between agencies the local authority SSDs should be given the lead role in community care. They should receive cash-limited funds and assess people who wanted state support to move into residential care or a nursing home. There should be a separate assessment of carers' needs. Services should aim 'to enable people to live in their own homes whenever feasible and sensible', emphasizing practical support. They should be 'needs led': that is people should have 'packages of care' designed in line with individual needs and preferences, rather than being fitted into existing services. The two most controversial proposals in the Griffiths report were that social services should become 'enabling agencies', restricting their role as far as possible to procuring and overseeing care and not its provision, and that central government should be closely involved in determining the priorities of a costed programme each year of its funding.

Community Care reform: legislation and implementation

Legislation

The government's response to the Griffiths report was fifteen months in coming, apparently taking so long because of its own hostility to local authorities and reluctance to transfer powers *to* them when its general strategy had been to work to the opposite end. However, the proposal to reduce the role of social services as direct providers of care was entirely in line with its philosophy.

All the main Griffiths proposals were accepted, with the notable exception of his suggestions that would have linked central government closely into the ongoing funding and performance of community care. Also rejected was his suggestion that a minister of state for community care be appointed. The proposals were enshrined in the White Paper, *Caring for People*, which finally appeared in 1989, and were embodied in the National Health Service and Community Care Act in 1990. (This is generally referred to in this book as the 1990 Act.)

In addition to the main proposals of the Griffiths report described above, SSDs as lead agencies were given responsibility, in conjunction with others, to publish clear plans for the development of community care services; they also were required to establish inspection units at arm's length from their own management to inspect residential homes in their own organization and in the independent sector. Further, there was to be a special additional grant to promote the development of social care for seriously mentally ill people. (*ibid*, p.6)

Preliminary reactions

The goals of the proposed reforms, to enhance the independence of people needing care and to centre services on their needs, met with widespread support. As one director commented 'How could one disagree with the rhetoric of community care?' (Wistow, *et al.*, 1994, p.52). Focusing the main responsibility for assessment and arranging services in a single organization also made sense to many people. But the radical change in the *means* by which services were to be provided, involving the transmogrification of social services departments from providers into enablers and all that entailed, was another matter. Many of the departments were proud of their services and were concerned at the nature of the changes proposed (p.59). They could point out that the main burden of the criticism of the Audit Commission was concerned with *policy* failure, not organizational incompetence. Further, the changes implied major upheavals in organization, the loss of many roles, the need for training in new skills, and the replacement of a cooperative with a competitive culture. All of these changes would be immensely costly in human and financial terms and could hardly fail to have an adverse effect on services while they were being implemented. There was also a general concern that the government would not make resources available on the scale essential for their successful implementation (*ibid*, p.53)

Perhaps the most extraordinary feature of the proposals was that they were completely untried. The government-funded research on care management at the Personal Social Services Research Unit (PSSRU), University of Kent was apparently influential both in the writing of the Griffiths Report and the White Paper. But, as its directors have pointed out, the research had been primarily concerned with a specific category of client, those at high risk of admission to residential care, not the wider spectrum of service users needing less but still substantial support. Care management had not been proved as a cost effective method in the treatment of other categories (e.g. Challis, 1992). More importantly, there had been no piloting to explore the general impact of the changes on departmental organization and services. The proposals were in these ways revolutionary not evolutionary, and the belief that they would work would seem to have owed more to ideology than reason.

Implementation

The timetable for implementation was a tight one. The legislation was passed in 1990. The main parts of the new system were to be in place within three years: inspection units and complaints procedures were to be established by 1991, local authority and health plans were to be implemented by 1992, and social security funds for new cases would be transferred from 1993 when assessment and care management procedures were to be introduced. However, it was accepted later that getting the system fully up and running would take longer and should be managed incrementally to minimize the disruptive effects of the changes on services (Wistow *et al.*, 1994, p.12).

Guidance poured out from the Department of Health on the details of implementation. A programme of monitoring the progress of every local authority was established using the regional health authorities and officers of the Social Services Inspectorate. A special support force was set up to advise departments identified as having particular difficulties in implementation (*ibid.*, p.11).

One of the most significant and controversial features of the implementation process was the decision of the government to insist that (in England) 85% of the social security element of the special transitional grant (STG) established to enable local authorities to take over responsibility for funding care from the social security system, must be spent in the independent sector. Initially, given the weakness of independent sector provision in many areas, the main effect might be to cushion the independent residential homes from the immediate impact of the changes. In the longer run, however, it was clear that the effect of the 85% rule would mean that departments had no choice but to build up private and voluntary provision and run down their own services, regardless of whether this made good sense or not in terms of local conditions or of establishing the most flexible and effective mix of statutory and non-statutory inputs.

The NHS reforms

The NHS reforms legislated in the same Act as those for community care had an equally strong ideological core. They aimed to replace the centrally managed, integrated health services by a more decentralized system in which an internal market took over the role of stimulating efficient and effective services. Formerly district health authorities, which had included members drawn from elected representatives of local government and professional bodies, were responsible for planning and providing a comprehensive range of health services to their populations. They directly controlled hospitals and community nursing services. General practitioners held individual contracts with the local family practitioner committee.

The changes were constructed to achieve more business-like organizations and management. District health authorities were to be concerned mainly with planning and purchasing services. Hospitals and community services were encouraged to become self-governing trusts, governed by boards of directors mainly appointed by the government and providing services which could be purchased by any district health authority in the country. GPs in larger practices were invited to apply for fund-holding status which would give them control over their own budgets to enable them 'to obtain a defined range of services direct from hospitals' (Secretaries of State, 1989b, p.5). They would also be encouraged to compete for patients.

There was strong opposition to the proposals from many quarters including the medical profession. By many it was seen as a covert attack on the very principles on which the service had been founded. The NHS Consultants Association, for example, feared that the changes would lead to escalating costs, the loss of strategic planning, destructive competition, the institutionalization of two levels of service, pressures to reduce the range and quality of services, staff demoralization, the industrialization of care, and a democratic deficit (NHSCA, 1995). The Labour Party also opposed many of the changes but when the Conservatives were re-elected in 1992 for a fourth term it became apparent that they would continue to be implemented. By September 1994, for instance, there were already 419 NHS trusts in England (*ibid.*, p.8).

New environments and new structures

Taken together, the NHS and community care reforms involved enormous changes for the organizations involved and the implementation of ideas which had previously never been piloted on any scale in a British context. It seems highly unlikely that any commercial enterprise would have taken such risks and adopted untested reforms across the board in this way. However, it appears that, even for a government claiming to place a high value on the disciplines of business management, public services were considered to be different; they can be safely reformed on the basis of little more than paper plans.

The case studies which follow describe personal experiences of these changes in health and personal social services as they relate to aspects of community care. In seeking to understand common elements in these experiences it may be useful, finally, to return to our earlier discussion of the relationship between the environment of organizations and their structures. The overall implication of the reforms was to substantially alter and complicate the environments in which the public services concerned operated. The government's detailed emphasis on process and output in health and personal social services began to create pressures on organizations to adapt their structures to something much closer to that of the factory, with primacy given to the coordination of the technical task. But the change was not as simple as that, for the previously dominant institutional environment, although modified in some respects (such as the removal of local government representation in the health service), remained. The managers of the new order, therefore, somehow had to learn to deal with the formidable task of coping with the competing and often irreconcilable demands of both environments at one and the same time.

Part 2

Views from the field: the case studies

The fourteen case studies which are presented in Part 2 are grouped into four chapters on the basis of the main focus of the work which they describe. Chapter 2 contains studies with common themes in management or a generalist perspective or both. Chapters 3 to 5 describe work with three of the most important categories of users of community care services: older people, people with learning disabilities and mentally ill people.

The purposive character of our small sample of people working in the community care field has been discussed in the Introduction. However, to fill out the context of the case studies further, it may be helpful to provide more detail on the composition of the sample and how the case studies were constructed.

The fifteen people interviewed represent four main professional groups: doctors, nurses, occupational therapists and social workers. In addition they included an untrained care worker and a user's guardian (who was a volunteer). Several held managerial positions. The case studies describe a wide range of settings including six health organizations, six social services departments and five independent sector agencies. They are situated in several areas of England and Wales.

The case studies are based mainly on face-to-face interviews but some have been supplemented by documentary material given to us by interviewees. We used a semi-structured interview schedule to explore experiences of working in the field of community care before and after the implentation of the 1990 Act (See Appendix 2). Most interviews took between one and a half and two and a half hours; they were taped and transcribed.

Case studies were drafted by the authors and sent to interviewees for comment, changes and corrections. They had full control of whether material should be used or not and of provisions for ensuring their personal anonymity. To protect their identity fully both contextual and personal characteristics have been altered. It is a telling comment on the nature of the worlds in which they work that by far the largest number of changes requested by members of the sample were to strengthen the anonymity of their contributions.

2

Managers and generalists

This chapter presents case studies involving the work of three managers and a general practitioner. Two of the managers are responsible for several different client groups. The third is a middle manager in a child care organization who does not fit the generalist criterion but whose management experience is highly relevant to the managerial issues raised by the other two management case studies.

Managers have been given a leading role in the public service reforms of the government, as we have shown in Chapter 1. They have the chief responsibility for getting the changes in place and functioning, even though they often have to do so with a reluctant or even hostile workforce. We have distinguished between two different types of managerialism which have emerged in this new world, the neo-Taylorist version based primarily on technical and economic imperatives, and new wave managerialism that regards the human factor as central to a successful organization. The three managers contributing to this chapter would all probably advocate something like the second kind of managerialism but their accounts show evidence of the growing strength of the more macho managers. The different approaches of their organizations to change and their abilities to cope with its demands make them particularly interesting to compare.

The assistant director describes a social services department reluctantly accepting the government's new policies but working in a carefully planned manner to implement a strategy of damage limitation fully supported by local councillors. The senior manager, in contrast, gives an account of a social services department where change seems far less coherent and there is an air of mistrust between councillors and officers. The middle manager in the independent child care organization explores the example of an agency deliberately adopting a version of neo-Taylorist managerialism in an attempt to equip itself to cope with its changing environment.

The general practitioner's case study is valuable both in providing views of the community care reforms from someone responsible for patients in all the three categories covered in Chapters 3 to 5 and for its account of the complex interplay of issues seen from an inner city practice.

Case Study 1

Damage limitation: managing the community care changes in a metropolitan authority. An assistant director

Background

This case study illustrates what happens when there are fundamental differences, in ideology and conception of the role of public services, between central and local government. It describes resistance and then adaptation to centrally driven change. It shows how managing change can be experienced as intrinsically rewarding even when the manager has major reservations about the policies concerned. Finally, it identifies serious concerns for the quality of services resulting from the community care reforms and for the survival of local democratic involvement in service provision.

Local authorities varied widely in their response to the community care legislation, in terms both of attitudes towards the principles involved and the strategies adopted towards implementing the changes. (e.g. Wistow *et al.*, 1994). The political affiliation of the councillors was not the only factor, although Conservative authorities were more likely than their opponents to be positive about the core ideas embedded in the changes. Councils were also influenced by their expectations of the outcome of the election following the 1990 Act and by local agendas of varying kinds.

This case study describes the response of a large Labour-dominated metropolitan authority to the 1990 Act from the perspective of the senior manager who was given much of the responsibility for introducing the changes. The authority, with a proud tradition of public service and a strong commitment to socialist principles, was hostile to the new legislation and especially its emphasis on the development of the independent sector at the expense of the local state.

The study first describes the attempt of the authority to ignore the changes and the battle of its officers to get it to accept the necessity to respond to them. The focus then moves to the radical reforms which followed the re-election of the Conservatives in 1992 as the local authority attempted to defend the core services of the social services department. Finally, it discusses the concerns for losses in service quality and for the very future of local authority services following the implementation of the legislation.

The changes are described by an assistant director in the authority's social services department. Initially appointed in 1990 with a brief for planning and service development, her first responsibility was to implement the provisions of the Children Act of 1989. Subsequently, she was responsible for making the changes in complaints procedures and inspection required by the community care legislation which had to be implemented by 1991. Finally, after the election of the Conservatives for a fourth term and when the council reluctantly accepted the need to implement the community care legislation in its entirety, it was her job to plan and manage through the changes, and then to become the overall manager of the community care services.

The metropolitan authority before the changes

Over the years the City had built up a strong, well-resourced public sector. Spending on public services was substantially above the national average. There was a strong anti-poverty programme focused on the most disadvantaged sectors, making active use of voluntary sector initiatives. In the view of the assistant director (AD) groups such as older people, people with disabilities, and black and ethnic minorities, were empowered by these policies and there was a 'sensible preventative programme that was heavily invested.'

Conditions of service for staff in the AD's view were excellent. Historically, a post with the City council was 'clearly perceived as a job for life and lots of jobs for lots of people and well paid compared with surrounding and comparable jobs.'

The AD felt that the main influences in running the City's public services were the politicians and the trade unions. Describing her perception of the ethos of the organization she defined it as a 'closed system'.

> I was quite surprised that many of the management had been born and brought up in the City, been to university in the City, stayed on in the City. It was very inbred and political and members of staff would be involved with the district Labour Party. It was very incestuous in respect to playing politics and very old fashioned, old fashioned politics, old fashioned City Hall.

While politicians and trade unionists were the main influences in this system, social workers tended to be held in low esteem; they were seen as élitists and troublemakers. Within social services, the groups with standing in the eyes of the Council were the largest: manual workers and people working in domiciliary and residential care.

For the AD the system as she found it when she arrived in 1990 had real strengths in terms of the level of provision, the anti-poverty policies, the empowerment of minority groups and terms of service for staff. The downside was the 'sense of paternalism' that went with it, the feeling that everything was in the gift of City Hall, and that 'there was little sense of accountability'. In 1990 the social services department was organized in a traditional structure, with separate fieldwork, residential and day care, and hospital divisions. Fieldwork teams were organized on a generic basis and there were strong community work and welfare rights sections as well as a network of voluntary sector initiatives which were grant-aided.

Although the community care proposals in the 1988 Griffiths report and the specific legislative plans published in the government White Paper a year later, clearly pointed towards major changes in the role of local authority social services departments including the move towards purchasing rather than providing services, the City made no preparations to introduce the reforms. Instead, the council decided to push ahead with its own favoured re-organization of the social services department, and to implement a much-discussed plan for a more localized and integrated service. The City was subdivided into divisions and each division was in turn made up of a number of localities. Each locality was to include residential, day, field and domiciliary services under a single manager. It was, in the AD's view, 'a good 1970s model of a restructure' although even in those terms rather over-complex, with a system of matrix management and lack of clarity about decision-making hierarchies. More to the point, in her view, it was out-of-date and did not relate to the new legislation.

The role of the AD

This was the position in 1990 when the AD was appointed. While her colleagues on the senior management team were completely absorbed by the task of introducing the new organization, she was given the job of making sure the department conformed with the requirements of the 1989 Children Act and, subsequently, those parts of the 1990 community care legislation covering complaints procedures and inspection which had to be implemented by 1991, before the likely date of the next election which was expected to save the day.

She described the importance of learning how her new authority worked in getting acceptance for the changes for which she was responsible and for their implementation.

> I had to try and understand the City's total decision-making infrastructure and the blocks, checks and balances within that, which was quite different from my previous authority. Once you've got an understanding of that framework, then you have to work sufficiently far in advance in order of principle, detail and cost, to start moving through these milestones. This includes staff consultation, trade union consultation, political consultation, and seeking the finances before you go to Committee for approval. Then come the stages of implementation.

The AD had particular difficulties in getting funds for the changes concerned with the Children Act and the inspection and complaints elements of the community care legislation.

> They wouldn't put any money into it. I had to fight tooth and nail. There was no budget whatsoever so I had to create one. Something like that seemed very simple but was very difficult here. Everything had to be negotiated with the trade unions, line by line, including simple things like finding accommodation.

The AD was ultimately successful, however, in managing through these changes. Although the timescales were short, and she had to work frantically hard and find ways of 'managing my exhaustion', she drew a lot of satisfaction from having 'a very clear task to a timescale with freedom in terms of defining the kind of quality and task'.

However, proposals from the social services directorate to the Council that the department should prepare itself for more radical change in the face of the full implementation of the community care legislation in 1993 were not successful. Right up to the 1992 election, the Council resisted the more radical elements of the reforms.

Change: the implementation of Community Care

When the Conservatives won the 1992 general election, the politicians were at last ready to accept that they would have to implement all the main provisions of the 1990 Act. Over the next two years the new organizational structure of the social services department, so recently introduced, was abandoned and was replaced by a structure which reflected the purchaser/provider split implied by the legislation and by subsequent guidance from the Department of Health. Charging for previously free services was introduced, and the department was increasingly purchasing services from the independent sector, whose growth it was now positively encouraging.

To prevent the closure of the local authority's elderly people's homes it was proposed to hive them off into an independent sector trust. In spite of the election results, it was no simple matter getting these changes through the Council and the department.

> To have to go to the district Labour Party and sell that package in an authority like this, which had had totally free services, a long, proud tradition of public service, – it needed quite a bit of thought about how to market that and to get them to go along with it. It took a lot of homework. You had to know your social policy and you had to know the community care business very well and you had to know the risk and the gamble and the alternatives and, in effect, that the people in the City had no choice. The political strategy was, 'We don't like it but we need to protect what we've invested in in the past'.

Given the nature of the local authority, getting acceptance for change was not simply a matter of convincing the district Labour Party and the councillors. Consultation with staff and unions was also an essential part of the process.

> In this authority a consultation is like a detailed dialogue. It was very time consuming and a little bit nonsensical on some of these things because, frankly, the blue-print was provided by the central government. But we've got a very politicized workforce and they wanted to debate the rightness or wrongness of the social policy.

The AD also had to deal with the private sector nursing and care homes which, on their side, were unhappy about the new responsibility given to social services departments by the 1990 Act in controlling the community care budget.

A central part of the strategy adopted by the authority (to prevent the services simply being privatized and run for profit) was the decision to create an independent sector trust to which local authority services could be moved. 'We had a very painful time of closing elderly people's homes, but we had large numbers of them'. Some people were transferred into the new trust where 'there's a sense that it's the preferred provider because it's a not-for-profit organization. It's a preferred provider partnership'. Once the politicians 'had been sold the idea and the necessity for it, they would have liked everyone to go there, just to keep them safe'. Similarly, once staff realized the situation and that given the financial position of the City, the only way to get investment into the buildings was by putting them in the independent sector, they, too, accepted the strategy.

The AD's experience of managing the change

Although the AD had little enthusiasm for the main direction of the reforms she was overseeing, the experience of managing the changes was in itself 'enjoyable and creative' for she gets 'a buzz from creativity'.

> To actually get a huge culture and organization to realize they had to move into protective positions was quite exciting. And then to see it happen, to see we've got a complaints procedure, and to see we've got an inspection unit, and to see we've got an independent trust organization, and to see what we've done with the home care service. If you've got something for it, you can look back and think: we have achieved change!

The new structure of the department

The department now has three divisions, each headed by an assistant director: community care, children's services and support services. The community care division is split, below the level of assistant director, into purchasing and providing organizations. Purchasing is sub-divided into services for elderly people, for people with disabilities and for hospital social work. The provider side of the division includes sections for physical disabilities, learning disabilities, mental health, home care, and residential services for elderly people – although most of the residential homes are in the process of being transferred to the independent sector trust.

The role of the AD in the new structure

Now that the main changes required by the new legislation are all in place and the AD is managing the community care division as a whole, her work pattern has changed. From managing innovation she now has the job of monitoring the new organization she has played such a large part in creating, taking a strategic overview, relating to independent sector organizations, working on joint commissioning with health and housing, and controlling the budget.

The pace of her work has calmed down somewhat from the hectic pressures of the last few years. Her strategic position in the organization gives her a comprehensive view of the operation of the new system and the opportunity to assess the advantages and disadvantages which it has brought with it. While she detects some gains, her overall conclusion is weighted heavily towards what she sees as the negative consequences of the reforms for both users and providers, as well as for the wider democratic process itself.

Advantages

The AD felt that the main gain from the reorganization was much greater clarity in the management structure. In the previous organization, there had been extensive complaints from staff about the complexity of the matrix system and the uncertainty as to who was responsible for what. With this went a feeling of lack of accountability. The new organization went a considerable way to meeting both kinds of criticism. It's a clear management structure, a clear system of accountability and dedicated specialist energy in the business. The home care service is given as an example.

> [It] is all managed under one lead manager and the whole business is managed under them. Everyone knows that and it's very clear. And we're looking increasingly at devolving budgets and devolving power and responsibilities. So, in effect, the home care service now sees itself as an in-house business which is expected to meet the same service specifications and contracts that we expect from the independent sector. They know they've got competitors who they have to match themselves against.

A second distinct advantage which directly benefited users was the improved response to referrals.

> When they make a referral, they can get a quick and speedy response, they get an assessment. Partly because we knew we were dealing with an unqualified workforce we've got a bloody good form that covers special assessment for carers, all major health and social care areas are clearly and simply covered. So I think the users get a quick and speedy response, they get an outcome that they can discuss and agree, and they get some service promptly.

Major investments have been made in building partnerships with users and carers. There is a user strategy and investment in user development; a carer centre has been opened in the city. There is a new consultation framework and a new sense of public accountability alongside that. Public information receives high priority.

The introduction of a planning framework is also helpful and multiagency work has received high priority, especially with health and housing colleagues.

The development of joint commissioning with the health authority has been an important new dimension in the social services and this has had an impact on the role of the local authority.

Disadvantages

The AD's criticisms of the changes reflected not the particular way in which her authority had implemented them, but underlying features of the reforms and their impact. They covered: the ideology; the effects of the new order on the organization, on users through deskilling of staff, on staff through deteriorating terms of service and in the creation of conflicts of interest between social services and elements of the health service.

Ideology

The AD's views on the changes were summed up by the one word 'appalling'.

> I think the impact has been appalling. Basically it is privatization. Local authority investments in community care services have been treated unevenly and sacrificed to the development of an untested and often unregulated market. It is covert privatization that's hitting many vulnerable people. The poverty gap in this city has been documented and is widening between the rich and the poor. The financial means testing supporting the new legislation has created new rifts.

The social services department has had to cut staff and focus its strategy on the defence of the most vulnerable users. The clarification of continuing health care needs should have underwritten the Department of Health guidance while social care has not been provided with a commitment to preventive work.

Organization

The rhetoric of the changes encourages the belief that they will produce streamlined organizations, far less bureaucratic than the pre-reform services. In the AD's view, in practice the opposite is true. At the heart of the problem is means testing.

> We've got 21 different financial assessment forms, because we've got so much charging and different ways of getting into charging and income. It's a checking and verification task that the benefits agency people used to do and it's an area subject to careful financial audit. So it is frustrating for qualified social workers to get bogged into that. I think that the paperwork has increased. A system that's supposed to be less bureaucratic is actually more bureaucratic.

De-skilling and the decline of social work

The changes have also begun to have a major impact in de-skilling aspects of the community care services and undermining the profession of social work itself, with serious implications for the standard of care that will be offered to users as a result. At the time of the reorganization on purchaser/provider lines, social workers in the department's generic teams were given a choice whether they went to the new children's services or stayed with community care. Most qualified workers went to the children's services. The remainder found themselves in the role of assessors rather than providers of care.

> Most of the social workers who are engaged in assessments pretty much full time are very, very frustrated social workers because they've got no time to do anything else. However, we are increasingly concerned about the growth of adult abuse and the management of risk in the community for increasingly vulnerable adults and pressurized carers.

There are very few continuing social work cases in the community care division, even with people with chronic problems such as enduring mental illness or lifetime problems such as learning disabilities. Where such users need continuing care, a plan is made by the assessor and then implemented by other workers. 'Social workers only come back into the case if there's a major change in circumstances, or a crisis.' The key worker in such cases may be a day care worker, a residential worker, or a home care worker, with little or no social work training or skills. 'If you look at the social work contingent in the field work teams, in some cases you haven't even got professionally qualified team leaders.'

The AD saw the causes of this situation as lying partly in the past where qualified social workers in the authority's generic teams had tended to prefer child care work and to concentrate on it. 'Consequently, when you restructure, that tends to have imprinted itself because people had preferences, had to make a choice.' But a second important factor, given the authority's no redundancy policy, was the need to find jobs for people who had to be redeployed as a result of the changes in local government.

> Every time there was a vacancy you had to look to the redundancy pool and you had to redeploy from anywhere in the city. In some areas of work such as administration, most of our staff are very low skilled and unqualified and the same applies to some of the fieldwork teams and service provider areas.

The response of the authority has been to introduce training for such people, and in particular for the assessors. But meanwhile, the AD said, 'Social work is disappearing fast. I don't know that social work will survive.' This was a situation which, as an advocate of the profession and a former teacher of social work, she was deeply concerned about, with its implied consequences for the deterioration of standards of fieldwork.

> I want to see a stronger and better profession, a profession which has been my life. I don't want to see the profession die under my nose when I'm in charge of it, for goodness sake! ... Talking to other authorities, they're also saying you don't need

qualified social workers, what you want is efficient assessors. It's the benefit agency work, financial assessment.

Staff

Quite apart from the threat to social work, the changes have had other negative consequences for staff. In particular, their security of employment has been reduced and, where they are now in competition with the independent sector, their terms of service are under threat.

Health service imperialism

Elements of professional social work have been lost from the fields of mental health and disabilities.

> Community psychiatric nurses and community learning disability nurses are picking up on the shortfall. You've got rid of one profession, you re-invent a lower order professional person like the assessor and you redistribute your professional skills to another profession.

From the perspective of the AD, in the whole notion of social care

> we're up against rampant imperialism on behalf of health. Holistic health has disappeared when they choose to describe it as having disappeared. When they choose to describe 'this' as now health care and 'that' as social care because we want access to your budget, they will do so with no questions asked. Otherwise, there's a sense that health is about everything. It's about prevention, investment, and health promotion.

Behind this imperialistic drive the AD identifies the health authority and behind that the national health service executive and the government.

> I think it's part of a possible long-term political agenda and I think it's about running down the local state entirely. I can quite easily see a scenario where we do not have any in-house services and pressure would be on to move purchasing into a community health agenda and local democracy is out of the window and it's all quango driven.

It was not surprising after this analysis to find that the AD rated her satisfaction with her job as rather lower than when she first moved to the City, and that she now felt quite insecure in her post.

> The message now is, who needs managers? Empower the workforce is the message. So I think there is a kind of sense of wobblyness and a lot of people are moving out of the organization.

A better future

The AD felt that any real improvements would require quite major changes in social policy, on the lines of a new Beveridge, to sort out the basic issues of income maintenance. After that, she was a strong advocate of the development of a locality based approach backed by a strong investment in increasing skills. Professionals from all the relevant services would work closely together in integrated teams serving relatively small local areas to provide coherent, accessible and relevant services.

Case Study 2

'We had done some excellent things': the undermining of specialist services in a social services department.
A senior manager

Introduction

This case study describes the impact of the community care reforms from the point of view of a senior manager with responsibilities for people with disabilities and mental health problems, working in a large social services department. It sketches the character of the organization and the specialist services it provided before April 1993, when the changes began to bite, and then shows how services started to be affected over the months that followed. The senior manager eventually became so unhappy with the impact of the changes on his job and the work which he believed in, that he resigned from the department and started his own private community care service. The last part of the case study describes his early experiences in this new role and reflects both on its challenges and his restored self-respect and morale.

The particular significance of this case study is its account of how the community care reforms, intended to improve standards of service, could create conditions likely to have the opposite effect for users and could undermine the morale of staff providing them.

Working in social services before the implementation of the NHSCC Act

Under the director, the general manager was in charge of all the services for people with disabilities and mental health problems including the adult training centres, hostels and day centres. He was responsible, as well, for all the social work teams which dealt with learning disabilities, physical disabilities, mental health and occupational therapy.

At this time he thought that the services had real strengths. The department was organized on a specialist basis but also had the advantage of a system of patches for services for older people and people with disabilities. Each patch covered a small locality and provided a good way for the population to make contact with the department. He valued the fact that specialism was available to users: 'It had really raised the profile of disability and mental health services'. In his view specialist expertise was essential for the kinds of cases his team dealt with.

> From my experience as a social worker, you don't want someone coming to visit you who's just a good hearted, honest person. You want somebody who's previously dealt with someone who's had brain injuries in a road accident, somebody who's met other people with epilepsy, other people who have Parkinson's, Huntington's. The parents and users look to you as special experts, non-medical, to call on a bank of knowledge that will help put them in touch with key local and national organizations, with coping mechanisms that are customized for them. You don't want people who say, 'I've never come across that. I had to look it up before I came to see you'. Whereas with specialisms you have great reassurance as a customer that somebody turns up who has experience of that specialism.

He was aware that in some areas where population is scattered there were not that many users with particular conditions and needs and the consequence was that the specialists had to travel. 'It will not look good on mileage charts, but it was in fact an excellent service.'

Over the previous ten years they had made real progress, having taken disability and mental health services

> from the lowest of the low up to a sort of professional par in credibility terms with services for children and for other adults. We'd done some excellent things and some of the things in our unit were excellent.

He cited examples of advocacy initiatives and the dispersal of the day centres. 'We would push things, user groups, user consultation days. We'd fly the flag in many ways.'

Users had the combined advantage of 'one stop' access through their local social services patch and specialist services that offered quite wide choice. The service was holistic with no division between purchaser and provider. Contact would be made with the reception service in the department; a social worker would visit and in part carry out an assessment and in part provide a service along the lines of: 'We will discuss these options and these options and I'll help you make a decision.'

It was a job he enjoyed very much, with a fair degree of freedom to do the work to standards that satisfied him. The main weaknesses in the organization were its lack of clarity in its budgetary systems which led to 'stop/go scenarios', and the frustration of working with senior managers who were 'not fighting for professional issues'.

Until 1993 he thinks the morale in his section was high because there was a sense of purpose, direction and carrying out the task. He contrasted his unit with some of the other services in his department at the time.

> Children's services were obviously always under the hammer; on the operational side, services for elderly people were already into cuts in homes, redeployment, changes in wages and conditions, thinking about contracting out. They were pretty pissed off really, particularly as they'd been promised rights for users, practice guidelines and quality services. I used to be able to look back on a year and say 'What have I done? Well, we've done this and we've done that'. A bit of a celebration really. They were really good days when the director used to come round and

we had a high profile in the department.'

Nor at this time, in his view, was there much feeling of job insecurity in his section; the people who left – voluntarily, or through redundancy – were people who were ready to go.

The pressures to split purchasing from providing

When the possibility of splitting purchasing from providing in the services for which he was responsible was mooted, the senior manager argued strongly against the move. In his view the current system worked well and the split would be likely to put at risk the specialist services that were so important to users. However, the pressures in favour of the purchaser/provider divide continued to grow. The local politicians of all parties, it seemed to him, tended to support the idea, as much from an established distrust of their officers and a desire to control them as anything. The dominant view of the politicians appeared to be:

> Officers couldn't manage budgets because they were so big and amorphous and there was a lot of waste that they couldn't really identify as a council because it was all disguised here and there. Whereas if they actually had a finite budget and clear unit costs and they knew exactly how many hours of home care went out, for example, they would feel more comfortable. But you might take a more cynical view and say that if budgets and unit costs were clear, they would know whether they were being conned or not. It depends whether you take a cynical or benevolent view of whether the council was genuinely wanting to see where their precious money was going. And I think there was a strong element of distrust probably around the way that traditionally they'd seen chief officers massaging budgets and robbing Peter to pay Paul. I think they were much happier with purchasers and providers rather than conglomerate services.

Pressures started to build up on the senior manager from inside the department to accept the split in services when the organization as a whole developed a purchaser/provider approach. 'There was a strong pressure for me to have my specialist team subsumed into an older adults purchasing team.' It was urged that 'all the needs were more or less the same, weren't they? You know, what's the difference between an old person of eighty getting home care and a young chap who's had an accident or someone with mental health problems?'

But the senior manager was not convinced. 'I fought very strongly, along with one or two others, to keep in specialisms because we were loath to throw away what we thought was a good service.' Initially, he managed to resist the changes although he acknowledged that he may not have won many friends in the process 'because I kept on, I wouldn't throw the towel in'. He is aware that he was not only defending specialism but also a job he personally valued.

> I was head of disability and mental health and I didn't want to become some kind of business purchaser or whatever, which I guess would have been the next step for me had my business unit as a provider/purchaser gone.

He knew people were saying 'Come on, let's just split. It'll save us money and what have you.' But in his view even that was not true and there would not be significant gains in terms of efficiency from economies of scale.

The split between purchasers and providers might have been acceptable in his mind if specialist skills and approaches had been safeguarded. The authority had previously clearly recognized the need for such specialist services. Now if there was to be a good service the purchasers must face and resolve the same questions which had led to the introduction of specialisms. In learning disabilities, for instance, he asked:

> Is it good enough that people are fed, clothed and watered and see the doctor once every so often? Or do we promote a much more fulfilling, integrated concept of what the county council expects of its learning disabilities service? The purchasing policy needs to reflect enough of that specialism ... If the purchasing side was sufficiently sympathetic to the specific needs of people with disabilities, young or old, then I think that as long as your providers are tooled up to providing that specialist service to meet individual needs, rather than just general good hearted social workers, then things will be satisfactory. Disabled people themselves don't want tea and biscuits. They want leading edge advice. 'I don't have to go into this home, do I? I can get ILF (Independent Living Fund), can't I? How do I get ILF? Can I hire my own staff?'

However, it seemed to him that saving money and accommodating plans for other changes in the department were uppermost in the developments which followed and the future for specialist services looked increasingly uncertain. Although he had successfully resisted the major structural change to purchaser/provider, posts at middle management level were lost. The senior manager felt that the decision was taken because it was easy to do. It was a change made 'in the interests of corporate simplicity, rather than meeting the needs of individual groups of people'.

> Two of the staff involved were over fifty and we amalgamated learning disabilities with physical disabilities, which may have made some sense in terms that they have one secretary and one data base of payments. In terms of professional skill, expertise, it was a backwards step.

However, the pressures for change did not stop there. New plans began to be made which would mean that his own section would be subsumed under a much larger section in the department providing services for older people. These services dwarfed the disabilities and mental health unit, with a budget two and a half times as great. It seemed increasingly clear that the specialisms of his team would be diluted or lost.

The impact of the changes on morale

The effect of these changes on morale in his section and on his own attitude to work began to make itself felt. There was less freedom to do the job to his own satisfaction, 'much more rigidity'. His enjoyment of the work declined. It was particularly frustrating that other senior managers were not fighting for professional issues and that they had to cope with politicians 'pretending they're businessmen'. Satisfaction became defined in terms of 'beating the ever more complicated system, especially when an issue was won on care issues rather than costs'.

He was aware that other staff in social services had begun to suffer from stress. He thought that overall in the last eighteen months the overriding pressure was that of not being able to deliver the sort of service that they had thought important. However, more recently he knew that the big stress was whether or not they would keep a job. In earlier rounds of reorganization there had been people in their fifties who had decided for themselves that they couldn't work to the new pressures and systems and took early retirement. Now, however, increasingly it was good younger managers who were facing job loss and did not know how they were going to pay the mortgage. Stress had begun to show in increased sickness. For example, one person who had never had a day's sickness in her life had had substantial periods off in the space of a few months.

He had come under increasing personal stress himself through the problems of managing the boundary between his unit and the department to enable his staff to have the space and security to get on with the job as he and they wanted it to be done. But there was a significant cost to his home and family life. His wife would say that he was constantly whingeing when he got home and he knew that that's what he did – moan about the social services organization. That was why she had backed him completely in taking the risk in setting up his own agency so that he could actually get on and do work how he wanted to do it. When it became clear that his unit's work was to lose its separate identity and be merged with that of services for older adults he decided the time had come to move out.

The perspective of the private provider

The senior manager's plan was to establish a private provider agency, employing his own care staff, which would give him 'an opportunity to deliver quality services in a way which was no longer possible, given current constraints, within social services departments'. From his own years in social services he knew 'that there were many cowboys around in the private sector who were delivering poor quality services'. His aim was to be in at the start and to provide *good* services. There was a niche market in relation to children with disabilities. On top of that, he intended to offer services for the range of adults wanting help, which could be either to provide personal care or could be jobs for older adults with money that would enhance their quality of life. 'If they wanted to have a companion to take them for a holiday to Brighton and home again, for example, I hoped to be able to supply that.'

The senior manager was aware of his motivation in his dealings with people in his new role. He was trying to provide a good service, but he knew that he had a commercial interest in doing so because there was the possibility that not only might people use his company again or recommend it to others, they might also ask him to provide services which they had not thought could be provided before they had come into contact with him.

This involved a complete mind change from work in social services where he had been trying to ration services; now he was trying to stimulate and develop them. To run a private company you have to attract enough business to cover your costs. He is experiencing from the other side of the fence the anxiety of providers who wish to get contracts from social services departments or health authorities: How do *they* make their decisions? Is the system fair? Will they take account of quality? He set out to get known by making approaches to social services at headquarters, writing to individual social workers, contacting GPs and some other people in health authorities.

He had made a bid for a contract with social services centrally and failed to get that, in his view because staff were uneasy about giving him a contract so soon after he had left. He knew that a lot of work was actually allocated by individual social workers and he didn't know the extent to which they would feel free to use his service. Some might be anxious that he, as a social worker himself, might be critical of assessments and he had seen two or three examples of sloppy work. In the same circumstances, as a social worker, he would want to try to make sure that users got access to the best possible service, and within the terms of obligations placed on him, to allow people to choose. He would try to find a way to suggest to people which was the better option, though he had to avoid using precisely those words.

The local social services department is to start a system of tenders: that is people must submit names and details of their way of working, to be followed by an interview, so that if acceptable they would be put on a list of approved contractors. He thought that would be to his advantage as this would mean that he would be openly listed and that there would then be full endorsement regarding use of his agency.

In terms of stresses of the job he thought that there were now far fewer, indeed people said how much younger he looked. The overriding stress was whether he could make enough money. He had chosen to rent an office and employ full-time office staff as a way of demonstrating that his agency was different from many others in terms of approachability. The home care workers were paid only when he used them and he'd been immensely impressed with the quality of some of the applicants, many of whom were working for other agencies and were dissatisfied with the arrangements within them.

The new market in home care: a concern for quality.

When he started his new job managing his own care business in 1995 the senior manager was astonished to find the extent to which price had come to take precedence over quality in dealings with the social workers representing his former employers.

> It surprised me how many social workers have rung up talking money first. They say 'Give me a price', as I would if I were buying a car tyre, Charlie Brown's against Kwikfit. I found it a bit of a culture shock.

Budgets have become a priority and it is now normal for people to act in this way and ask for a price list first. 'One presumes that they get the funding and then, perhaps, worry about whether your organization can actually meet this person's needs.'

From what he had learned about other independent sector providers he had formed the view 'that a lot of them are not up to the job and I wouldn't want them through my front door. Because, as I say, they've got no policies, no procedures, no insurance, no back-up, and no culture of care'.

He thought that there were a lot of concerns about the running of some agencies, for example, in terms of details like insurance cover but also in terms of a lack of any regulations to ensure that they could produce the type of service that was wanted. In his view too many people just took on the work regardless of whether they could provide what was wanted.

He contrasts the work conditions and expectations in his firm with that of other private agencies. Some of the people who have come to work for his firm

> have seen that we pay decent rates. Some have shock-horror stories about their previous employers: the hours they're expected to work; the pay they get; cash in hand; some get paid in IOUs. They go out to meet people 'cold', as it were. They get a list through the door: 'Your clients this week are Mr Smith (bathing), Mrs Jones (take to the toilet, give her breakfast, etc.)' and you turn up and do that. That's not the way we operate but it's clearly a cheap way of doing things.

The comments of a local councillor to him recently suggested that there is some political awareness of such quality issues in private domiciliary care.

> She said that she'd picked up one or two anecdotes about these agencies. In one, the worker couldn't get to a client so they sent their mother or their daughter. Nothing had gone wrong but the level of unprofessionalism is incredible. We've tried to be the quality end. But to date, albeit it's early days, it hasn't paid off in terms of business being put our way.

Looking back on the professionals still working in the department he had left, his predominant impression was of individuals unable to relate to their changing organization and unsure of the new protocols and expected standards of professionalism in the new purchaser/provider world. At least in his brave new world, his role as an independent provider was unambiguous and he was now clear about where responsibility and accountability lay.

The future

The senior manager was clear in his mind about the immediate reforms he would like to see in the running of the statutory services he had left to achieve improvements in community care. First, individual social workers should be given their own budget and their own patch in which to work. If they managed the job well they should be praised, if they didn't they should be fired. Second, the volume of paperwork should be halved. Third, chief officers should be appointed who are able champions of social services and it should be ensured that all senior managers on the operations side of providing/purchasing should have care backgrounds and qualifications. Fourth, the independent sector should be more rigorously monitored. Finally, local authorities should be given enough resources to be able to compete with the independent sector.

Case Study 3

From moving spirit to managerial ethos: change in an independent child care charity.
A middle manager

Background

The changes described in most of the case studies in this book were imposed from outside on the organizations involved and they had little choice but to respond and adapt. This case study, however, describes an organization that was faced with no such imperatives and where the changes were, in the words of the middle manager whose experience is described here, 'entirely self-inflicted'.

The organization is one of the larger national voluntary sector charities. It both raises funds and undertakes development work in the field, mainly through a system of projects; the field work is managed on a regional basis. Each region has its own regional manager, assistant regional managers and project managers. Assistant regional managers are responsible for initiating and managing a group of projects.

The case study describes changes in the organization and management of the charity over the past few years, as seen by an assistant regional manager. While accepting that a case for some measure of change existed, he believes that the reforms actually adopted were influenced more by pressures to conform with the fashionable managerialism of the day than the underlying objectives of the organization. In his view, the changes have seriously damaged middle management commitment and morale, and shifted the dynamic of the charity from a central concern for children to an obsession with the well-being and growth of the organization.

Before the changes

The organization of work

The main work of the organization was and is to create and run projects to develop and provide services for children in fields where there is no appropriate statutory provision or such provision is clearly inadequate, and in so doing to provide models for practice. To manage this work the organization has a regional structure which covers the whole country. Before the changes described in this study, each of these regions had its own budget. The assistant regional managers (ARMs), working under the supervision of the regional manager, were responsible for identifying suitable projects, negotiating with the other parties that might be involved in setting them up, establishing the projects, appointing their staff and overseeing their management once they were up and running.

Projects focused on a wide variety of areas. To take a few examples, they might provide care for severely physically disabled children or for children with learning disabilities. They might be concerned with working with children and families where there was risk of sexual abuse. They might involve the establishment of a family centre or schemes to help tackle homelessness or offending amongst young people.

The assistant regional manager's work

There were two main components: negotiating new work and overseeing existing projects. Most of his projects were set up through negotiations with local authorities and involved varying proportions of local authority money and the organization's money.

> As a result of networking I would get ideas for projects that mostly were initiated by local authorities. They would come to us and say, 'We've got a problem, we've got a need. Have you got any ideas?'

Alternatively, new projects grew out of existing projects:

> We'd have a project on the ground and then it would change and it would evolve into something new, or it would spawn a new service.

Decisions on initiating new work were taken between the regional manager and the assistant regional managers. The regional manager knew how much money was available in the local budget and might say

> You can spend £80,000. If I got back having spent less than £80,000, then we'd got a bit more money to spend on something else. If I had spent £10,000 more on it in the negotiations I knew that was alright because I knew what we'd got left in the regional pot. I'd have to have it approved but I knew what I could do while I was out there negotiating. Final approval depended on head office in London but was seldom refused if a good case was made.

The second part of his job was operational management. This included the details of setting up the new projects once they had been negotiated.

> We had an interesting job in that, unlike local authorities at the equivalent level, we had total responsibility. We had responsibility for premises, we'd work with the architects on the premises; we'd have responsibility for staffing and personnel, so we'd do a lot of personnel work using headquarters personnel people as our advisors; we'd do a lot of financial work.

Once the projects were set up, the project managers would take over day-to-day responsibility for them but the ARMs continued to oversee their work, frequently visiting the projects and providing personal supervision and support for the project managers.

Advantages and disadvantages of the pre-change organization

The great advantage of this system in terms of the objectives of the organization, in the view of the ARM, was that it gave the assistant regional managers substantial scope to set up creative projects and it put no bars on their freedom to develop work with the most disadvantaged children, regardless of their ability to find external sources of finance. The freedom and responsibility given to the ARMs encouraged high levels of commitment and participation, with beneficial effects on the quality of projects and their management, and their ability to identify and promote work with children and young people in the greatest need.

The disadvantages of the organization at this time, in his view, were that in spite of the discretion given to the regions in setting up and managing projects, certain matters like staffing establishments and the replacement of cars were still controlled by the national headquarters and decision-making on them was slow. In addition, the ARMs were blitzed with paperwork from the centre, much of which he felt was irrelevant. Project managers in their turn were officially controlled by a number of bureaucratic rules which were experienced as inhibiting their effectiveness.

Aims and ethos

The ethos of the organization before the changes was defined by the ARM as a 'central commitment to kids.' Everything flowed around this commitment, he said, 'so that people were passionate about services, passionate about issues; kids were highly regarded even if they were loud mouthed nuisances'. It was totally unacceptable then, in his view, to regard working for the organization as nothing more than a job.

> The pressure was to be very committed; old fashioned ideas like going the extra mile were very real – staff who would stay on duty if a kid was ill; nobody rushing off; people providing out-of-hours cover without pay and without thinking about it. You ran the service and did what you had to do to keep the show on the road.

Experience of the job

While he found the bureaucratic elements of the work frustrating the ARM's general level of satisfaction was very high. There had been a positive draw to come to the organization after the constraints of working in a local authority:

because there was the opportunity to specialize, to have the resources, take the risk, to be innovative in an organization that says; 'Alright, achieve it then as you say you can, do it, and we'll resource you, and we'll cope with the risks.'

He particularly enjoyed negotiating new work:

I thought that was a real thrill. To start from nothing, negotiate and see it happen. When the projects were established I actually used to like walking the shop floor. Just being around and seeing kids. When things worked well there was lots of pride, lots of fun, lots of people really pleased with what they were doing – a real buzz about it.

He felt he had all the freedom he needed to do the work well and was secure in his job. He could speak out about the job without constraint: 'Everybody felt that you could say what you wanted and people listened. It was a very noisy sort of organization then.' Relationships with the regional manager were good and with senior management away in London were 'much less oppressive than in a local authority where management could be geographically near'.

The Changes

Origins and consultation

Discussion of the need for radical change in the organization began early in the 1990s. In the ARM's view, objectively the condition of the organization was very healthy at the time and there was no pressing reason such as declining funding or a loss of confidence on the part of its statutory partners to trigger the debate. Instead he felt that the impetus for change, which came from the top of the organization,

was about responding both to the local government environment and the whole environment of the eighties and, I suppose, the introduction of new management theories and thinking to make sure we don't get left behind, to make plans for the twenty-first century.

By this time, too, many of the managers had been on externally run management courses and had been exposed to the new organizational philosophies with their emphasis on managerial rather than professional concepts and leadership.

In addition, the ARM said there was a more immediate incentive for change: the organization had identified the possibility of growth yet it was clear that the existing bureaucratic structure would not readily accommodate it and some kind of reorganization seemed the necessary precondition of achieving it.

Before any plans were formed about *how* the organization might be reformed, however, an extensive programme of consultation was launched amongst the staff. There was widespread participation in this process but, in the ARM's view, what emerged was a list of criticisms rather than proposals:

I think that most of the staff responded and it became the largest grievance procedure in the world because, when you look at what staff actually did say, they didn't look at the twenty-first century, they looked at the here and now. Very little was about saying what they wanted for the future but they did write about what they didn't like now!

The changes

The ARM felt that the proposed changes which emerged after the consultation had little to do with the views expressed by staff. While staff said they wanted a loosening of bureaucratic controls and faster decision making, 'the actual way it changed and the solution that was proposed wasn't proposed by the consultation' but emerged from the steering group set up to organize the consultation.

The ARM described the main changes as involving decentralization but went on to qualify this as a 'Thatcherite decentralization' which to him meant devolving responsibility but centralizing power. The most important features of the decentralization, in terms of the formal structure, were that the final say about the funding of projects was passed from headquarters management to the regional managers meeting as a group, and that project managers were to assume more direct control of the day-to-day decisions in the running of their projects. At the same time, however, the need was identified for far more emphasis on performance measurement to provide quality assurance. A system indicating what proportion of a project's funding should be negotiated from stakeholders outside the organization was introduced.

Impact of the changes on the work of the assistant regional managers

The first consequence of the changes for the ARM's job was that the individual regions no longer had their own pot of money on which the plans for the region could be built. All the organization's development money was held by the regional managers' meeting and allocated by their collective decision on the basis of individual proposals for new work.

The ARM recognized a certain logic in this move as it meant that it was now possible to have an overview of development work in the organization as a whole; regions would be able to learn from each other more easily and it should be possible to cut out needless duplication of innovatory projects. But this gain was offset, in his view, by the introduction of a great deal of uncertainty in his work negotiating new projects. Whereas in the former system he and his manager knew just how much money was available to the team and that if they put forward a sound proposal it was highly likely to be funded, today the decision is out of their hands. 'Now we negotiate a project without the slightest idea whether you'll get the money.'

The ARM's work is further complicated and handicapped by the new rules categorizing projects by how much money he is expected to raise for them from outside his own organization. *All* projects, even the most innovatory and difficult to fund, are now expected to have a substantial element of such funding.

> In the past I could negotiate a project that was 100 per cent funded by the organization, or 50 per cent or whatever; I've now got categories. So on new work, for example, utterly non-statutory street work which no local authority has a duty to provide and wouldn't provide, I've been set a target of 50/50 statutory funding.

The result is that such work, if it is to be funded at all, takes far longer to get going and is at much more risk of collapse. The ARM gave an example of streetwork with teenagers at risk he had eventually succeeded in getting funded:

> I've got the most amazing combination of money all tacked together. It's taken me much longer to negotiate. It's bits of secondment, bits of money, bits of this, bits of that. The whole pack of cards from the local authority could collapse at any minute. And under the old system we could have decided to 100 per cent fund it.

The ARM felt that the pressure was on to generate income

> so you've got to do work in the high income-generating bands now. You get involved in things being attractive because there's a lot of money attached to them, rather than them being attractive because of the nature of the work.

An example was projects with children leaving care which the organization had pioneered and for which now local authorities often have their own service. It is

> ancient work, we know it, we've done it, we've proved it but if somebody's prepared to fund 100 per cent or 105 per cent to do it, it's very attractive. It actually has no *new* professional or dissemination value but it's quite interesting to us because it's big money.

Another change in the job of the ARM resulted from the increased devolution of responsibility to project managers. Formerly, the ARMs had been responsible for supervising their work quite closely and for keeping in frequent touch with their projects. As part of the process of increasing the project managers' ability to take more decisions without elaborate consultation above them, the ARM's managerial role has become much more arm's length. This has meant that there is now only general oversight instead of hands-on management, and quarterly reviews of work have replaced personal one-to-one supervision and frequent visits.

The ARM felt that this aspect of the new system was flawed in at least two respects. First, he now did not have enough knowledge of what was happening in the projects to oversee them effectively.

> Most of the time things don't go wrong but when they do go wrong it's so long before we find out about them that they're far worse. So the problems are much bigger and take longer to sort out.

Second, the loss of supervision makes life more difficult for both the ARM and the project manager. Supervision had given the ARMs the opportunity to share their experience and knowledge with the project managers: 'Then you could nudge practice. Now you have no input at all. All you pick up is when things go wrong.' The project managers themselves feel the need for continuing supervision and continue to get it when they can on an *ad hoc*, unofficial basis. The ARMs, however, are not meant to be giving such supervision anymore and are meant, as a result, to have overall responsibility for several more projects than before. The result is an overwhelming pressure of work.

The quality assurance measures

While much of the old bureaucratic undergrowth was cleared away in the changes, to the relief of both ARMS and project managers, a new systems of controls, in their own way tighter than the system which preceded them, has begun to take shape. Further, in the view of the ARM, the main criteria now used often fail to include the success or failure of the project in terms of the underlying objectives: 'They have impact objectives, service outcomes and outputs but none of my project managers is assessed any more on "Is the work any good?"' Taking as an example the new street project with young people, he said,

> We would have lots and lots of charts and graphs. How many contacts on the streets? How many contacts for accommodation? How many contacts for health advice? We have absolutely everything but we wouldn't know whether the staff liked the kids, whether the kids liked the staff enough to come, whether it made any difference to them.

The ARM's objection is not to having relevant measures of performance and accountability but to the proliferation of what he regards as *irrelevant* measures which are applied on a standard basis to all projects. These tend to focus on process rather than purpose. So, for instance, in a project helping young people with serious mental illness learn to live in the community, the manager's official statement of objectives is about having a particular service operational by a set date, setting up a supportive lodging scheme, having information available to families. Quality assurance is about service targets; the maintenance of standards laid down; key policies and procedures; accountability to funders, service users, and the organization; and responsiveness to users and referrers.

> Nowhere does it say that the *aim* of this project is to get kids into independence and see they've a good quality of life and that we support them until they don't need us any more. Which is what parents would say about their children.

The emphasis on procedures when they are unrelated to the central purpose of the project is, in his view, counter-productive. The organization, for instance, insists that all projects have three ways of consulting users and evidence that they have been implemented must be presented. But it does not follow that the project manager has to do more than go through the *form* of consultation. 'What we have done is to put onto a professional operation a commercial structure and pattern of operation.'

The impact of change on the project managers and the projects

Project managers initially welcomed the greater autonomy the changes promised them. To some extent this autonomy has been realized in practice. But they are now experiencing new forms of control from the centre which they never anticipated, as the quality assurance system brings in 'very tight accountability', sets standards of performance, and so on.

> They get surprised when the next set of regulations and rules comes out, when the standards come out and they realize that their scope for activity is getting less and less.

One of the strengths of the old organization, in his view, was the very lack of precision in definitions:

> The boundaries were beautifully fuzzy and, I think, fuzzy boundaries enable you to do good practice. If you tighten the boundaries you actually restrict the capacity for innovation.

That fuzziness was fast vanishing. Finally, the project managers are missing the regular supervision and close support they formerly had from the ARMs.

The knock-on effect of all these changes on the service provided by the projects themselves is more difficult to assess. The ARM tends to believe that the front line workers may not as yet have been much affected by them and that they are carrying on their work with clients much as before. But if the morale and commitment of the middle mangers is failing in the new system, and their ability to develop truly innovative work is reduced, it seems inevitable that these factors in turn will eventually affect the nature and quality of the projects themselves.

The assistant regional manager's personal evaluation of the changes

The ARM's experience of his job today is largely negative. He feels that he has lost the freedom to do the work to his satisfaction, that the ethos of the organization has changed, that relations with senior management have deteriorated, that there are pressures against speaking one's mind and for conformity. In sum, there is little enjoyment left in his daily tasks.

The freedom to do his job to his own satisfaction has gone with his loss of frequent contact with the projects.

> I do have to see the purpose. I do have to hear that the purpose of my work is happening, that things are happening for kids and nice things are happening, that you have an influence on that. All of that has been removed.

The ethos of the organization is now centred on itself rather than children. It's about the organization growing and perpetuating itself. While it always had a vested interest in keeping going, that's much more prominent now: 'The vehicle just happens to be children and families.' He saw this as the principal disadvantage of the changes to the organization, using the words of the Archbishop of Canterbury who has been quoted as saying that he was worried that the larger charities 'had imposed a managerial ethos on what used to be a moving spirit'.

Relations with his manager changed virtually overnight when the new organizational structure was introduced. Before that date, as was common practice in the organization, he had received regular personal supervision from his boss which focused on his professional development and was quite separate from operational management. He had greatly valued such supervision and the opportunities it gave to share problems informally and to learn and to grow. In the new order, it was replaced by a formal quarterly 'performance review' – a highly structured process that was part of the management control system.

Further, in his new role, he found his manager who had always been tolerant of his outspokenness in the old organization, now would allow no criticism: 'Challenging the new order is seditious – you are wrong and you are told to shut up'. Even when some aspect of the new structure is clearly not working, management does not want to know. He and his colleagues

> are actually told to shut up in regional management meetings. If you challenge the party line, it's very threatening and people are holding very firmly to the party line.

The result of such reactions to criticism is a strong feeling that you have to conform:

> It's a sort of local authority paranoia that I've never seen in this organization before. People will do something unspecified to you if you don't conform. That was never, ever the ethos before.

Perhaps the 'unspecified' threat is redundancy since feelings of job security, too, had been undermined by the changes and the possibilities of 'delayering', particularly at middle management level.

The combined effect of the changes on the ARM's personal experience of his job has been drastic. He says he now gets no enjoyment from it:

> If you mean enjoyment in the sense that it used to be; fun, heady, roller-coaster, stimulating fun. Lots of people laughing, lots of tears as well, all of that. Real gutsy stuff. It's all gone.

And he feels this is true too of the feelings of the other ARMs. 'My colleagues are stressed, miserable, unhappy. No fun to be with. Lost.'

The future

The ARM had no ready solutions for the many self-inflicted problems he had identified which had resulted from the changes in the organization. But he was not entirely pessimistic about the future and could see 'glimmers' of improvements:

There's been a lot of pain over the last two years and a lot of people have been hurt in the process but you can see the glimmers. The saving grace about the organization is that it does learn and I think it is essentially responsive. People are now beginning to say, 'Yes, perhaps our work load is too high. Perhaps we ought to have smaller standard control. Yes, the management training needs to be better. We need to equip people who've now got authority to do the job better.'

It was an irony, however, which the ARM enjoyed pointing out, that the reformed organization prided itself on being a 'learning organization' but had been singularly slow about proving it: 'It has actually not learned. It's taken us eighteen months to begin to start learning again.'

Case Study 4

Order from chaos? Change in an inner city general practice.
A general practitioner

Background

General practitioners occupy a central place in the front line of the caring services. They are the first port of call for people who often have social as well as health problems. They are not only gatekeepers for entry to secondary care in the hospitals but also may act as intermediaries for their patients with social services, housing departments, and other service providers. In their day-to-day work, they collaborate closely with other primary health professionals including community nurses and health visitors.

In the 1990 Act, their key role in providing primary health care was spelt out and reinforced. The Act and other government policy decisions have favoured the development of primary care and a more preventative approach within it, and, as a part of this strategy, a shift of resources from secondary care.

GP fund holding, initially in larger practices, was encouraged by the new legislation as a central element in the creation of a purchaser/provider split in the NHS and the introduction of an internal market.

This case study focuses on the experience of a general practitioner (GP), working in an inner city area in which many of the inhabitants face problems of unemployment, low income and poor health. The study indicates the importance of context, differing professional priorities and rising expectations, as well as the impact of the 1990 Act itself in understanding the issues facing GPs. A combined response to the new legislation amongst GPs in the city concerned seems to be offering a collectivist twist to the market oriented direction of the 'reforms', which offers hope for a more collaborative and planned service, while at the same time strengthening the bargaining power of primary care.

The practice and its work before the implementation of the changes

The practice and its environment

The practice is a small one serving part of an inner city area. Its staff, throughout the five-year period covered by this account, include in addition to the GPs, a practice manager, practice nurse, receptionists and secretaries; a community nurse and a health visitor are attached. The area served by the practice has high levels of unemployment, with 20 per cent or more out of work, and, as the GP says, 'all that that implies in terms of social disadvantage and effects on health'. About 10 per cent of the practice population belong to an ethnic minority group.

The typical daily work round

The structure of the GP's day before the 1990 NHS reforms was very much as it is today and so this account of his current work round covers both periods. He starts at 8.30 am with a non-appointment or 'open' surgery. The GPs run an open surgery because they find it suits many of their patients better.

> The problem with full appointment surgeries, particularly in an area like this part of the city, is that a lot of patients don't have telephones and they aren't used to dealing with the whole business of making appointments. Even if they do make appointments, they're often not very good at keeping them and they also have a perception that when they have a problem it needs to be dealt with there and then. So if there isn't an appointment, they come in and demand to be seen and that creates stress for the receptionists.

In addition, in his experience the patients quite like 'the culture of the waiting room where they sit and chat and discuss the world, including their doctor!'

'Depending on what time you finish the open surgery – and sometimes it goes on until 12 o'clock – you then go out and do visits and come back in time for the afternoon surgery.' The day finishes between 6.0 and 6.30 p.m. During that time the doctor will have seen about 20 people in the open surgery, from 12 to 15 in the booked afternoon surgery, which will, together with visits, make a daily total of about 38 to 40 patients.

Typical cases and the problems they involved

The GP described typical cases which might be encountered in some of the main client groups in the practice. With elderly people

> a common problem is somebody coming in who is becoming increasingly disabled and is having problems with mobility and self-care. You need some sort of therapeutic assessment, inasmuch as you are looking at how you might intervene to improve somebody's mobility and to decrease their level of dependence by therapeutic intervention through drugs. If, for instance, they've got Parkinson's disease, and that's why they're having problems of self-care because they can't do up their buttons and dress themselves, then medication may well help.

If this only improves things to a limited extent the GP might then find himself looking for social care – perhaps a home carer, meals-on-wheels, an assessment by an occupational therapist to see how aids and adaptations might improve arrangements in the patient's home. So at this stage he would refer the case to social services.

Social services

In dealings with the social services, the GP typically encountered two kinds of problem. The first was simply one of poor communication about referrals and allocations of cases:

> You'd send off a letter or you'd ring up and it would go into a black hole called the allocation meeting and you never got any feedback or information or discovered quite what had happened.

The second problem was that often social services 'would not accept a GP's say-so in terms of medical assessment and would only accept a referral from a specialist'. This response seemed to be rooted in a 'rather negative perception of general practitioners' in social services, a perception which he also felt operated in the reverse direction.

The root of these differences lay, he believed, in differences of 'philosophy' represented in the medical model of care and the social model of care.

> The medical model of care is about making objective diagnoses and not making value judgements whereas the social model of care is about making value judgements about worth and standards.

A further point of difference between the two worlds of the GP and social services was that while

> general practice is a demand led service and general practitioners are reactive and responsive to people when they present, social services are much more of a rationed and planned service, which is about allocation and management of service to a much greater extent.

Referral to hospital

This was mainly for episodes of acute illness where physical conditions were concerned or 'sub-acute' cases where 'someone has multiple pathologies of one sort or another where everything seems to be going wrong at once'. In the instance of someone with dementia, however, referral might take place to get a 'more formal assessment, a management plan, and access to a greater range of resources' rather than for any therapeutic intervention.

The GP emphasized the limits of the relevance of complex hospital treatment, as far as some patients were concerned. A considerable number of elderly people say: 'Look, I've had a good innings. I don't want people prodding and poking and probing. I'm quite happy to meet my maker'. That should be respected and it's not down to rather élitist physicians to say that if we do that we're being ageist.

The GP's evaluation and experience of general practice before the changes

Four or five years ago, in the opinion of the GP, the advantages of the way the general practice itself operated, leaving aside the issues of relationships with other services, lay in the response to the individual patient. The patients who came for treatment, in his perception, 'got a reasonable level of service'. However, turning to the the disadvantages, he points out that at that time there was 'very little thought of looking at the practice population and priorities within it and going out and identifying people'. As a result 'clearly, a fair number of people didn't turn up' who might have benefited from the doctors' help.

The GP felt that he had been free to speak out about his job both inside and outside the practice. Inside the practice there was an acceptance that disagreement on issues could often be healthy. Externally, 'GPs have always had that freedom because they are independent contractors'. The Family Practitioner Committee (forerunner of today's Family Health Services Authority) was mainly concerned with administrative matters and put few, if any, pressures on the GPs which affected the way they did their job. He got considerable enjoyment from the work, finding the most satisfaction from 'the whole business of being responsible, doing the job that at the end of the day was down to you, and the satisfaction in terms of feedback from patients'. The most frustrating aspect of the work 'was and still is, just the level of demand: the fact that you can't possibly deal with all the problems that they present'.

The changes

The rationale for the changes and the GP's reaction

The GP perceived the main rationale of the changes involved in the 1990 Act as combining a number of goals: moving health and social services from being service-led to being needs-led; curbing the spiralling costs of the NHS caused by the development of high-tech care; moving the balance from secondary to primary care; giving the consumer a greater input; and using the purchaser/provider split and the internal market as a key part of the strategy to achieve all of this.

His own reaction to the proposals was mixed. There were clear positives in his view in 'looking at the needs of the population base and looking at GPs having more control in terms of purchasing cost-effective secondary care'. He also recognized the strength of the case for greater accountability in general practice. But he was highly critical of the means chosen to achieve the latter through market mechanisms and competition, at the cost of collaboration and cooperation. He felt it was perfectly feasible to introduce a purchaser/provider divide between primary and secondary services without the market. He was also critical about the lack of dialogue in preparing and implementing the changes, the lack of coherent planning and the apparent failure of those responsible to think through the effects of the interaction of the different elements in the strategy.

The changes implemented

The implementation of the changes in the last few years has to be seen, in this practice at least, against a background of rising demand from the patients and increasing pressures on the doctors and the other practice staff. Part of this, the GP felt, could be put down to the government's explicit encouragement of consumerism and the increased expectations of patients. But as significant, if not more so, were the increasing problems of the inner city:

> Within inner cities you are talking about communities which are under enormous stress and that generates all sorts of problems around mental health and stress generally which increase levels of demand. And general social fragmentation and breakdown, levels of crime, etc. have a knock-on effect in terms of the demands that are made on general practice.

With this context in mind, five aspects of the experience of the GP since the implementation of the changes are reviewed: the needs of the practice population; relations with the hospital sector; inter-professional relationships and effectiveness; health–social services collaboration; and the successful resistance to fund holding.

Targeting and the needs of the practice population

The GP feels that the case for the practice to look at the needs of the whole population it serves, and not just those who present themselves at the surgery, is entirely valid. The use of incentives in this area has clearly worked, as for example in the case of programmes for screening for cervical cancer and for immunization. But in other cases the initiatives have not been thought through properly. The classic case is that, as part of their contract, they are supposed to offer all people over 75 years old an annual review appointment in the surgery or a home visit. The GP believed that most of his profession felt this was a waste of time since it wasn't focused on those whom the practice staff were already in a position to identify as likely to benefit from regular contact. It positively encouraged the cynical response that the obligation could be met with a doorstep visit without setting foot inside the house.

The problem is not simply that this kind of assessment has not been thought through adequately and is not cost-effective, but that it leads to the increased expectations of the patients concerned and has led many elderly people to believe GPs now have a statutory obligation to visit them, which they don't.

Relations with hospitals

The GP felt that the shift of resources from the secondary to the primary sector
had yet to be realised, partly because the government has 'washed its hands of
that so that it is down to the purchasers and health authorities' to achieve. A
further difficulty is that the information systems to demonstrate the outcomes of
primary care do not exist in the same way that the hospital can show finished
consultant episodes and outpatient episodes. The position is not helped by the
emphasis in the Citizen's Charter on questions such as speed of response, rather
than quality of care:

> It's all about waiting times and how quickly you see people and cramming more and
> more people through the machine. The Secretary of State does it all the time: 'The
> health service has seen χ more patients this year.'

Interprofessional relationships and effectiveness

The attempt to bring waiting lists down by increasing throughput, the GP pointed
out, 'gets you into the whole business of whether you can provide adequate
support for earlier discharge of people at home'. This logically should involve
exploring ways of making those support services more effective.

> Do you actually need an H or G grade district nurse to do some of the things that
> might be required for somebody who's at home or can that be provided by a home
> care assistant? And how do you change from one system to another? Clearly, there
> are professional vested interests.

Yet these issues remain to be tackled and meantime the pressure for throughput
is maintained.

Another issue involving the interrelationship of different professional groups
and different definitions of priorities for care, which remained unresolved by the
reforms, was illustrated by the example of services for mentally ill people.
Following central directives, the mental health services are taking their main
responsibility to be to work with the long term, severely mentally ill.

> The primary care services are saying: 'Hang on a minute, there's a whole group of
> people out here who don't have long-term and continuing problems but clearly have
> mental health needs in terms of counselling, stress management and depression, and
> anxiety states.'

A study of the problem in the inner city area, part of which is served by the GP's
practice, has shown that even many of the long-term mentally ill are not receiving
help from the mental health service: 'Over 50 per cent haven't been seen in the last
two years by anybody from secondary care. They're solely dependent on primary
care.'

Health–social services collaboration

The GP felt there had been modest but real gains in relationships between the practice and social services following the changes.

> I think the community care changes have produced much more discussion and communication between primary care and social services than there has been in the preceding ten years. So we are talking to one another much more than we have in the past.

The discussions have concentrated on 'focused response to identified needs' and have included, for example, joint concerns such as the care of people in residential and nursing homes. The improvement has also gone some way towards tackling the problem of social services assesments of practice patients: 'I think it's easier to get access to assessment than it was in the past and you get feedback about assessment'. But 'that doesn't necessarily mean it's easier to get access to services'. Limited resources and sometimes differences in priorities in the spending of these affect what is actually available. In particular, 'there aren't necessarily the resources even to keep the baseline services going'. For example, the GP noted, aids and appliances have been a major problem during the year; social services have 'used up most of their budget by January and we haven't got anything left for aids and appliances'.

Successful resistance to fundholding: the locality purchasing model

The practice took a stand against fund-holding from the start on two main grounds. The first was the preference of the partners for collaboration rather than competition. In the inner city

> there were a lot of professionals going in there who were stressed, who were under pressure. We felt there was a need for those professionals to work more effectively together and support one another more effectively.

The agenda for them was about inter-professional and inter-agency working, not fragmentation through fundholding. The second reason was concern about the sheer cost of fundholding, in terms of administrative costs and other expenditure.

The practice's reservations about GP fundholding were shared by the large majority of practices in the inner city area. They had successfully stood out against this reform and banded together to work out a viable alternative in the form of locality purchasing. Subsequently, they had persuaded the DHA to work more closely with them with the result that each group of a dozen or so practices now has its own representative appointed by the DHA to coordinate their work and manage a locality purchasing budget which will eventually be built up to the level of fundholding.

The locality purchasing model not only gives the group of practices involved more muscle in negotiating with providers of secondary care. It also enables a more collective approach to analysing common problems and devising common strategies in response. The practices in the scheme had recently undertaken a needs assessment in the area, working with local community groups to identify priorities for action.   Collaboration with social services in joint planning and purchasing is a possible next step.

The GP's experience of the post-reform practice

The GP still feels as free as before to speak out about his job and as secure in his post. If there have been more pressures to conform, they have been to apply for fund-holding status, and that they have successfully resisted. He feels somewhat less freedom in *how* he goes about his work because there is greater accountability to the FHSA than there was to the FPC. But he accepts the need for that and does not feel unduly constrained as a result.

However, the stress involved in the job has undoubtedly increased. Indeed, the GP characterizes the ethos of the system now as one of 'survival'. He explained that what he meant by this was survival in the face of:

> Increasing pressure from both sides: in terms of patient-led demand which is perhaps fuelled by things like the Patients' Charter, but equally there is increasing pressure in terms of meeting targets, with the production of various things for management at the centre of it.

The GP mentioned research showing that 50 per cent of GPs were suffering measurable levels of stress and talked of signs of such stress in his own practice:

> There are occasions where the pressure does get very intense and people crack. People blow a fuse. There is just so much less slack in the system than there used to be. There is a limit to how much you can tighten up a system which, at the end of the day, is dealing with people. If it's about production lines and bits of inanimate machinery, then you can make that system fairly efficient. But if you're talking about a system which has got people in it, people have differing expectations.

It is not suprising in this context that the GP rates his current level of job satisfaction rather lower than it was five years ago. There is a need, he thinks, for GPs to consider seriously whether 'we really want to have this level of income if this is the job we're going to be doing and would I rather have less money and a bit more time?'

A way forward

Several improvements are implied in the discussion of the various issues reviewed by the GP. However, a single theme is clearly dominant, that of locality.

> I would go strongly, more and more strongly for locality development. There are

enormous opportunities for involving social services in that and looking at more effective joint commissioning of services. The final agenda is about involving the local community in that and getting agreement with the local community.

His own locality group had already begun to show what was possible with a new project, using some of its locality money earmarked for the care of older people to set up a special team of a GP, a community geriatrician, a social worker, a district nurse, a speech therapist and a physiotherapist. This team has the job of focusing on residential and nursing homes for elderly people and examining the issue of quality of standards. Current evidence suggests this varies widely. Registration and inspection tend to concentrate on bricks and mortar issues. This team will begin to engage with the crucial dimension of process.

3

Working with older people

Both in absolute and proportionate terms the number of older people in the population in Britain has grown significantly over the last hundred years. It is estimated that in 1991 about three million people in the country were between 75 and 84 years old (7 per cent of the population) and about 800,000 were 85 years old or over (1.6 per cent of the population) (Coleman *et al.*, 1993, p.4).

The increasing longevity of the population is a cause for celebration. However, it brings with it new challenges to the health and social services. People over 75 make significantly greater demands on their resources. For instance in 1993–4 the personal social services in England and Wales committed 38 per cent of their gross expenditure to elderly people (CIPFA, 1994) and the incidence of poverty and deprivation amongst elderly people is higher than in other age groups (Walker, 1993).

The case studies focusing on older people in this chapter are all concerned with health care professionals: a geriatrician, a community nurse, a qualified carer in a nursing home and a community psychiatric nurse (CPN). However, all the cases illustrate relationships with social services and the CPN describes the experience of becoming an independent provider of home care services for her local social services department (Case Study 8).

All the studies recount major changes in the work of the interviewees which have resulted from the 1990 Act, most of which, in their views, have led to a deterioration in the services concerned. They appear to demonstrate, in particular, the failure of those who have planned and implemented the changes to understand the interrelatedness of the different parts of the system of services they were reforming. Thus, for example, the requirement for hospital trusts to increase the throughput of patients in turn increases the pressures on the community trusts that must care for the patients on their discharge from hospital but have inadequate resources to cope with larger numbers of sicker patients (Case Study 6). Similarly, the closure of long-term care beds in the hospitals increases the flow of very ill and dying patients to nursing homes, undermining the morale of the staff and the care of the long-term residents (Case Study 7). Nor does the supposed advent of more powerful and rigorous managers succeed in curbing the self-interest of consultants when it clashes with the progressive development of holistic, preventive services popular with the primary carers (Case Study 5).

Case Study 5

The politics of disintegration: the demise of a department of geriatric medicine.
A geriatrician

Background

Geriatrics is the branch of medical science that deals with the health and welfare of old people. Its origins in British medical practice are traced back to the period between the wars when Dr. Marjory Warren worked with the inmates of chronic long-stay workhouse wards. She found that by applying medical assessment with the aim of diagnosis and rehabilitation, many were able to leave these institutions. With the founding of the NHS it became an accepted part of the new service.

The argument for a specialty dealing with a category of patients defined by the ageing process is set out quite fully in this case study by the geriatrician who is its subject. Basically, it is that the problems of the disabled elderly person are typically quite complex and that medical diagnosis and treatment are often not enough.

Until recently practically all acute hospitals had a department of geriatric medicine. The consultants in such departments would normally have, in addition to their own beds in the acute hospital, a number of beds in the smaller community hospitals, providing places for recuperation after an episode in the acute hospital. They also might have their own long stay beds where patients not fit enough for discharge could be placed.

In recent years the position of geriatric medicine has changed in a number of respects. The specialty has lost most of its long-stay beds as the NHS has withdrawn from this provision and the nursing homes have moved in to replace it. The close relationship between the acute departments and the community services has been put under strain with the replacement of organizations integrated under a common district management by separate acute hospital and community health service trusts. More radical still has been the move in an increasing number of acute hospitals for geriatric departments to be integrated with general medical departments and to cease to exist as a separate specialty.

In this case study a geriatrician describes his firsthand experience of these changes and the generally adverse effects he believes they have had on the provision of health services for elderly people in the area in which he works. This is not, however, simply an account of the effects of the implementation of the NHS reforms on a particular area of medicine. It is as much a story of medical politics and the play of ambitions in a period of organizational upheaval, and of how status and security can take precedence over the interests of patients.

The geriatrician, whose view of events this is, has been a consultant for about a decade in an English district general hospital (DGH). About two years ago, under the new arrangements, the hospital became an acute hospital trust.

Before the changes

A philosophy of service

The geriatrician had decided that he wanted to work as a geriatrician since his years as a medical student. He described himself as 'something of a religious geriatrician' in that he *believes* in the good that can be achieved by application of a particular philosophy to the problems associated with disability in old age. He explained:

> The philosophy I have always adopted is that the typical disabled elderly person is complex. Someone who's got more than one thing wrong with them, often the different things interacting together or the treatment for one condition having an effect on another. On top of this are changes in mental state such as depression and confusion as well as the problems carers have in coping. So complexity is obviously the rule.

As a result the geriatrician makes a point of distinguishing the process of diagnosis from that of assessment. Diagnosis is concerned with 'symptoms, physical signs and the results of investigations'. Assessment, as he conceives it, *includes* diagnosis but also 'contains all the add-ons, the extra information one requires to actually describe the full picture'. This is the logical starting point for any health or social service intervention.

Although committed to this approach on the basis of personal experience and philosophy, the geriatrician also sees firm scientific evidence supporting the benefits to be achieved. A large 'meta analysis' incorporating the results of all the relevant research on comprehensive geriatric assessment has demonstrated this quite clearly (Stuck *et al.*, 1993).

The implementation of this policy has major organizational implications, including the need for multidisciplinary teamwork and a close relationship between the hospital department and community services.

The geriatric service in the early 1990s

The geriatrician by this time was clinical manager of his department. He felt he had built up an integrated service for the area covered by his hospital.

> The service integrated the care required in all phases of illness, from the acute phase

(the major doorway to admission for the geriatric service) to rehabilitation and then community follow-up, with community hospitals used for both rehab. and convalescence and, to a limited extent, long term care.

The organization of the service

The geriatric department in the DGH was managed by a team consisting of all the senior staff in the department: the geriatrician (as clinical manager), the two other consultant geriatricians, a nurse manager, two sisters from the acute wards and one from the day hospital, a senior physiotherapist, an occupational therapist, a social worker, and a business manager. This team met on alternate weeks and addressed all issues relevant to the department. In addition a weekly business meeting was held, including the clinical manager, senior nurse and business manager. The style of management was based on consensus and all decisions taken were subject to discussion, often over a protracted period.

The department had two wards in the DGH, together with a day hospital and out-patient clinics. Each consultant also had a number of beds in the community hospitals. The allocation of cases to consultant was by geographical area. In this way consultants could build up a knowledge of their patients over time, as well as of the range of community services available in their area.

Referrals to the department were, at this time, entirely a matter of GP choice. They could choose between sending their patients who were over 75 years old to the geriatric department or to the general medical department.

The service in operation and its advantages

The admissions procedure to the hospital involved the GP phoning a doctor on the team of the consultant responsible for his or her area and arranging for the patient to come in. Where an admission was made out of normal working hours, admission would be to whichever team the admitting doctor belonged with a transfer to the geographically appropriate team the next day.

The geriatrician described what he saw as the advantages of this system:

> First of all, the GP chose who should be under me. I believe that there is no one better placed not only to judge the immediate needs of an acutely ill patient but also to predict the resources which will be required to organize discharge. Second, it provided a high degree of continuity of care both within one episode of illness and between episodes. Once the philosophy of detailed holistic assessment has been applied, much of that assessment remains valid for the lifetime of that patient. Of course, this applies not only to the medical details of the patient but also to the patient's family and carers. Efforts made at an early stage bore fruit, sometimes many years later, and allowed a sense of trust to develop. In addition if errors were made, for example with discharge arrangements, there was a near certainty that if something went wrong, they'd automatically come back under me and I could learn from the mistake. This system also had the advantage of allowing me to become very well acquainted with GPs and other key community staff and to

be able to have a clear overall view of the service needs in my area.

Continuity of care was therefore one of the key features determining quality of care.

As a result of this method, complemented with close cooperation with services in the community, the geriatrician was able to achieve a shorter stay in hospital for his patients and a higher rate of discharge directly to the patient's home, rather than to a community hospital before discharge, compared to his colleagues.

The success of the department and the problems that it created

The clearest evidence that the department's methods and service was appreciated lay in the GPs' preference for it over the alternative of the general medical department. As the geriatrician put it:

> The GPs had a free choice and this tended to be on the geriatricians' side, such that we were not only getting a lot of frail elderly but also a lot of 'fit' elderly with, for example, heart attacks and so on. We were victims of our own success in that the workload of the geriatric department built up, its bed occupancy rate was very high, and at times it could only cope by overflowing into the general medical department. In the winter months anything up to between ten and twenty general medical beds were being used for care of the elderly. Unfortunately, one consequence of this was that the team approach, with doctors, nurses, therapists and social workers sharing joint assessments, could not be applied. Paradoxically, quality of care became impossible to achieve as a direct result of the success of the department. Our inability to provide an adequate quality of care for our own patients in a situation which was obvious to the general physicians, greatly weakened our position in the ensuing negotiations. It now seems tragic that our failure to solve this problem resulted in the destruction of what was otherwise a high quality service. In retrospect it is clear that an agreement to limit a consultant's responsibility to within his own ward, that is not to have accepted patients as 'outliers', would have been far preferable.

The geriatrician's personal experience of the job

Overall, the geriatrician enjoyed his work and got considerable satisfaction from being able to offer patients what he felt was a high quality service. He felt secure in his post and able to speak his mind about his work without constraint. The ethos in the department was one which 'clearly related to the frail elderly group who needed a special service that was multi-disciplinary and holistic'. There were frustrations from the excessive workload. There was also a perceived danger for some patients in that referral to a geriatric department might mean they would miss out on other medical expertise they might need. But his general experience of the job was clearly positive.

Change

About two years ago the decision was taken to integrate the geriatric department with the general medical department and the high quality system of care developed over several years by the geriatrician was effectively abandoned. In the view of the geriatrician, three factors in particular played a major part in bringing about this decision: the success of the geriatric service itself; the existence of an alternative model which was being promoted quite widely in the country as a whole; and a lack of external control over what he saw as the self-interest and ambitions of the consultant, general physicians and the other geriatricians.

Victims of their own success

The positive image of the geriatric department with the community services was reflected in the high referral rate from GPs. This created increased workloads for the geriatricians and all their staff and resulted in the overflows from the department into the beds of the general medical department. For the geriatrician,

> The obvious solution was that we should have resources from them, that we should be given an additional ward, an extra consultant and more junior doctors. Clearly, that was very threatening to the general physicians.

The alternative, it seemed to the geriatrician, since there was no prospect of getting the general physicians to give up resources in favour of geriatrics, was to find ways of

> juggling with the admissions policy to see whether we could reduce the number of people who came to the care of the elderly and increase the number that went to medicine. Instead of matching resources to patients, which is clearly what should have happened, we were shifting patients to resources.

This could be achieved, the geriatrician thought, if the geriatrics department restricted admissions to frail elderly people (the disabled or potentially disabled), who should be its core group anyway, and the people who were previously fit and not disabled but simply had a medical need – perhaps pneumonia or a chest pain – should go to general medicine. This solution would have had the additional advantage of dealing with the criticism over access to other medical expertise.

At the heart of such a change of policy was the need to define the client group for which the geriatric service was intended. If there was one single reason for the eventual demise of the department it was the failure of the three consultant geriatricians to agree on this matter. To the study geriatrician it was obvious that a specialized service could only be justified on the basis of providing a high quality of care for a client group with needs which were in some way defined as special. Unfortunately however, his two colleagues found this solution 'totally unacceptable'.

They both felt that association with a full range of acute medical specialties, not just the frail elderly, was vital, as I would put it, for their status. The cynical, or maybe the realistic way of saying this is that if you've got patients who are perceived as second rate, then the staff who work with them are then perceived as second rate also.

The integrated model of hospital care

An alternative solution was suggested to the geriatrician's colleagues in his department and the general medical department by the promotion of a model of hospital treatment integrating geriatrics and general medicine. The idea of integration of geriatric with general medicine is associated with the name of Professor Grimley Evans in Newcastle upon Tyne (Grimley Evans, 1983). It involved pairing consultants from general medicine and geriatrics, with shared teams of junior doctors. In this way, it was argued, elderly people would benefit from both kinds of expertise.

The model had been developed in a teaching hospital where there were sufficient consultants in the two specialties to create such joint teams. In these circumstances, in that it should bring a wider range of expertise to bear on each case, the model had much to recommend it. However, in the typical district general hospital, (or, later, acute hospital trust) such staffing levels might not exist and there was evidently a risk that instead of joint teams of general physicians and geriatricians caring for all the elderly patients, the geriatricians would simply be absorbed into the new integrated departments in the role of general physicians and there would no longer be any guarantee that all patients with special needs would be seen by a geriatrician.

Although initially the geriatrician favoured retention of departmental autonomy, it became evident that the lack of common objectives with his consultant colleagues made this impossible. He therefore came to favour a policy of full integration, according to the Newcastle model. To be successful this required the support of all the consultants involved. He also advocated nursing mechanisms within the acute hospital and a new community geriatrician post to compensate for the loss of service which would result from the change of policy. Unfortunately not only was the full model of integration not implemented, but these other conditions were not met.

The interests of the consultants

In the view of the geriatrician a key factor in the decision to integrate his department with the general medicine department was the attitude of the consultants in that department and of his two geriatrician colleagues. It was important to see these attitudes in the context of the low standing that geriatrics tended to have in the medical pecking order:

> The history of geriatric medicine is that it comes through the poor laws and the work houses, whereas general medicine comes through the voluntary hospitals. There's always been this question of status, that a geriatric consultant is lower status than a general physician, so generally attaching a lower value to us.

The geriatrician found that his two colleagues were attracted to the idea of integration with the general medical department. He believed this was not only because of the workload problems of the department but also because 'they both had personal ambitions within the hospital where to be in with the general physicians favoured these aspirations'. One of them, in particular, he felt wanted the 'kudos' of the general physician.

> Being one of a small group of three consultants who spend a lot of time in the community in a somewhat peripheral activity is different from being one of a large department. In fact, as soon as this change took place, he changed the title on his notepaper to general physician and stopped calling himself a geriatrician. Clearly, to have achieved that status change for him was vitally important.

The attitude of the general physicians was grounded, in the geriatrician's opinion, in a complete lack of understanding and sympathy for his holisitic approach. 'They think I'm completely mad. They simply don't understand what I'm talking about.' When he had tried to explain his philosophy to them they muttered 'that I was doing the GPs' work'. One reason that the care of the elderly service was not valued by the general physicians was that they were not users of the service.

> A few of their people who develop strokes or severe disability they might have referred for rehabilitation but it would be no more than two or three a month, if that, and some of them virtually never referred.

Given these views on geriatric medicine, the general physicians could see no objections to the integration of general medicine and geriatrics and welcomed the extra resources it would bring.

The geriatrician's attempt to defend his specialty

The geriatrician could not persuade his colleagues of his view that the integration of the specialties would have adverse effects on the care of elderly people. So he attempted to prevent the change by other means.

> I tried various last ditch methods to stop it happening. I contacted the Regional Health Authority who agreed at one stage to invite the Health Advisory Service (HAS) in but this was then overturned at a higher level. Eventually the District Health Authority agreed to this and a preliminary visit took place. I have never, despite repeated requests, seen their report but I am told that they were very concerned by what they saw. But their advice was *advice* to the trust and basically the local managers paid no heed to it whatsoever. They considered it all a total waste of time. HAS offered to return and carry out a full enquiry but no further action was undertaken.

The District Health Authority was almost completely absent from the negotiations between the two departments. Although some of the health authority officers were verbally supportive, only one meeting was held with no subsequent action.

> This was all happening at a time when the role of the DHA was changing, first by its new 'purchaser' role and second by proposed amalgamation with the FHSA and the neighbouring DHA to form an entirely new authority. The senior officers were understandably preoccupied with these changes and seemed completely unable to focus on this issue. Although their local health policy documents referred to services for the frail and disabled elderly, they were unable to specify the service they required in the form of a contract or service agreement.

The third possible external influence was the GPs' local organization. On the basis of their referral habits it was reasonable to assume that the GPs would have supported the maintenance of the service. But

> the GPs have enough troubles of their own and although they would individually express great concern at what was going on, collectively they seemed completely ineffectual. In any case, the way the matter was handled within the trust, they were given no opportunity even to express an opinion ... As far as the senior officers in the trust were concerned, when the new chief executive and new chairman were appointed, I went to see them. They appeared concerned about the issues but played no active part in the discussions.

The general physicians were in a powerful position to promote the move to integration, holding the key positions of chairperson in the local medical executive and the hospital management committee, and later the medical director in the new trust. When nothing came of his attempts to get external bodies to intervene, and when his two geriatrician colleagues gave their open support to the general physicians, he decided there was little point in continuing the fight and resigned his appointment as clinical manager of the department. The integration of the two departments then went ahead.

The integrated department

The organization of the new department

In the integrated department, all the consultants (both general physicians and geriatricians) treat patients of all ages. The geographical allocation of patients has been abandoned (after a twelve-month phasing out period). Now the geriatrician becomes responsible for a particular patient according to the day he happens to be on call. He is as likely to find himself treating a twenty-year old asthma patient from any part of the county as an elderly person from a particular area. Further, although the Grimley Evans model was quoted in the arguments for change, joint teams of general physicians and geriatricians were never set up. The geriatricians do continue to have their own rehabilitation beds in the community hospitals and there are some 'secondary' referrals of cases from the other consultants, mainly on the basis of difficulty discharging the patient, rather than according to assessed need for a particular service. But most frail elderly patients now do not get to see a geriatrician since there are more general physicians than geriatricians.

Consequences of the reorganization

For most of the consultants the reorganization has been experienced as positive. The larger number of consultants means that each one of them is less frequently on call. The general physicians have inherited the resources of the geriatric department and no longer have the humiliation of facing the evidence that GPs tended to prefer the services offered by that department to theirs. The two geriatricians who supported the change have raised their status and made it easier to follow their ambitions within the hospital.

However, in the view of the case study geriatrician, the change has been predominantly detrimental to the interests of the elderly patient. First, the GPs no longer get to choose between the general medical and geriatrics departments. Second, the predominant method of treatment becomes that of the traditional medical model focused on diagnosis of the presenting problem, rather than the holistic approach which the geriatrician argues is much more appropriate for the elderly patient. The general physicians 'are quite happy to manage the frail elderly: if they come in, give them antibiotics and send them home again'. Finally, most elderly patients are not only not being seen by a geriatrician; as a result they are also being denied access to the other services still controlled by them.

> Previously 30 to 40 per cent of my patients would have gone on to a community hospital where they may have stayed for anything from a week or two to several months for convalescence, rehabilitation and discharge planning. A high proportion of those people no longer come under my care and therefore do not have access because the access is only through me.

A further negative consequence for community services of these changes was a fall in the utilization of the geriatricians' beds in the community hospitals and ultimately a loss of several of these beds.

The creation of the trusts and its consequences

The period during which the integration of the general medicine and geriatrics departments was being debated was also the time when plans for the organization of the acute hospital trust and the community trust were being developed. The pressures and complexities of the change from district health managed services to trust management created an unstable environment in which, in the geriatrician's view, it was easier to push the integration of the two departments through.

Further, the subsequent consolidation of the separate trust organizations for the acute hospital and the community has led to rivalry and competition between the two which has made the maintenance of any kind of continuity in treatment between the acute hospital and the community infinitely more difficult.

> Clearly, in terms of service, what one requires is a high degree of cooperation between the two. But the opposite has occurred – they see themselves as rivals. There have been several examples of active non-cooperation between the two, justified as 'conflict of interest'.

The geriatrician put the rivalry down partly to what he called the psychology of management. With newly appointed managers 'you get what is really a sort of muscle flexing'. This could lead to petty minded decisions with adverse effects on staff and the services they could provide for patients. The rivalry could become much further developed, the geriatrician thought, since basically the two trusts were vying for the same limited cake provided by the district health authority. An aggressive community trust might well seek to provide in their community hospitals many of the services currently offered in the acute hospitals. Conversely, managers in the acute trust tend to place a low value on community services and would be only too pleased to gain control with a view to diverting resources into acute services.

At the same time the decline in overall planning for the medical needs of elderly people has reached its nadir. From a situation ten years ago 'where we had highly focused specific planning' it has moved to a 'very chaotic situation' today 'where a specific client group is no longer identified or planned for'.

The geriatrician's personal experience and evaluation of the changes

The geriatrician is in no doubt about the sharp decline in the quality of services available to elderly people in the area his hospital serves as a result of the changes of the last few years and the abolition of the department of geriatric medicine. For him personally this has been a depressing and difficult time. The ethos in the hospital now, he feels, is determined in a setting governed by irrational forces, and so is characterized by people trying to make head or tail of what is happening and to justify it. His specialty has gone and he is doing a job he doesn't want to do. He no longer has the freedom to do the job to his own satisfaction. He feels his job is much less secure, not only because it is well known that he is unhappy in his post and would rather move to the community trust, but also because his contract is no longer held by the DHA with the assumptions of career-long tenure but by the medical director of his own hospital with whom he has crossed swords in attempting to keep his department alive. Nor does he now feel so free to speak out about his work for he has experienced overt attempts to stop him doing so. For example, when his plan to give a paper on his personal view of these events to a professional conference was retailed to the medical director, he was forbidden to give the paper.

A way ahead

The geriatrician feels that the needs of elderly people demand that his specialty should be reinvented. It may not be possible to do this under the old title. With

> what I see as the demise of geriatric medicine and the whole problem of ageism and using age as a criterion, my approach increasingly now is to call it a disability service and the next phase of our service development is going to be an adult disability service.

More immediately, still working with his focus on elderly patients, he believes it should be possible for geriatricians to work much more closely and effectively with community services to intervene early in cases and substantially reduce the proportion of acute hospital admissions necessary for this group. If successful, such a programme would be a decisive move towards shifting resources from acute hospitals to the community and to the development of preventive practice. Perhaps the ultimate irony of his situation is that he feels the trust is trying to prevent him from developing this new model of service. He attributes the reason simply to 'malice'. 'I am a minority of one in the acute hospital and I am known to be hostile to what has happened there.'

Case Study 6

Quicker and sicker: the impact of change on community nursing.
A community nurse

Background

Community nurses provide nursing care for people living in their own homes. Formerly known as district nurses, they complete training to the level of registered nurses and then undertake an additional year of training to qualify them to work in the community. Until the changes introduced by the 1990 Act, they were employed by district health authorities. Today most of them are part of community health trusts and are contracted to provide services to the patients of a general practice. Their referrals are mainly from the general practice concerned, or from hospitals when patients still needing nursing care are discharged. They also take referrals directly from relatives and from home care if patients are having problems.

This case study describes the experience of a community nurse with eleven years' experience in her job. It begins by focusing on her work before the recent changes in organization and the increased pressures of work which have accompanied them. It then outlines the changes and describes the community nurse's impression of their impact.

The central significance of this case study is its account of how the changes of the last few years have relentlessly increased workloads and stress and diminished the rewards of the job. The study also shows clearly how the quality of inter-professional and inter-organizational relationships has declined and contributed to the problems faced by the community nurse.

Community nursing before the changes

Setting and organization

In 1990 the community nurse worked in a community nursing team, part of the nursing service of the local district health authority, which was responsible for the patients of a large general practice serving a mixed urban and rural area, with a substantial retirement population. There were four community nursing sisters (CNs), four state enrolled nurses (SENs) with district nurse training and four auxiliaries. Each CN had her own patch and her own small sub-team of an SEN and an auxiliary. The team, which worked from a clinic close to the

general practice, was managed by a senior nurse. She was based in a neighbouring town but would come out every week to chair a meeting of the nurses
and discuss any management matters with them.

Most work was referred to the nurses either by the general practitioners or
directly by the hospitals when one of the general practitioners' patients was
discharged and needed some continuing nursing care. While the nurses did work
for the practice, they were not employed by it and exercised independent judgement about cases, when they felt it was necessary.

> We did blood tests for the doctors, dressing for the doctors, assessments for the
> doctors, but we weren't their handmaidens. If we didn't agree with something that
> they requested, say for example an enema, when perhaps the patient hadn't been
> seen by the doctor, we'd go in there and say 'I think this patient should be seen'. We
> weren't like puppets and we aren't like puppets.

The daily round

The community nurse would plan out her day and that of her SEN and auxiliary
colleagues in advance. She would alternate the calls between herself and the SEN
so that she was in touch with all the patients on her patch. The day started officially at 8.45 am and finished at 5.30 pm. It might involve visiting between a
dozen and fifteen patients. She went straight from home to her first call, because
'if you go into the surgery you tend to get delayed there' but would call in later
in the day to pick up any messages and requests for visits for the next day. She
planned her breaks round the pattern of the day:

> You're meant to pull over to the side of the road and have a break in the morning.
> But I tend to work it in with one of my visits where they make the best cups of tea
> – when it's an advice and support type of visit when people like you to have a cup
> of tea with them.

Her lunch break was an opportunity to catch up on paperwork.

Typical cases

Most cases involved relatively short calls at this time. Typical cases involved
blood tests and injections, and also dressing leg ulcers. The community nurse
would also monitor cases on the bath list. People coming out of hospital would
be visited but, because they seemed to be in hospital longer then, they would
come out without the problems which are more common now. 'A referral to
"check wound" would *be* a "check wound" and that would be all.'

There were then also more of what the team called 'general nursing calls'
when the community nurse went in and washed and dressed a patient. This was
partly because they had such a high number of cases needing bathing and general
nursing care and there were not enough auxiliaries to cover it all. But in the
community nurse's view it was important that she should do such visits because

it was difficult to assess patients properly without them.

> It's very difficult to just go in and look at a patient who's dressed and sat in a chair and call that a full assessment. To really assess a patient you have got to see them when you're washing them or whatever, and you see their mobility and everything doing that."

The community nurse's evaluation of the job

The main limitation to the job at this time, in the community nurse's view, was that they needed more auxiliary help. Working in a retirement area the lists of people needing help were building up and building up 'and they were not going to get any better, so it was a continuing thing'. Otherwise, she felt she could do a good job. 'In those days you were more in control of what happened to the patients. I was sort of in charge'. The community nurse felt she was secure in her job. She could speak out if she wanted to but didn't need to so much then. 'I don't think I was so bolshy then as I am now.'

She was positive about her manager. 'She was very good. She was strict but she was understanding at the same time.' The team now miss her regular weekly meetings with them when 'you could vent your feelings rather than have them build up after so many weeks'. Describing the ethos of the team at that time she said: 'We wanted good care for the patients' and remarked that they were not so swamped by paperwork that it was impossible to give it. 'Now,' she added, 'they talk about standards of care and quality of care and all this, that and the other, but people are so busy writing about it that they've got no time to do it! It all seems a bit crazy to me.'

The Changes

For the community nurse, the important changes in the formal structure of her work and her profession during the last few years were: the new organization of community care; the restructuring of the health service; a new grading for nurses; and the increased in-service training requirements for nurses.

While the overall organizational reforms had the greatest impact, the changes in grading and training added their own complications. The new grading system seemed complex to the community nurse and had created numerous anomalies so that, for example, 'in the hospital two sisters working alongside could both be different grades. It turned nurse against nurse and there were appeals'. The community nurse welcomed the increased emphasis on training to update nurses' skills and to enable SENs to become Registered General Nurses. The problem, though, was the failure to provide the additional resources to facilitate this:

> It's a good thing, but they're not providing the resources, they're not replacing the nurses who aren't in the community or on the wards when they're out doing studying.

The changes involving community care and the structure of the health service have made their impact more gradually. The most immediate organizational change was the replacement of the DHA by two separate bodies, an acute hospital trust and a community trust. The nurses were now part of the latter. It has made little immediate difference to the day-to-day management of their work except that they have lost the regular contact they had with the hierarchy above them. The senior nurse who used to supervise the team through regular weekly meetings has retired and the manager who has replaced her is too pressured to have the time to continue with the meetings. A further change has been the granting of fund-holding status to the general practice which the nurses service. Again, this had made no direct impact on the nurses pattern of work so far. However, the doctors did make an attempt to get the nurses to contract their services through a neighbouring trust which had apparently offered to provide the service more cheaply. The team had resisted and the proposal had been dropped but had left them feeling insecure about their future.

The changing working world of the community nurse

The community nurse's daily round remains, on the surface, much as it was five years ago. She continues to be responsible for planning her work and that of her SEN and auxiliary colleagues working in her patch. But over the intervening years the *experience* of her daily work and that of her team has altered quite dramatically as circumstances in their environment have altered. These changes relate in particular, in the community nurse's view, to changes in discharge practice from hospitals, resource issues, relations with social services, staffing matters, and the build up of pressure and stress. Combined, these factors have taken much of the satisfaction out of her job and led her to take an openly critical view within the trust that employs her.

Changing hospital discharge practice

Before the community care reforms it was normal for the community nurses to be fully involved in all cases needing their intervention. The hospital would send through a message requesting an assessment and the patient would be visited either on the day of discharge or the following morning.

Under the new arrangements, in many cases packages of care are prepared by a social worker in the hospital or by somebody appointed as case manager for the particular patient. As a result, the community nurse has found, there is no longer any certainty that patients needing her help will be referred to her. If the case is a clear cut medical one the referral will still come through from hospital nurse to community nurse but where a package of social care is to be arranged, the hospital social worker has the lead role and medical needs may be misunderstood or overlooked. 'They are not seeing the caring as a skilled task ... and the home care girls, as wonderful as they are, are not skilled.' The community nurse is now finding she is getting some referrals from home care managers *after* people have been discharged from hospital like the terminally ill man 'where I heard about him because the home care girl found he had a colostomy and didn't know what to do with it'.

Some other referrals provide quite inadequate information and reveal care packages in place which suggest to the community nurse that the social workers constructing them have failed to understand the needs of the patient. The community nurse gave an example of a woman she was asked to visit after her discharge from hospital with the request to 'check bowels', something which could normally be completed within half an hour. She arrived to find an 80-year-old woman who 'was a severe stroke patient. She was chair-fast, in other words she couldn't stand'. On top of this she was heavy (over twelve stone) and by EU regulations required three people to lift her. Her husband himself was over 80 and could not help.

> The care package involved one home care girl going in in the morning and one at night and a private agency carer going in the same, morning and night, at the week-ends and we'd not been informed at all although the woman needed a full nursing assessment. It was a catastrophe.

In the worst instances patients

> are discharged and there's been no preparations made at all. None at all. They are just sent home. And what happens is that they end up going back a few days later. But it looks very good for statistics. Virginia Bottomley's having champagne when that happens because it looks wonderful. But it's no good for the patients.

The other change in discharge practice which has become increasingly apparent is that, since patients are staying in hospital for shorter periods and less convalescent care is available, when they are discharged they often need more intensive care from the CNs.

> Quicker and sicker discharges, as we often call them. Things do take longer, the visits do take longer and I think sometimes patients, when they're in hospital now, the nurses haven't got the time to give the advice that perhaps they did in the past. So that when we go, and it's one to one, they need that advice and support, so that can be time consuming.

Diminishing resources

While the throughput of hospitals was being increased, the resources needed to cope with it, in the community nurse's view, were either static or diminishing. Long stay beds in NHS hospitals were being closed. It was now planned to close the local community hospital, although it was not only valuable for convalescence and respite care, but much more acceptable to some patients 'who will agree to go in there when they will not go to the acute hospital'.

Getting hold of the aids that are essential to enable some people to manage at home – zimmer frames, bath board and bath seats, for example – has become much more difficult and long drawn out. In one example given by the community nurse a patient 'had gone off her legs and it was 4 o'clock on a Friday afternoon and I needed a zimmer there and then'. She rang social services, whose job it is to provide such aids. 'They said it would arrive by next Wednesday. The poor woman died by the following Tuesday.' For other aids an assessment by an occupational therapist is needed and you find there may be a six months waiting list for this.

Another aspect of the resources problem, in the community nurse's experience, was the cutback in hours of social carers. In one case, one of her patients had her home care reduced from half an hour to fifteen minutes. 'Fifteen minutes to light the fire, do breakfast, help the patient dress and give emotional support.' The community nurse urged the patient to write to protest and her half hour was restored but she asked 'What about the people who don't write ?'

Beleaguered social services

The community nurse found it increasingly difficult to work with social services, not because of any hostilty but because they seemed to be overwhelmed. A lot of her time

> was spent trying to contact social services and trying to arrange things and banging my head against a brick wall because I couldn't get assessments done. I couldn't even get to speak to the social worker.

Yet without the assessment such practical things as bath boards and bath seats were not available and without those she couldn't send a nursing auxiliary in to bath somebody. She also found now that as a self-protecting device, social service staff are very reluctant to put anything in writing: 'They won't put it in writing, nothing ever is in writing, because you've got them over a barrel.'

Increasing pressure and stress in the community nursing team

The effect of the deteriorating working conditions of the team has told in the build up of pressure and stress. Unlike social services, who have a waiting list for their services, the community nurses have no way of controlling the rising demands for their work. As the community nurse put it,

> Everywhere that you look at has a waiting list. But we don't and we just keep absorbing and absorbing calls. It's just taking it out of the nurses because it is just putting more and more pressure.

As a result, she said, they can't meet the standards they are supposed to achieve. They are meant to visit within 24 hours of referral but simply haven't the resources to do so. In her view unless staffing is increased, these commitments should be withdrawn. As it is

> you're squashed in the middle of providing a wonderful standard of care for so many patients as well as having to do your paperwork to say you provided that standard of care as well as updating yourself. All these things are just closing in.

The impact on the team is to create 'a lot of confrontations in the office because you feel completely stressed'. There is no opportunity to talk to management about it 'because they are stressed too'. The health of the team is affected and more people are away sick, more often. 'And if people are not sick, they are showing signs of stress. People are getting irate'. She has discussed stress with others in the team and admitted 'waking up at 4 o'clock in the morning, I work through all my patients, I work through all my calls. I should have done this or that for that patient'. She found that they all do the same and that one girl hardly ever sleeps for worrying. She believes that as a result of stress 'the job suffers. I think some people don't put their heart into the job any more'.

Role dilution: a management solution

The response of management to the growing pressures of the job seemed to be to try to find ways of increasing the role taken by the unqualified nursing auxiliaries. The community nurse said she was being asked if there were any of the jobs she undertook that she could pass on to her auxiliary.

> Because they are bringing in the NVQ they are trying to say, 'Couldn't you teach the nursing auxiliaries to take blood? Couldn't you let them do dressings?' Well you could, you could hand over all your care. But ultimately who would suffer?

The community nurse felt that while there might be a case for extending the role of auxiliaries in a hospital setting where their work could be overseen by qualified nurses who would also be keeping an eye on the condition of the patient, that could not be accepted in the community where the auxiliary would be on her own and unsupervised when treating the patient. She gave the example of dressing a leg ulcer. An auxiliary might be trained to do such a dressing but much more is involved in good nursing.

> When I go into a patient's house, just to do a leg ulcer, I'm looking for signs of infection, I'm seeing if they've had a reaction to the dressing that they had on before, I'm seeing if it's healing. I'm looking at the patient as a whole. I'm doing things you don't write down.

All of this requires knowledge and skills that go far beyond the process of changing a dressing and which are essential for the effective treatment of the patient. For such reasons the community nurses in her team were not prepared to agree to the devolvement of these aspects of their work to the auxiliaries.

Fighting back: the community nurses demand action

Some of the CNs took their response to their deteriorating conditions of work to direct confrontation with the general practitioners and management. One of the CNs, in desperation, has informed the GPs on a number of occasions that the district nurses are too busy to take extra calls. 'But the GPs don't appear to see it as their problem. Besides, they are all overworked and stressed themselves.'

However, the community nurse has also been driven to the point where she feels she must go beyond such token action and make her concerns officially known. When she has raised problems of work stress informally, all she has heard from management has been 'There isn't any money, there isn't any money. I wake up screaming "There isn't any money!"' The time for conforming, in her view, is over.

> I think if patients are suffering and colleagues are suffering, I have been pushed into a corner now, and I feel something has got to be done.

In the past, she recognized, nurses would 'fight for patients' rights but they've lost their fight'. Possibly this was because their solidarity had been broken by the new grading and many 'now think of themselves and beggar the rest'. Whatever the cause, she felt that 'now nurses are afraid'.

Nevertheless, the community nurse began to write to management about her concerns, in spite of warnings from a colleague who felt she risked being branded as a 'trouble maker.'

> The first letter I wrote, I had this rage in me and I just felt, I am not a great believer in God but I thought this is a sign, this rage. I went and typed like crazy and I just sent it straight away.

Her first letter expressed her concerns about increasing workloads, less and less time for each patient, no time to write-up her records, growing problems in collaborating with social services who are facing similar problems, and her resulting concerns for the adverse effect on patients and nurses. After several months she wrote again, this time emphasizing her concerns for her patients' and colleagues' well-being as stress levels were becoming unbearable.

The response she received suggested that the team should undertake an analysis of nurses' caseloads. But by then a few members of the team had left for other jobs and the remaining nurses were so overstretched covering for them that there was no time even to meet to discuss the proposal. So things became worse rather than better.

The community nurse's evaluation of the job

The community nurse now gets very little satisfaction from the job. She characterized the current ethos as one of 'gloom'.

> People are just so fed up I don't think there's anybody, including the GPs, who's not

just completely had enough of it all. You are not providing this wonderful care they say you should be providing. It's frustration. We are definitely all burnt out. There's a lot of anger because we are the ones facing it, the ones having to go out and say, 'We haven't got it, we can't provide it'. The senior managers and politicians are up there away from it all.

Ways of improving the service

'You feel you need to throw everything out as it is and put it all back !' was the community nurse's predominant feeling about improvements. At the same time 'you need the people at the top to listen to the people on the front line'. At present it seems they just want to cut things back all the time to save money.

Apart from the major issues of providing better organization and adequate resources for the caring services, the community nurse had three specific proposals for improvements. The first concerned the involvement of CNs in hospital discharge.

> Community sisters should be allowed the time to go up to the hospitals to be included in the assessment of patients, to be included in the preparations of care packages.

Her second suggestion related to closer links with home carers, currently separately managed by social services.

> The home care girls are providing hands on care. Community nursing sisters are the experts in hands on care. So they should be based with the community nursing sisters.

Thirdly, she felt that community nurses should become closely involved in the residential homes on their patches. 'Going in, visiting, developing a friendship with staff in these places, and trust' would be a better way of raising standards rather than relying on inspectors whom people tend to fear and hide problems from.

Case Study 7

'Where else can I go?' The effects of the
Community Care changes on the regime of a
nursing home.
A qualified carer

Background

For many elderly people too frail and dependent to cope at home or to be
accepted as residents in residential care, the nursing home may be the place
where they spend the last years of their lives.

The changes introduced by the 1990 Act were intended to ensure that only after a
thorough assessment by social services could an elderly person be supported in residential care at public expense. The preferred goal, wherever possible, would be to
provide care to people in their own homes. The early impact of the changes, when
the relevant provisions of the Act were introduced in 1993, was to reduce the
numbers of new admissions to residential homes and, in some instances such as the
case study reported here, to increase the proportion of very ill patients in nursing
homes.

This case study describes what happened in one private nursing home as the
Act began to be implemented and the home concerned started to experience
problems in filling its beds. The case study illustrates how the operation of the
social market can lead to unwelcome consequences for the regime of the home
including a marked deterioration of standards of care. The study also raises
issues concerning the nature of the regimes in such homes and the difficulties
facing staff as well as patients, residents, and their relatives in criticizing and
changing them if those in charge become no longer effective in providing an
acceptable level of care.

This account is based on the experience of a qualified carer (referred to
throughout as the carer) who worked part-time in the home for nearly five years
and saw the changes being introduced.

The nursing home before the changes

The home has beds for 30 patients; it is privately run. Before the changes trig-
gered by the 1990 Act it drew most of its patients from the local area. The
majority of them were physically disabled, typically as a result of a stroke or a
heart condition. However, only two or three patients were mentally impaired and

showing the early signs of dementia. About half the patients had their own room; the others shared with one other person.

The daily pattern of life in the home

The carer described the pattern of life in the home at that time:

> They'd be got up and have their breakfasts at about 8.30. During the morning there'd be the physical side of things seen to – all the bathing and everything would be sorted out in the morning. And they would have their coffee and read their papers. They didn't do an awful lot in the morning. Sometimes the staff would do a little bit of movement to music or something like that.

In the afternoons

> they used to have visitors, quite a few visitors would come in. There was very little else. At about 4.30 it was tea time. Most of them had televisions in their own rooms or they could stay in the main lounge if they wanted to.

The quality of care

In the carer's view the physical quality of care in the home at this time was good, although she had reservations about social aspects of the regime which, in her opinion, restricted the quality of life of its residents.

> When I first went there it was considered one of the better places, definitely, if you needed that sort of care. It was a good quality of care. The food was excellent. There were never any grumbles about the food. In fact, we were encouraged to do a questionnaire about their favourite recipes. And that was encouraged by the kitchen staff and by the management so that they got feedback about what people liked. On the comfort side, it was a comfortable home. Homely and clean. Everyone was well cared for, well groomed.

The reputation of the home in the local area was good and there was always a waiting list of potential residents.

However, for the carer, some aspects of the physical treatment of patients were undesirable and the social life of the home was impoverished by the over-protective, paternalistic and closed character of the regime and a lack of understanding of the psychological needs of patients.

Her concerns about the physical treatment of patients related mainly to inconsiderateness sometimes exhibited by the staff. She did not feel that care assistants were unkind. They seemed to want to do the best they could. It was simply that they 'just didn't know any better'.

> They weren't actually rough but coarse-mannered. They'd upset the patients, shout back at the patients, move a patient without telling them and it would make the patient jump. Or they'd put something down in front of the patient or throw something into their lap or something and make the patients jump. They might laugh or make a joke of the patients at inappropriate times.

When the carer complained to the management she was likely to get the hopeless response of 'What can we do about it?' Communication between the low-paid and mainly unqualified care assistants and management was poor and relationships were not made better by the contrasts in their terms of services and working conditions.

In terms of the social life of patients, the carer felt that over-protectiveness was reflected in a desire to avoid risk. For instance, on behalf of a particular patient, the carer asked that she should be allowed to make drinks in her own room, because she felt it would benefit her. The management refused on the grounds that it was too much of a risk. The closed nature of the home may have also been related to risk in that the matron discouraged activities which took the patients into the outside world, although she was happy to allow people to come into the home to enrich its social life. But this aspect of the regime also seemed to be linked to a curious notion of fairness. When the carer was trying to arrange trips for residents she found the attitude of management was 'that it wasn't fair that some of them were allowed to be taken out and others were not well enough to go'.

These attitudes were consistent with the carer's view that management's conception of care was mainly confined to the physical – good food, good accommodation, cleanliness and safety. The possibility that patients might have other needs beyond the passive entertainment offered by television seemed to escape them.

The work of the carer

The carer saw it as her role to try to help fill the gap in the lives of patients left by this largely physical approach to their care. She attempted to do this both by the activities she introduced into the home and by developing richer links between the home and the local community.

Inside the home she worked both with individual patients and with groups. She contacted the local hospital so that she could back up what they were doing for individual patients.

> Each time I would see everybody because I felt it was very important to make that contact. For some that was what they needed more than anything else, just the contact. I'd bring them things in that they were asking for. I'd do the library, I'd bring tapes, talking books and things like that. I set up all that. For some that was what was needed.
>
> For others, and that was quite a large number to begin with, they needed to be in a group and feel the support, the group support. We did a lot of reminiscence work. We did movement, a movement session. I'd sometimes organize games for stimulation. We started cooking sessions. It was a case of getting the wheelchairs sorted out and the stroke patients needed a lot of assistance but it was so rewarding when they made their own things. Just the smell of being in the kitchen again. And there was a lady who was very keen on gardening and I took her in little cuttings.

Externally, the carer set up

> a lot of different things to involve the community in the home – concerts, schools, to try and draw the community in. I managed to take patients out a number of times to different things in the community.

Staff attitudes to the carer's work

The carer felt that her work was appreciated by the patients but not the staff who seemed unable to understand that an activity might be evaluated on any other grounds than its output, that it could be enjoyable and fulfilling in itself.

> I never really felt appreciated or understood by the other staff. They seemed to judge what I was doing by the *result* of the activity they saw. So they judged what was going on by the end product, perhaps a small article that the elderly person had made, a small craft article. That was their criterion. They never seemed to fully understand what was behind it even when they were doing some of the NVQ assessments and they actually came in and were with the group and saw the aims of what I was trying to get from the group. It never seemed to get across, especially to the senior members of staff. They acted as if they knew what I was doing, that they 'knew the lot', and they didn't. They weren't particularly interested. They couldn't see the value of it. So I found it very frustrating, really, from the beginning.

The carer added, however, that apart from this difference in attitude to what were the 'ingredients' of quality care, she got on well with other staff at a personal level.

The Changes

Following the implementation of the community care legislation, the more rigorous assessment of people needing support and the switch to the provision of more support in people's own homes, the character of the patient population of the nursing home gradually began to alter. As the elderly people living there before the changes died, new patients who were mentally much more deteriorated and who were often physically ill, took their places. Today the frail elderly person in full possession of her or his faculties (the predominant type of patient only a few years ago) is in a small minority. Most patients are very confused or very ill or both.

   The owners have found it increasingly difficult to recruit patients, following the community care changes, and now, as the carer put it,

> are searching to keep the beds filled. They're bringing in people from quite a long way away into what isn't their community. They are getting in very, very dependent patients. They've got a lot of patients that need feeding, they've got a lot of patients that need toileting and that's all they've got time for, feeding and toileting these patients. And some of the people that are coming in, come in from hospital and they're only there for a number of days before they die. You can't understand why they've been moved into a nursing home. They're there for such a short time.

Impact on staff

The switch to a more highly dependent patient population in the home was not matched by a parallel increase in the numbers of staff. The existing staff were expected to cope with the increased demands without any extra help. As a result they were increasingly pressured and had little time to spare for anything beyond feeding and toileting. The carer observed that these changes 'caused terrible dissatisfaction amongst the staff. The turnover in staff is incredible'. She attributed this turnover to the 'depressed state' of staff and added 'I do feel, as well, that the mangement have lost interest. They're definitely not putting in the effort that they were.'

The carer found that the activities group grew much smaller. She tried to work with some of the very confused patients on an individual basis and felt she was getting through to them but was rewarded with a hostile reception from the staff.

> I would go and see somebody who was very, very confused and take work with me for stimulating and talking to that person. The other staff would feel that I was completely wasting my time. They would have just stuck this person in front of a television. They would huff and puff and sail right past me because I was just one person with one patient and they were rushing round. I couldn't get through to them the value of what I was doing or interest them in continuing this type of work.

Impact on patients

The influx of very confused and sick patients meant a deterioration in standards of care for everyone. The carer commented on the consequences for the surviving group of patients who had been in the home before the changes made their impact. They were severely disabled but not ill. 'It's hard for the ones that have been there that do need nursing care, that need constant nursing care, that aren't sick people and aren't quite so dependent. They're being put with very, very highly dependent people and the level of stimulation is very, very poor'.

Patients began to confide their unhappiness about the home to the carer.

> I found that the ones that were really very able to express themselves were telling me things about the home and about what was upsetting them about the home. There'd be somebody crying out to go to the toilet and they'd be left, or the staff would shout at them 'Oh, you've only just been'. They'd hear one of the staff say 'What are you doing that for? Because you haven't got a mind?' The patients would say how unhappy the staff were, they could see that the staff were unhappy and they'd say 'Everyone is leaving us'.

But most of the patients had no such choice. As one of them, who had once been happy in the home, said to the carer, 'Where can I go from here? There's nowhere for me'.

The experience of two patients, in particular, epitomised for the carer the loss in standards of care and concern she witnessed in the home, and drove her in the end to resign her post.

Negligence and neglect

The first case was of a long-term resident who had been a very active person but needed nursing care.

> Her quality of life was a very good quality of life. She was very involved in what was going on. She had good communications with the community and people were visiting her. I first noticed that there was something wrong with her behaviour when she became flushed and sweaty. First of all I mentioned this to the senior nursing staff on duty. Nothing was said afterwards and I mentioned it again when it happened again. Then about a month after that I began to notice that she really didn't seem very well and I mentioned this first to the nursing staff and they said they had noticed that she wasn't herself and that it was probably constipation. Then I mentioned it to the matron that I wasn't happy with how she was and she said they were going to be running some tests.
>
>   Then, unfortunately, somebody died within the home who she knew quite well and it was said that her physical state was a reaction to this. Then I went and saw the qualified nurse and she said 'She's putting it on, it's all put on. It's all a big act to get attention'. She wasn't that type of person to be demanding attention so I wasn't at all happy with the way things were going. About a couple of weeks later the doctor was informed and he did some tests.

The tests were inconclusive and the matron started saying that she thought the patient had had a small stroke. The carer was unconvinced and felt that the symptoms were not consistent with that diagnosis.

> They ran all these blood tests and things and the tests came back clear and so as far as they were concerned she was alright. But you could see she wasn't. She was really beginning to look a sick person. And when I said something to the matron she said, 'Well, she brought it on herself because she went out and it was cold outside and I have got no sympathy for her, she brings it on herself.'

The carer went off to talk to the patient and she told her how worried she was and described specific serious symptoms. When the carer retailed this information back to the matron, the matron was angry and asked '"Who told her that? Who gave her that information?", implying I had said something to her.'

The patient became sicker, collapsed and was taken to hospital. Even the decision to transfer her to hospital was insensitively handled, in the view of the carer. When she visited her in hospital the patient explained how distressing it had been on the morning of her admission when the nursing home staff had gone into her room and said 'Come along now, you're going into hospital' and that was the first she had heard. So she immediately thought there's something desperately wrong with her. Within five minutes of her admission to hospital they had worked out that she had a serious cardiac condition.

The needs of the home versus the needs of the patient

The other patient whose treatment at the home deeply disturbed the carer had decided that he wanted to return to his own home for the last part of his life. As he said to her, 'I want to go home. I want to die in my own home'. In the carer's view, with adequate support, he was fit enough to live on his own again but the carer felt that

> the managers did all they could to try and prevent this. They were telling the social worker and people that came to assess the patient that he was dangerous on steps, that he needed more supervision, and constant care. Social services were setting up care packages to let the patient go back into the community but it would have meant an empty bed and these beds are becoming very difficult to fill. So there was a real conflict of interest.

The carer felt torn between her loyalty to her employers and to the patients concerned. 'The home didn't want me to be involved. They tried to put up a barrier.' But she felt it was the right move for the patient to go back home and told social services that she believed he could cope. Eventually he was resettled in his own house and the carer felt she herself could no longer keep her job at the nursing home:

> I felt in a terrible dilemma in that there were these people that were dependent on my going there and yet I just wanted to get out. I felt that I was compromising my ideals by being part of this system that I didn't agree with.

After leaving her post, however, she did continue to come into the home regularly to visit the patients and keep up contact with them on a voluntary basis.

The difficulties of speaking out and the inadequacy of inspection

The carer had spoken out on a number of occasions when she had seen staff behaving badly or inappropriately towards patients but she felt she couldn't speak freely 'partly because often when I did speak out I seemed to get a very nasty reaction'. She gave the example of an occasion when the home's nursing sister was in charge.

> I'd seen something that I felt wasn't right and I had gone to her and told her. I mean, she was in charge of the nursing auxiliaries and care assistants. And I had actually gone and told her that I felt something wasn't right. I think it was over toileting a patient. And she shouted and shrieked at me – like a fish woman – and she said that if I'd got any complaints, to take them to the manager, that it wasn't for her to deal with my complaints. I did take them to the management, particularly towards the end but was told: 'What can I do about it? We train these girls; they go on these NVQ courses, and I can't *make* them better.'

The atmosphere in the home made it equally difficult for other staff, patients and their relatives to voice their criticisms openly. Amongst the staff,

> very few people spoke up because there could be such nastiness, so everybody tried
> to avoid this nasty tongue. Rather than stand up to it, people looked for other jobs
> and there was a constant turnover of staff.

Patients often confided their concerns about the deterioration of standards in the home to the carer but didn't feel they could speak out for fear of the consequences. Relatives likewise were worried that any criticism could rebound on patients. As one said to the carer, 'I can see so many things wrong I just have to bite my tongue because if I say anything I'm frightened it is going to be taken out on my mother'.

Inspection of nursing homes by the health authorities might be expected to detect just such poor standards of care. However, it was no help in this case where it seemed to focus on the physical condition of the home and involved no discussions with patients or staff.

> I don't know what these inspectors look for when they go in. I was there when an
> inspector came and as far as I saw the inspector looked in the kitchens and at what
> boards were being used for what foods, that sort of thing. They looked in a
> bedroom. They glanced in the dining room. They were shown round by the matron
> which I don't think is a particularly good idea.

For the future

The carer had several ideas how the organization and management of the home could be changed to radically improve the quality of life of its residents. These included much greater resident and staff participation in decision-making, a far greater emphasis on the training of staff and enriching the daily life of the home. She pointed out that such changes would involve relatively little financial outlay. However, she was well aware that they would require, if not a change in managers, a significant change in the attitudes of management.

Case Study 8

The price of caring: from trust employee to private sector employer.
A community psychiatric nurse

Background

This case study centres on the experience of a community psychiatric nurse (CPN) who had worked for many years in the NHS, but who became increasingly alienated by her experiences following the reorganization of the service in the early 1990s. She decided to change her role from employee to employer, leaving her job with an NHS trust and setting up her own company to provide caring services in the community. Her aim was not simply to create a job where she once again had a degree of autonomy and responsibility, but also to show that it was possible to establish a high quality service that really was responsive to the needs of its clients.

This initiative could almost have been designed as a copybook example of what the government hoped would happen after the new legislation was introduced: the skilled and committed professional rejects the constraints of the public service bureaucracy in favour of the challenge of independence and enterprise and, as others do the same, the market, with all its anticipated advantages, is born. However, the case study suggests that while in the right hands such initiatives can produce high quality services, they may have a high price tag both in terms of costs to the entrepreneur and in their reinforcement of the low wage economy and all that goes with it. Further, the study appears to indicate that in less scrupulous hands, where profits are the main driving force, quality may well be sacrificed.

The CPN was trained first as a Registered General Nurse (RGN) and then as a Registered Mental Nurse (RMN). She was never happy with the 'starched pinnie and frilly cap' approach of general nursing with its keeping-your-distance from patients methods, but discovered during her training, when she spent eight weeks on a psychiatric ward, that she loved mental health nursing.

Working with those described as elderly mentally infirm (EMI) appealed to the CPN firstly because she liked them as people. 'You could get the odd one who was awful but most of them were lovely. Some people claim elderly mentally infirm patients have no idea what they want, or who they are'. In her view, that is absurd. They may not know the day of the week, but they still know what they like. They can enjoy themselves, retain a lively sense of humour and be fun to work with. It was a great challenge to find out what they *could* do and how to help their carers.

This study begins by summarizing the CPN's experience in the NHS and the reasons why she finally decided to leave the service. The main focus, however, is on her new role as a private sector care provider and her evaluation of the working of the community care reforms from that perspective.

Organization of the work

In the early 1980s the CPN was appointed to a post working with the elderly mentally infirm with responsibility for a large area served by an EMI Assessment Unit in a district general hospital. She was based in the unit where she also had a role as a clinical nurse specialist. Essentially, she managed her own work.

Her cases were referred by the psycho-geriatrician in the Unit and by GPs throughout her area. At any one time her caseload would be about sixty strong. On a normal day she would see about six of these patients, visiting them at home, and spending an hour in the unit first and last thing.

Her main work was with the carers of elderly mentally infirm people struggling to cope with maintaining the person at home. Typically this would involve getting the carers to keep a record of the pattern of problems that arose in providing care during the day, analysing that, and then helping them to find effective ways of dealing with them. Crises tended to occur round particular events, especially dressing, feeding and toileting but there could also be more general problems such as shouting and demanding attention when the carer or carers and others in the house were trying to get on with their lives. The CPN would work with carers over weeks or months or even years, helping them to develop strategies for handling such difficulties. She would also be on the alert for any signs of elder abuse by the carers, who were often under considerable stress, and in such cases work with the person concerned to prevent its recurrence.

The CPN found the work very satisfying, especially because she felt it enabled her to enhance the quality of life of the carers and her patients. Her only real frustration was that she never had enough time but was always rushing from one job to another.

The creation of the multi-disciplinary team

Towards the end of the 1980s, the CPN helped to plan a multi-disciplinary mental health team consisting of four CPNs, two social workers, an occupational therapist, a physiotherapist, a psychologist and a psycho-geriatrician. The team did not really gel in its first three years. There was a weekly meeting but little joint work developed. It had no common base and its members were scattered in different locations round the area it served. The system of referrals was to individual members of the team, not the team as a whole.

The CPN's work broadened from elderly mentally infirm cases to the whole range of mental health. This came as a bit of a shock after nine years concentrating on elderly people with dementia but she welcomed the challenge of being pushed to brush up her knowledge and skills in other areas. While multi-disciplinary work by the team did not develop as hoped, patients gained by the general increase in professional resources made available.

Why the CPN left the job and set up her own business

The CPN says there were three main reasons why she decided to quit her job as a CPN and start her own caring business: the management of the team, the growing control of her work, and the creation of the community trust.

The management of the multi-disciplinary team

In 1994 it was decided that the team needed a manager rather than a co-ordinator, a role the CPN had filled until then. The CPN applied for the job but was passed over in favour of another woman. The CPN felt that she was perceived as being too close to the team and not having the directive approach to management favoured by the trust. She believed that they wanted someone ready to be an authoritative leader, ready to impose unpopular decisions if necessary, and not a participative leader with a strong sympathy for the point of view of the team members. She would not have minded the decision so much if the person who was appointed had not been someone who had previously held her job but had left it because she had a strong dislike for working with elderly people!

Encroaching control of the work of the CPN

With the aim of acquiring greater control over the work pattern of the CPNs, management introduced a small portable computer – 'Com Care' – which CPNs were required to take out with them on all their calls. On this they had to enter the time of the start and end of each visit to a patient and the nature of the visit (using precoded categories). These data were then fed into a computer at headquarters and used by management to analyse the CPNs' work patterns.

The CPN did not object in the least to being held accountable for what she did. Her work had been audited ever since she had taken up her post and she believed she had nothing to hide. What she did object to was the particular use management made of the data. Their predominant aim, it seemed to her, had become to increase throughput and, to this end, the patient discharge rate. Long term care was no longer allowed. Nor was her own practice of using her own judgement on when to close a case.

To her mind the CPNs knew their patients well and were far better judges of these matters than managers. But they were trying to reduce involvement to time limited 'episodes' of care and had no sympathy for an approach in which CPNs got to know patients and treated their needs holistically.

The community health trust

The development of the multi-disciplinary team overlapped with the development of the new community trust. The CPN disliked the new world the trust represented with its emphasis on management, money and markets. The first thing that happened, she said, was a doubling in the number of managers and she had wondered what services had had to be cut to fund their salaries. Then it became clear that 'the management of the trust was chaotic'. The first year the managers appointed a whole lot of nurse advisers and then twelve months later dismissed them. More savings were needed and so it was decided that some of the locality managers, not long since appointed by the trust, must also go – and there was a fight for survival amongst them. The main driving force seemed to be money. The decision to reduce the work of the CPN to measurable and controllable episodes was determined, it was said, by the need to shape the work so that it could be contracted by fundholding GPs.

The combination of these three factors led to the CPN's decision to quit and start her own caring business. Her plans were laid well in advance and her company was registered the same month as she resigned.

The caring business

Goals

The CPN's goals for her organization were threefold: to make a profit, to provide a good quality of service and to be a good employer. The challenge, as she was quickly to find out, would be to make these goals compatible with one another since it became apparent that you would probably make the biggest profit if you could largely ignore quality of service and the work conditions of staff.

The organization

The CPN decided to focus the work of the company on local council districts closest to her home, which was to be the company office. The structure of the organization was developed and adapted over the first few months in the light of experience. It was soon found essential, for example, to devolve the day-to-day management of the recruited care workers onto three team leaders, one for each of the district council areas. Each team consisted of eight to ten workers. The team leaders drew up work rotas, did preliminary visits to clients and supervised the care workers.

The workforce

The recruitment of staff is carried out carefully with all applicants being inter-viewed and two references taken up in each case. The references are followed through with telephone conversations with referees when sometimes significant reservations are expressed by the referees which they do not feel can be committed to paper. The large majority of the 31 people recruited so far are married women with working husbands. There are only two men amongst the carers. Apart from the CPN, who says 'I'm 24 hours a day, seven days a week', the staff are part-time. The hours worked by carers each week range from as little as three or four to as many as forty or fifty. The average, however, is about eleven hours.

Training and supervision

The aim of providing high quality care means that the CPN has given a priority to training and supervision. All new staff receive training on the basics of caring when they are recruited. The training programme has been devised by the CPN and is carried through by one of the team leaders who has a gift for teaching. Subsequently, staff are encouraged to take NVQ training, for which the CPN is the assessor. If they achieve NVQ Level II they receive an increase in pay. All the cases are regularly visited by the team leaders to check on client and carer satisfaction with the service.

The client and the cases

In terms of paying the piper, the main client of the company is the county social services department, not the individual people cared for. The implementation of the community care legislation has led the social services department to create a purchasing division which contracts both the social services' own providers (home care) and independent sector organizations to provide specific 'packages of care' for people who have been assessed as in need. The main points of contact between the company and social services are the care managers who are responsible for most of the budget for care. The care managers will ask the company for a quotation for providing a specified input of services. Although some cases are time-limited most are with people with long-term needs and are open-ended.

A typical case would be a referral concerning an elderly lady being discharged from hospital in a week or ten days' time. The case manager would phone with details describing her problems and needs: 'whether she's not able to do her meals, or change her clothes, or attend the bathroom without support. And usually they indicate what they want doing, the hours and the times'. The range of services offered by the company cover all aspects of personal care except nursing care. This includes, for instance, washing, dressing, toileting, shopping, cooking, feeding and some cleaning.

When a case is first referred to the company a visit is made to the client to decide whether or not to take the case on. Once a case is accepted, the team leader introduces the care worker to the user and arranges the details of the service. Subsequently, she makes regular visits to check that the user and her principal informal carers are satisfied with the service received.

Formal monitoring of the service by the social services, as far as the CPN can ascertain, seems to be very limited. Her impression is that they are only likely to intervene if the user complains to them or if there is some obvious crisis. Otherwise the company is left to get on with it. The CPN believes that her staff provide a good standard of care and she says that she is 'quite proud of them'.

Issues and dilemmas

The initial experience of the caring business has made the CPN acutely aware of several issues at the heart of the new system deriving in particular, but not exclusively, from its economic rationale.

The economics of the caring business

The primary pressures in the new system are those of price rather than quality. Launching the new business 'you tend to keep your prices a bit low so that people take notice of you and try you out'. The problem then becomes how to raise your prices once you are accepted, as the CPN discovered when social services criticized the company for having missed some calls. She fully accepted that they were at fault and that improvements in the management system were required. But when she later pointed out that these improvements would cost money and that would have to be reflected in increased charges, she said:

> I never got any response at all. When I actually sent them information about the changes they thought I was being grossly unreasonable in saying that I needed to kick up the prices by as much as I'd asked for. So I sent them an analysis of where that money was going to go. I think they had a real shock. Perhaps it's because they are not actually in business. The purchasing manager is a purchasing manager. It's not necessary that he should know what a company like ours costs to run.

A key factor influencing the economics of the business is the nature of the competition. There are five or six other private businesses offering services in the area the company covers. Their prices are very similar to those charged by the CPN but, as far as she can find out, they invest much less in ensuring the quality of their services. Two national agencies, in particular, seem to provide little in the way of training and provide minimal support for their care workers. For example, when a care worker is allocated to a case for the first time:

> the agencies just send them. They don't know who they are going to. They don't

know what they are expected to do when they get there apart from providing personal care or for companionship or whatever. They don't get an introductory visit. They don't get anybody meeting them there to introduce them.

This contrasts with what the CPN regards as essential good practice on such occasions when 'We try hard not to let people "go strange"' and she ensures that her care workers are introduced to their clients by the team leader. But such good practice costs money, for the supervisor must be paid for the occasion. Unless social services are prepared to pay extra for a higher quality service, which so far there has been no sign they are willing to do, the company must find the additional costs from its own slender profits.

Costing care

The social services as virtually a monopoly purchaser is in a strong position to insist on its preferred method of costing cases. Although the costs of individual cases can vary considerably, as a result, for instance, of the different location of clients and the mileage involved in visiting them, the SSD normally insists on a standard price-per-hour. This is particularly difficult for a new business to calculate, not knowing how referrals will average out over a typical period of time. Further, the expected cost level is so low that it clearly assumes that care staff will be treated as casual workers and that no provision will be included for holidays, sickness or pension, and at best minimal amounts for training and supervision.

Care managers and social workers

Most of the care managers in the county were social workers before the reorganisation and the CPN felt that 'they don't always have the right sentiments to be a good manager'. While they were often very good at evaluating a client's situation, they were sometimes much less able to understand the managerial problems of a business providing the care needed. For example, she was asked at short notice to provide someone to visit a client five times a day. She couldn't meet this request since for a case as demanding as this she would require time to recruit and train a new worker.

> The care manager involved couldn't understand the problem: it was like, 'What the hell's wrong with you? What's the matter with you, woman?' But his manager was completely different and rang up and said 'I've just heard about that call. Is this a care plan problem? Have we got the care plan wrong?' He actually stood still long enough to ask why we had difficulty with it and to establish that we didn't have time to recruit.'

Employment issues

The most salient effect of the pricing structure of community care on the company was in its impact on the wages which could be offered and the effect this, in turn, had on both recruitment and retention of staff. The company paid £3.00 per hour to new recruits, £3.50 when they had successfully completed the basic training provided, and £4.00 if they gained the NVQ Level II qualification. In addition a mileage rate was paid for the care workers' travel from their homes to the clients' homes. There was no provision for holidays, sickness or retirement pension. Wage levels and mileage rates were markedly inferior to those for home carers employed directly by social services, who also had fringe benefits.

These levels of pay and terms of service were simply too low for many potentially good workers who were currently on income support. The CPN commented:

> My biggest headache is this damn benefits trap where you can't get people to come to you. They're safer staying on the dole. The state is all back to front. There's no encouragement, is there?

She picked out the rules governing housing benefit as the particular problem, for those who have it lose pound for pound if they take on any paid employment. She gave the example of a potential recruit she had just interviewed. She was

> really just the job, enthusiastic, good personality. She would have been a gem. Just a little bit of training and we'd have a real good one there. She asked about her housing benefit. As soon as she found out what was going to happen to it, she was gone!

The low wages were also a problem in keeping good staff. Turnover amongst carers was quite high and when the CPN analysed the main factors leading people to leave, she found that money was the top of the list, followed by hours and mileage. Both hours and mileage had an economic element in that some people left because they couldn't get enough hours to make the job worth while, and the mileage rate was very low.

The ethics of a low wage business

The CPN's ambition was to provide better conditions for her staff:

> I've got this thing in my head about being a good employer, which probably isn't good for business. It probably makes me a lousy business woman! I'll never be a millionaire. But the people who work all weekends for us, they're up an down all day Saturday and Sunday when everybody else is lying in bed or going shopping. I believe they should be paid a little bit more.

Commenting on a recently suggested minimum wage of £3.60 per hour, she added:

> We're the kind of company that's actually paying people sub-living wages and I'm

not proud of it. We're actually furthering it by not saying to social services that we're slave labour in this market.

Her response is to try to bargain for better rates from social services but she acknowledges that, given the competition with the big private agencies in the field, this may not be successful.

Evaluation

The CPN felt that while the new system of community care had created the conditions for a low-wage provider service, it had also brought some gains for those who were assessed as needing care.

> They definitely get more choice in the way that they get care and certainly if they don't like the firm that they've got, they can have a new firm instead.

However, she pointed out that some people were frightened to ask for more care because they felt they would be forced to pay for it. She also felt that there could be a downside to choice. The old home help system had provided 'stability where you always knew what was going on'. If care was switched from one agency to another, you lost such continuity. Further, choice could provide the unscrupulous carer with opportunities to manipulate the system for personal gain. She instanced an elderly client whom her workers had been supporting successfully in her own home, enabling her to continue to get out, go shopping and maintain an element of independence. The woman had had a stroke.

> We were maintaining her activities to the best of our ability. Some days she was good, some days she couldn't be bothered. A lovely relationship was formed. At some stage her daughter spotted her mum's vulnerability and decided she was going for power of attorney. She moved her from the house she was living in to her house and turned her into an invalid. She decided she didn't like what our carer was doing. She kept saying, 'My mother needs nursing care.' We kept saying, 'No, she doesn't. She's fine. Leave her alone. She's getting on alright.' In the end she won because they have the right to choose. Our girl gets wheeled out and a nursing agency went in. The next thing we know is that the mother's house is on the market and I have a funny feeling that mum is heading very rapidly towards a nursing home.

In spite of these difficulties and having periods when she wonders why she has chosen her new career, the CPN enjoys her work very much and finds it more fulfilling than her job in her last years with the NHS trust.

> Ninety-nine per cent of the time I enjoy what I'm doing. It's a heck of a challenge and I've learned so much. Mind you, I love learning. It's an expensive way to learn sometimes, but I suppose that's what business is all about really.

The future

Two kinds of changes seemed particularly important to the CPN if the caring business was to be improved, one at the micro level, the other involving social security policy. The first concerned improving the standard of management in the front line of the social service's purchasing division. The care managers needed management training if they were to understand the providers' problems and work more effectively with them. The larger social security issue was that of the benefits trap. If that could be somehow be abolished 'We'd get a load of people back off the dole train' and, taken together with a national minimum wage, the basic problems of recruitment and retention of good quality staff should be resolved at the same time.

4

Working with people with learning disabilities

The term 'learning disabilities' is used to describe the condition of people whose mental functioning is impaired either as a result of congenital conditions or by brain damage. Since in most instances the conditions exist from birth, health and social services work with those concerned over the whole life span.

Until the 1960s it was usual practice to confine people with moderate or severe conditions of what was then called 'mental handicap' in long-stay hospitals for all of their lives. Since then, aided by advances in drug treatment (as we have noted in Chapter 1), successive governments have followed a policy of deinstitutionalization, aimed at resettling as many patients from such hospitals as possible in the community. While it was recognized that they would continue to need considerable support, it was believed that they could live in much more normal conditions than in the hospital and have a quality of life much closer to that of the rest of the population.

The process of resettlement in the community has continued over the last three decades, gathering momentum in recent years with the growth of support for the rights of people with learning disabilities to a normal life, and with the increasing pressure on economic grounds finally to close as many as possible of the emptying long-stay hospitals. The method of resettlement has generally involved a gradual process of preparation, starting in the hospital many months or even years before, as patients have been encouraged to learn the skills of more independent living.

Local authorities have extensive responsibilities for supporting people with learning disabilities living in the community. For example, in 1993–4 there were about 18,000 people with learning disabilities living in social services or independent sector residential accommodation in England and Wales, and over 43,000 attending social education and day centres. In total the English and Welsh local authorities devoted over 13 per cent of their personal social services budgets to people with learning disabilities (CIPFA, 1994).

The case studies in this chapter include experiences of services for people with learning disabilities from the perspective of a hospital involved in resettling its patients in the community (Case Study 9), a social services team responsible for providing continuing support in the community both for people resettled from hospital and those who have never been admitted (Case Study 10) and a voluntary organization running a supported housing scheme (Case Study 11). The fourth case study, uniquely in this book, concentrates on the experience of one user of the system as seen through the eyes of his guardian and a care assistant (Case Study 12).

A common view runs through all the cases: that the community care changes, expected by some to strengthen the dynamic of reform in services for people with learning disabilities, have had the opposite effect, replacing the ideal of user-led choice with the reality of budget- and service-led decisions.

Case Study 9

Resettlement in the community: fighting for principle-driven change in hospital and social services.
A nurse manager

Background

The policy of resettling patients from long-stay mental handicap hospitals in the community, which we have discussed in Chapter 1, set challenges to both the hospitals and social services departments to ensure that they were carried through in a way that gave priority to the needs of the patients rather than the convenience of the organizations. This study vividly illustrates the nature of these challenges from the point of view of a nurse manager who was responsible for resettlement programmes first in a hospital and later for a social services department. The study is also a good example of the implementation of community care policies which long pre-dated the changes brought in by the 1990 Act but which were later affected by it.

Key themes in the case study are the resistance of hospital professionals to change, the commitment and persistence of the resettlement team, the conflict between principles and resources, and the impact of different management styles. The influence of the 1990 Act was particularly evident in the last two of these.

The nurse manager was a graduate and a trained nurse. He worked in the mental handicap hospital from the end of the 1970s until 1991 when he moved to the local social services department to handle the other side of the resettlement process.

The hospital: principle-driven change

The hospital

The mental handicap hospital was a large establishment which had been built in the last century to serve the surrounding counties. Its work was affected by a number of external policy changes made before and during the time covered by the case study. Most important of these were the government directive to close most wards in hospitals for people with learning disabilities; the RHA's (regional health authority) development of principles and a code of practice; the new management system with unit general managers, resulting from the Griffiths report of 1983 (DHSS, 1983); and the 1990 Act introducing the separation of purchasing and providing.

The nurse manager was responsible to the director of nursing services who, in turn, reported to the unit general manager of the hospital. The RHA had the responsibility of driving through the closure programme, though, within any one hospital, its *direct* control over individual staff members or individual decisions was minimal. Its influence was most powerfully exercised through allocation of funds.

The need for change and resistance to it

The nurse manager was strongly convinced of the need for the resettlement programme. 'You couldn't defend the hospitals,' he said, 'they were gross places.' When he first came to work in the mental handicap hospital he had been appalled at what he found. There were

> dreadful conditions for the clients. A lot of violence going on to staff and unfortunately the other way round as well, and between clients. It was overwhelming. I nearly walked out straight away. I couldn't believe it.

He had only stuck the job because of the feeling of being part of a team trying to improve things and fighting for clients' rights.

Many of the other professionals in his hospital, however, did not share his view and did all they could to resist the resettlement policy. 'A lot of the staff used to think: "We're the only ones who can manage them. They'll go out there and they'll run amok and children will get raped." All the worst scenarios'. The nurses had come out on strike against the changes and in the early days of the closure programme, in the mid-1980s,

> the consultants were dead against it and were telling parents that people would be left roaming the streets and this sort of thing, getting parents against it. They were vetoing resettlements and they'd no authority to do it. But no structure was there to challenge them because up to that point they had held total sway.

Beginning the changes

Against this level of opposition the first steps in introducing resettlement were cautious ones. This was a period the nurse manager described as 'cloak and dagger stuff' when resettlements were largely *ad hoc* 'as finance departments weren't releasing people's money'. But he and his colleagues were driven by a strong belief in the value of what they were doing. In the light of his experience in the intervening years he commented:

> I can't believe now the extent to which it was principle-driven. At the time I thought it wasn't good enough but then I look at what's been going on since and realize it was quite an outstanding model of support that most people got. Everybody went into homes of their own, never in groups of more than four.

The resettlement programme rapidly gathered momentum after the unit general manager came out in support of it:

> He wanted resettlement to happen and he pulled everybody into line. The consultants totally withdrew from the process which was helpful. All we required them to do was to sign the discharge papers and that worked. The social workers were glad to be working to a structure because they were no longer sort of enemies of the hospital. They've done a difficult job.

Keeping up the momentum

The nurse manager and his colleagues worked hard to maintain the momentum of the programme and to keep it on course. The strong support of his line manager and his own tendency to speak out and say what he believed in were important factors in the process.

> I had plenty of supervision both with the director of nursing services and with the unit general manager. They both had a large number of questions they wanted answering. It sounds as if I am blowing my own trumpet, but I think it was that I was trusted to get on with it and that it was more a basis of me going to say 'I'm having trouble with this' and they would go and sort it, if it was something that was beyond my authority. Initially there was a resistance from the wards. People were trying to sabotage resettlements early on and the director of nursing was very tough on that.

He stresses the importance of an organization being able to have an open debate. Indeed, he strove to create a management system in which people for whom he had responsibility could say what they thought. The precondition for this was their attitude to the fundamentals of the job.

> I tried to engender a feeling of confidence among the staff, where if they stuck their necks out for the clients, I'd stick my neck out for them. In that atmosphere it's about the middle managers creating the right atmosphere for people having the bottle to speak out, to speak their mind.

Power

Power is a central theme in the story, perhaps particularly significant as new systems were being established and individuals and organizations struggled to assert their positions. For example, people wondered whether the hospital could stop a resettlement if they thought that the receiving agency had not produced a good enough service.

> There was a test case early on where the hospital tried to stop a resettlement to a district because there weren't enough support services in place. The RHA made it quite clear that we could make a noise about it and point it out but we had no power of veto. It was the responsibility of the receiving districts to set the service up. So all we could do in the end was to make a noise. But, having said that, we did hold up

several resettlements because we made enough noise and embarrassed people into improving what was on offer.

Power lay with the RHA which could, and in the early days did, refuse money to those providing resettlement if the schemes did not conform to the model district plan. Fighting for control of money was central to negotiations and central to the establishment of power bases. Thus the fine calculations could spell success or failure for the future of schemes. This particular area had a dowry system: 'They worked out the average cost of keeping someone in a long-stay hospital and that went on the back of the person when they were resettled.' The money was not paid by the hospital to the receiving authority. The RHA would withdraw money from the hospital each year and then re-allocate it to the receiving authorities. 'When a person resettles you hardly get a reduction in costs at all, so the RHA had to top it up.' He talked of 'an annual battle for the unit general manager to resist the money that was being taken out'.

Significantly, the principles that were established at the beginning related to money systems as well. Each party had fears: the hospitals, that money would be transferred from their budgets and not used by the agencies which received it for the purpose for which it was allocated; the receiving departments, that the money would be too little to provide adequate support for the individual once in the community; further they feared that there might be money for the person coming out of hospital, but not for the person with learning disabilities who never went in to hospital.

Outcomes

Within the hospital, the nurse manager worked with others to establish a system which focused on 'what this person needs and then trying to create a service', rather than 'here's a house, let's bung everybody in it'. So he tried to 'keep updating and improving the Individual Planning (IP) system'. Immense energy was being directed to that end.

> There was no test of course, but I used to wonder what real difference IP ended up making. We were all swanning around thinking we were behaving in this principled way, and sometimes I thought that we had to put gallons of extra effort in for the slightest drop of improvement. Could we justify it? But at least it kept everybody on their toes and they knew what they were meant to be doing.

He contrasted the much greater investment of staff time in working on the detail for people moving out by his hospital than by others. He wonders now if they were a bit 'precious' but thinks the pay-off for the time spent may be that out of 130 people who were resettled from the hospital, only three returned.

For him, there was the 'pleasure of working, trying to work, in a principled way. It feels right, it feels nice to have people around you prepared to stick their necks out over the same things'. At the heart was his belief that the hospitals 'were infringements of people's rights'.

Defending the principles

He thinks that the hospital where he worked was disliked by regional staff because negotiations with other hospitals which were not so insistent on principles were more straightforward.

> At 'B' hospital you went in, you were told what to do; it was the same routine every time. The RHA didn't like our flexibility. We were the only ones speaking out. At the regional meeting I'd say something and you would see everybody's eyebrows raise: 'Here we go again, the same old rhetoric from "C" hospital'.

In one heated interchange he referred back to the 'grandiose base': 'normalization and rights and local, comprehensive services'.

> I kept calling them back to those principles and was accused of being precious. They replied: 'Yes, that was '84 and we're now in '89'. It was a really angry meeting. I'd stood there accused of empire building and the rest and I'd accused them of being unprincipled and driven entirely by finance, not the model district service. But we always used to go back to those principles and there were a couple of occasions where people round the room were telling me to shut up because they were already toeing the party line.

He got particularly angry when there was talk of targets for each district, in the sense of setting an allocation of a number of people who were to be resettled in that area.

> It looked as if people's wishes to go somewhere other than the place allocated by the district had been thrown out of the window. We managed successfully to get that modified. We said that as a hospital we weren't prepared to negotiate with districts which weren't prepared to work to individual needs.

A retreat from standards

Towards the end of the nurse manager's time in the hospital the effect of the 1990 Act began to make itself felt and the funding on which good resettlement schemes depended became increasingly difficult to protect. Looking back to that period he is convinced that within the hospital the purchaser/provider split 'worked against the interests of the clients'. For example, he had to go to regional meetings 'basically to outbid others, that was what it was about; nothing to do with individual need. It was an essential part of the job but I used to absolutely hate it'.

More importantly, the ring fencing of resettlement money began to break down.

> When the resettlement first started with the regional funding, the exact words were,

> 'The money is ring fenced, index linked and in perpetuity'. That was a commitment made by region. Region for the purpose of resettlement has now been dissolved. And region was the policing agency. They had minimum standards that had to be met. Region has now gone, so there's nobody policing.

The control and use of money has been a central debating matter from the inception of resettlement. As has been mentioned, the RHA was concerned that SSDs might use funds specified for people with learning disabilities elsewhere in their budgets.

> Social services ended up saying 'Bugger off'. So at that point everybody was criticizing social services because the money was starting to leak out. But then when health trusts were created, they did exactly the same thing. So in 'X', which used to be one of the best districts from the point of view of a principled way of working, they openly siphoned off some to their acute services. And region protested about it, but trusts don't have to take instructions from region. They're independent. And region's disappearing anyway in terms of its monitoring function. So all those early commitments that they made are now sort of meaningless.

Social services: the impact of the new managerialism

A promising beginning

In 1991 the nurse manager moved to his new job in the local social services department in the section which had the task of overseeing the accommodation and services for people who had come out of hospital. The changes following the passage of the 1990 Act were beginning to make themselves felt in the department but there was for some time a measure of insulation from them because the work of the section was seen as a discrete function with funding from the health authority.

The nurse manager believes that in this initial period his job had four features which made it possible for him to be creative. First, he had direct responsibility for service provision; second, they were setting up a new service from scratch; third, he had the sort of manager 'who leaves you to get on with it but is there if you want her'; and finally, there was the measure of freedom already identified in that their funding was coming from the health authority – all that social services was doing 'was basically laundering it and processing things we wanted to do'.

The consequence was that they established different practices than in the department as a whole. 'We did lots of things they didn't like but, to their credit, they worked with us.' Thus, *at that stage*, the administrative, personnel and financial staff were willing to set up new systems, such as budgets, that didn't exist anywhere else.

The differences between the two systems are found in the detail. There was no precedent for the development of the new service. Staff were supporting the clients in the clients' houses but they were not based in the houses in the way that hostel staff were. So some facilities were needed for staff in the clients' houses, for example access to a phone or shower, or having a meal with clients. Money was paid from the social services department into the clients' household budget to cover the things like the rent of a phone which was for the staff benefit. Funds were also included for the costs of support staff when clients went out or went on holiday. In the early period of his work in the social services department, the administrative and finance staff were anxious about the development of different systems but they came down and held meetings. The outcome was that these staff made clear that they wanted to work with the new ideas but that the responsibility was not theirs: 'Be it on your heads'. He had to work for this co-operation. On a couple of occasions 'I took some of the clients in that were really full of their lives to sort something out about their money. And once the administrative staff were able to put faces to names, they were really committed'.

Disappointments

This promising start was not to endure. It was followed by a reorganization 'which basically wiped out all that we'd done'. New administrative systems were imposed, managed from a town which was far more remote, and negotiations were with someone far more senior who had been a personnel manager in industry.

> Locally we had an ethos based on 'Trust your staff and they'll do their job'. I think we were thought of as really naïve. Several practices that I thought of as good practice, they thought of as wishy-washy with the staff taking us for a ride.

So, practices were changed and staff goodwill was lost. The nurse manager is clear that going on holiday with clients is hard:

> You are at work and away from home for long periods. But the view of this guy was, I remember his words, 'They're pissing up your back; they're getting all these free holidays'. It was quite clear he'd never been in a support service. I couldn't believe the attitude.

A similar attitude was expressed towards the other practices established to encourage staff integration with clients such as having their meals with them. This made a more natural environment than the sort of hovering that happens with supervising other people eating; staff were to model behaviour and the result would be a more homely atmosphere. There was a notion of the staff being in the clients' house as guests. The new line was that "Nobody else in social services got a free meal so why should these staff?' The fact that they were working was not acknowledged. Inevitably many staff began to bring in sandwiches and the nature of the meal was changed.

The examples could be multiplied. The nurse manager sees the vital aspect of work with staff in these settings as being the quality of the work that they do in the vast amount of time in which they're not supervised. 'The quality of what goes on is almost entirely about the self-monitoring by staff who want to be there.' Some of that quality he stresses is related to 'planning and setting up systems' but it is the staff motivation that he considers fundamental.

Old and new values

The evidence grew that in the new order in both social services and health the influence of the values which had guided them in resettlement had disappeared:

> The social service staff for the service that I was involved in setting up had all these consistent values about funding and everything else. They were all committed to that and we spent a lot of time on training; they shared the values and then, suddenly, within a year social services changed it all. The staff are having to see these dropping standards.'

The new managers were contrasted to the former personnel and finance staff. They had said:

> 'Well, basically, we're here as your tool, particularly as you're taking responsibility for the cash now'. Later, when new staff were involved and there were administrative delays in resettlements we said 'Surely, you're here to facilitate'. The reply was: 'No, that's an old fashioned view. We're here to manage'.

Dealings with the purchaser on a resettlement plan for an individual client showed the value shift even more starkly. In earlier years every proposal of this kind had to adhere closely to the principles of normalization and clients' rights. Now, when the resettlement team talked about the quality of life as a guiding principle the purchaser replied, 'We're no longer talking about quality of life' and added that they were only concerned with minimum standards. 'So purchasers don't even talk the same language now.'

Speaking out and honest relationships

While the nurse manager still felt that he personally could speak freely, his view is that in general in both the health authority and social services there is less freedom than before. The situation has deteriorated over several years and is linked to fear of losing one's job, a fear that is now prevalent in social services.

The notion of 'speaking out' should not be seen only as being able to say what is wrong. He thinks staff should be able to be open about the strengths and limitations of the services they provide, whereas some requirements imposed on social services staff since 1991 have demanded dishonesty. He knows of staff who have to go out and re-assess clients to make cuts in services.

> But they have been told to say that it's a re-prioritization; they aren't allowed to say to their clients that it's a cut. It's a cut. That's exactly what it is but they've been told they're not to say it. Quite direct. So, speaking out will put their job in

> jeopardy. And this is people who have been used to speaking out and I don't know what they are going to do.

Circumstances change the terms of the debate. The notion of service deficiency had been an attempt to chart the difference between 'reality and the dreams'. Now, in one part of social services the idea was dealt a death blow as there was 'no longer to be such a thing as a service deficiency form'.

His notion of open debate is linked to honesty. If there have to be cuts which will have consequences for services:

> Let's be honest about the costs. I can never understand the need to dress it up. Why was a Labour council concerned about hiding the truth? At a local level an issue has been that the council endorse documents stating the values and aims of the service. Those are still the same, but the policies that they implement are in conflict with those values in lots of areas.

The decision to leave

The cumulative effect of these changes was to make the nurse manager decide to leave social services. There was no prospect that the deteriorating situation he had described would improve. Indeed, the local authority was seriously over-spent. He could see that tough decisions would have to be made and the quality of life of users would suffer. But he in no way regretted his time in the job and its continuing challenge. He captured the essence of what he had striven for:

> When we bring this down to the individual client level, we're trying to envisage a life which can probably never be achieved. But you need that to know where you're going. It's been described as the North Star. The early sailors steered by the North Star, never thinking they were going to land their ship on it. I think there's a lot of cognitive dissonance when you've got this. You know you're not going to achieve it but you're still trying to achieve it.

Case Study 10

Learning disabilities: a service in jeopardy.
A learning disabilities team leader

Background

This case study describes the experience of the impact of the community care reforms through the eyes of the leader of a small learning disabilities team in a shire county. Its starting point before the changes is with a combined mental health and learning disabilities team operating with growing success in a bureaucratic organization, looking forward to the greater flexibility and responsiveness apparently promised by the reforms. The reality, however, from the team leader's (TL) perspective has been sadly different and the very future of learning disabilities as a front line service now seems in doubt.

Before the changes

The organization of the department and the team

The county social services department was divided into geographical divisions, each of which was virtually a mini-social services department embracing field, domiciliary, day and residential care. Field work was organized in area teams each of which consisted of three sub-teams dealing with children, mental health and learning disabilities, elderly people and physical disabilities. While all ongoing work was covered by the specialist teams, initial referrals were received by duty officers, drawn in turn from these teams. The duty officers were expected to have the generic skills to take any immediate action needed on referrals and, if appropriate, then pass them for further work to the relevant specialist team. In the case study TL's area, such referrals were normally in the hands of the senior of the appropriate team by the end of the day in which they came in.

The work of the mental health/learning disabilities team

While the team was responsible for both kinds of clients, over the years there was an increasing emphasis on specialization, with different workers concentrating on mental health and on learning disabilities.

When a referral of someone with learning disabilities came into the team, the social worker to whom the case was allocated did an initial assessment and plan.

> With our clients there was seldom any immediate rationing based on rigid eligibility
> criteria. There was clarification of the department's role and the initial assessment
> would go on over some weeks because LD clients are a lifetime commitment. You
> are not into spot provision. You are into a life plan.

Social workers had increasing discretion in setting about finding appropriate
services. Assessment was seen as an ongoing activity, taking place alongside
provision. Where that provision involved other professionals such as community
nurses or day care staff, it could take on a multi-disciplinary character. The
work of finding appropriate placements and building or supporting care systems
for people with learning disabilities, was aided by a growing cooperation
between different parts of the social services department and with different agencies with responsibilities in the field; by an increased devolution of
responsibilities and access to resources by workers and carers; and by the
creativity of workers encouraged by these developments.

Inside the social services department the specialist learning disability services
in field, residential and day sections were becoming more cohesive, aided by the
appointment of a manager for learning disabilities at divisional level. Work with
the health service was enhanced by a joint strategy at the local level and common
membership of the community mental handicap team. At the individual level,
workers from different agencies routinely worked together on the same cases.
There was also considerable co-working with private and voluntary homes in
seeking to adapt the care provided to individual needs.

Intra- and inter-organizational cooperation was made easier by the increasing
devolution of decision making to the social workers and operational managers
such as day centre managers. Social workers negotiated directly with day
services and hostels for places. Once regular short-term care was agreed and set
up, carers could themselves take on arrangements for hostel stays or family
support, within an agreed limit.

Relations with senior management tended to be positive. At the divisional level
managers regarded the LD services as 'the flagship' of the development of
needs-led services aimed at developing potential and minimizing dependancy.
Further, while the team did not control access to scarce outside resources, it did
at least have a voice in decisions made about their use. For example, the county
succeeded in freeing some of its resources, previously used to support LD clients
in out-of-county placements, to facilitate creative and imaginative work by social
workers to support clients and their carers in their own homes and to access
community facilities for them.

Further, the team leader said, sometimes management would find ways round
the rules, for example making it possible to switch money from a residential
establishment to support work in the community.

> Now management would say that the old management colluded improperly with the
> workers to make these things happen. From the perception of the workers, manage-
> ment was being supportive, creative and actually using their commonsense about

delivering a good service. It's funny how we yearn for those nice people in division! We used to mutter about them then!"

These positive aspects of work in the LD field were, nevertheless, offset to a considerable extent by the inheritance from the very different approach of the old mental handicap services. Many resources were tied up in existing buildings and services, and controlled under rigid budget heads. Old ways of working often persisted, too. In addition, there was a lack of the range of appropriate specialist services needed if the aims of making it possible for LD clients to live in the community in small groups or on their own were to be realized. In particular, the department's home help service could seldom provide the services needed by LD clients, objecting that they were too difficult, or required specialist skills, or needed help at the wrong time of the day.

Advantages and disadvantages

The team leader felt that there was much that was positive about the LD services in his area before the changes. There was a strong feeling that they were steadily improving as increased specialization was introduced, cooperation with other agencies was strengthened, more decisions were devolved to the team, and workers were becoming increasingly creative in shaping needs-led services. The frustrations facing the team focused centrally on the legacy of the bricks and mortar approach of the past and the lack of appropriate services to allow the full development of normalization. In that context, the community care legislation with its emphasis on supporting clients in their own homes and freeing up the resources for such needs-led services was seen as holding positive promise.

The team leader's personal experience of the job

The TL got considerable enjoyment from his job, particularly prizing the feeling that he had his own territory, that he understood the world he was operating in, and felt that he had his place in it. He could say then

> I've got my manor, I know the people who I'm serving. I've got an overview and most of the people I know personally and I know I can often respond to them because I know a lot. It was the individuality and flexibility, the feeling about the relationships with a relatively small group of clients.

Having his place in this world, he said, 'gave me a certain degree of power and I knew where to go for the next bit of power'. The frustrations of the job were related to the difficulty, in the bricks and mortar culture, of freeing up the resources the team needed to help its clients, his own personal dislike of the generic work he had to do in the area team whenever it was his turn to do intake duty, and the at times overwhelming workload.

He felt secure in his work and able to speak out freely in the organization. He was not aware of pressures to conform and noted that even this bureaucratic department was prepared to tolerate eccentrics whose administrative work might be poor but whose work for clients had wide respect.

The Changes

The promise of the reforms

The TL and his colleagues, when they read about the community care reforms, formed quite specific expectations about how they would facilitate their work. What seemed to be promised was an organizational structure which would help them to provide

> just those 'ordinary life', community-based developmental services which LD professionals had been trying to implement in the old 'bricks and mortar' environment. The purchaser/provider separation was intended to liberate clients from the bad old ways of services providing what they had, rather than what people needed.

Specifically, they expected to see far more resources available, initially through the special transitional grant, to buy services the clients really needed for their independence; the creation of more independent services to meet these needs; and empowerment of client and carer in needs assessment and through choice.

The organizational changes

The early implementation papers following the 1990 Act suggested different ways of introducing a purchaser/provider split in SSDs. This county chose the most radical, implementing the split at the front line by separating the assessment of cases and decisions about what provision should be made, from the provision of service itself. The authority was divided into separate purchasing and providing sections for all services except child care. All existing staff were required to apply for jobs in the new organization and there was no guarantee that they would be able to keep the same kind of work as they had been doing.

The county was sub-divided into divisions. Each was headed by a purchasing manager who deployed a number of assessment teams. Many of the social work staff, especially in the elderly and physically disabled teams, were transferred to roles as social work assessors in these teams or as care managers. The bulk of the other front line staff of the authority – in the residential, day care, field and domiciliary services – were transferred to provider teams, within a different organizational structure.

Learning disabilities was preserved as a provider service. The TL was appointed to head a social work team specializing in LD, covering territory previously served by two area teams. Other LD specialist services from the department as well as from health were also located in the same building.

Experience of the change process

The manner in which the reorganization was handled provided the first evidence of a quite dramatic shift in management style in the department. Most staff felt that the consultation process was perfunctory and gave them little effective say. The team leader characterized the handling of the process as

> macho-management. A lack of consultation, a series of edicts. There's been no nego-tiation, no recognition that there is any input to come from professional staff. They know what they are going to do and do it. If you objected you were told that you were old-fashioned and that you should 'get real'. We were de-skilled in the process.

The actual mechanics of slotting people into new jobs was long drawn out, left some people in limbo for months on end, and concluded for many with an unsat-isfactory outcome. However, the members of the LD social work team felt lucky. All had worked in the field before, in the same general area. They were based in a familiar office and with the whole array of LD services for the area.

After the Changes

The first phase

During the first year following the changes the experience of the new LD team was a mixture of positives and negatives. On the down side, the team had to contend with a complex and unhelpful referral process. Specialist long term social work was to be commissioned following assessment by a social worker in one of the case assessment teams (purchasing). If a client required a complex package of care he or she was to be referred to care management (purchasing) instead. If clients were under 18 they were to be the responsibility of the special needs chil-dren's service. As a result, four teams could be involved where before the changes there was just one. But on the positive side, most of the new organizational arrangements were slow to come into effect and informally the team continued to act to a considerable degree as both an assesssor and provider of services, and benefited from the arrival of the first tranche of special transitional grant money as well as from co-location with other colleagues working in the LD field.

At this stage the new assessment scheme was quite relaxed. The LD team was able to take on cases from amongst previous clients, and others they knew, with minimum formality. Some satisfactory packages of support were put together with the care management team for LD clients who needed intensive support at home.

The second phase

Early in the second year, the real implications of the new system became increasingly apparent to the TL. This was partly a result of the full operational-ization of the new structure but the whole process of change was given a violent impetus by the financial crisis which hit the department, along with other shire counties. According to the management of the social services department, this was caused when the government changed the rules affecting the amount of the STG paid to the counties. The sum involved was drastically reduced with only a few months' notice. The new organizational structure had to rapidly find means of cutting several millions of pounds from its budget. It was in this context that the LD team became sharply aware of the deficiencies and contradictions of the new system and in which it found itself confronting a management that had once seemed sympathetic and friendly, if paternalistic, but which was now recast almost as an opponent to be fought and outwitted in the struggle to provide clients with a decent service.

Key issues identified by the TL are the problems of the purchaser/provider split, the damage to interagency relationships, the sidelining of social work, and the character and behaviour of the new management.

Contradictions of the purchaser/provider split

For the TL

> the division of the department into purchasers and providers has virtually resulted in two departments. There has been little common agreement about service objectives and principles. At times there seems to have been more effort put into fighting each other than in providing a service. Since the purchasers hold the purse-strings, specialist provider social work has little influence.

The concept of separating assessment from intervention is, in his view, 'fundamentally flawed'. Its contradictions are particularly clearly illustrated in the case of LD clients for whom a long-term and holistic perspective is usually required. Ironically, the introduction of quasi-separate assessment has not resulted in needs-led, individually designed services. Instead,

> people have been 'slotted in' and subjected to disabling and limiting generic regulations far worse than before the Community Care act. Case assessment social workers have usually little specialist knowledge or understanding of learning disabilities and have little time to carry out an assessment which they were generally expected to complete in a single visit.

The result, from the point of view of clients and carers, is that services are

> complicated, fragmented, and delayed by the split between case assessment, care management, and social work. They are left confused and irritated. It is even worse for a child transferring to adult services. Enormous amounts of time, effort and paper go into just making the system work rather than providing a service.

Further, the hoped for new specialized services for people with LD have not emerged. Support available through the care management section of the department is limited to providing strictly personal care and is not available to help clients to develop independence. Independent sector alternatives have not materialized and are unlikely to since the 'ceilings' imposed by the department's purchasing managers on hourly rates of pay and the price of total packages remove any incentive to potential providers with appropriate expertise to become involved.

The decline of inter-agency cooperation

The purchaser/provider split, which has taken place in the health service as well as in social services and the separate assessment of social care needs

> has colossally undermined formal inter-agency working. Colleagues in health feel excluded from assessment and planning. There is now a major social/health care argument with little of the mutual help and cooperation that existed before. Clients are losing out on services as a result.

The old flexibility in which workers from different departments or services cooperated together to support and cover for each other in working with a client is no longer possible.

> A community nurse might only be allowed to do things to do with the maintenance of someone's health through advice on diet and personal hygiene in contrast to the system before the changes when she might call in to see if they are OK and perhaps advise them how to manage their bills. Supposing the social worker was on leave, the community nurse might cover all the things the social worker had been doing. In return the social worker might check the medication was being taken. Now they are not supposed to do it.

Marginalizing social work

These processes have had the effect that, in the TL's words, 'social work has been totally sidelined'. Its status is reduced to 'counselling' which 'should occasionally be used to render some of the more difficult customers a bit easier to manage. If they are still difficult, the social worker has failed'. The social workers in LD are now labelled providers and are not responsible for decisions as to whether clients should get a service or not.

However, when the TL pointed out to a purchasing manager that he didn't believe, therefore, that his team should be expected to say 'no' to a client,

> The manager got really angry at that point and said 'Yes it is, it's social workers' responsibility to say no. That's exactly what it is'. The catch phrase in the department is 'the providers should own the department's budget'. The purchasing manager says: 'The trouble with your team is that they don't own the budget'. Owning the department's budget means, apparently, not advocating for your clients' needs.

Advocating for resources for a client, or even drawing attention to unmet need, which once would have been accepted as the job of the social worker (whether or not the resources were available to help), are now, according to the team leader, likely to be seen as hostile acts.

> Nowadays they say you are disloyal. It's as though they have no respect for your judgement. In the past people respected that you were making a professional judgement and giving them your advice on your considered view and they received that in that spirit. Then they said 'yea' or 'nay'. Nowadays they resent us making such requests and are in effect saying 'What the hell are you doing coming up here and saying this to us? What you are saying to us is absolutely subversive and a sacking offence'.

Most recently, the whole future of the LD teams in the county appears to be in doubt as it has become known that the director feels there is no longer a need for a specialist provider service and would like to see the social workers in the existing teams remustered as generic care managers in the purchasing part of the department.

The making of macho management

These interchanges with management are typical of the much more abrasive style of leadership that began to surface from the beginning of the changes. 'It was as though they had been briefed to suddenly introduce that kind of style to social services management.'

It became increasingly clear that a new culture was developing in the management of the department which was driven first and foremost by the budget and the need to balance the books, and which was to be delivered in a new managerial style, wrapped in the language and style of a commercial business. Behind it all was an overriding demand that appearances should be maintained, and that the department should present a picture of an organization that was coping.

The problem of government under-funding is widely recognized in the authority and is the source of many of the problems faced by the social services department, the TL believes. He finds it extraordinary, then, 'how little outcry there has been from officers and members' and to what degree certain managers have at least appeared to throw themselves with gusto into the crisis, eager to prove their ability to 'manage' the budget. LD clients may not have suffered as much as some other client groups, given there is less 'new business' than with other client groups. 'Nevertheless for new clients or newly occurring needs the outlook is bleak. As a member of the divisional purchasing team said, "We are here to preserve life, not to enhance it".'

His cynicism about management motivation has been reinforced by memorandums emphasizing various 'let-out' clauses in the community care legislation and Department of Health directives. In particular, it has been emphasized that the Department of Health 'Choice Directive' only applies to residential care, and then only if it does not result in the department exceeding its resources. Advice has been given about covertly delaying both assessments and the subsequent provision of service in order to save money.

His explanation of how managers who were themselves once social workers can now take this view of the profession and its work is simply that they are

> small people in positions of power who see their main activity as controlling the budget, not providing services for people.
> [His social worker wife adds] They are just thinking very mechanically. There is a sense of counter revolution, a switch in the ethos of the organization. The whole business of the market has undermined everything that the social workers up to eighteen months ago stood for. It is as though their thought processes, the way they deal with matters, are no longer valid to the organization.

The TL's summary evaluation of trends in LD service provision since the 1990 Act

His overall view of the impact of the Act in his organization was extremely negative. There was decreasing recognition of specialist needs; decreasing cooperation between workers and external agencies; decreasing emphasis on needs-led, individualized services; a concentration of power and decision-making in the hands of the purchasing managers; services were finance-led 'to an astonishing degree'; no value was placed on professional judgement which was being replaced by rules and 'tick the box' evaluations. The result was an extremely demoralized staff.

The declining standards of service to clients: a case study

The team leader cited a recent example which summed up the devastating effects of the changes on the quality of services which can now be provided for clients.

The placement of a learning disabled man in his thirties, who had been a client of the department since his childhood, was breaking down. A few years ago he had been helped to move into a private house with two other less severely disabled men. Since then one of them had died and the client's capacity to cope had deteriorated badly. In the view of the social and health services workers who were supporting him he urgently needed to go back into some form of residential care, a view the client, who was 'absolutely miserable and is longing to be cared for', shares. A highly suitable place, fully acceptable to the client, had been found in a small home run by a social worker who was very used to dealing with difficult behaviour.

In the pre-1990 Act days, at this stage the team would simply have applied on behalf of the client for social security funding for the new placement and it would automatically have been granted. Instead, the purchasers first did all they could to delay a decision on the move and then refused it. Initially, they required a couple of months to consider the paper work. Then they sent a care manager, with no training in learning disabilities, to reassess the case. When her report supported the move, the purchasers ruled that no new placements in independent residential services were to be sanctioned and the proposal was refused. The only alternative to the client's present accommodation that could be offered was a place in a large hostel for people with learning disabilities run by the department where a number of people live whose behaviour is known to have an adverse interaction with their client.

Subsequently, the client was helped by his social worker to make a formal complaint which was also taken up by a voluntary organization (which had been informally contacted by the team leader). The social worker was accused of 'not acting like an officer of the department' by an angry purchasing manager but the placement was finally agreed to after four months of wrangling and proved highly successful. 'So much,' commented the L, 'for the Department of Health's choice directive.'

The team leader's personal experience of his job after the reforms

It is not surprising, in the light of these experiences of the new organization, to find that the TL rates his enjoyment substantially lower than before them. In particular, he misses the very element he prized under the old system, his sense of control. It frustrates him that he has 'no real power at all to do anything to effect any change for the positive'. He doesn't feel that he now has the freedom to do the job to his own satisfaction because

> I need to seek permission from another part of the organization which doesn't even share the same values whereas previously I felt the organization broadly shared the same values, even if in detail it wasn't always quite the same. I have very, very little freedom. I'm stopped at every corner.

Speaking out now is a high risk strategy. The TL cited the case of a colleague who was given a reprimand for speaking to the Mental Health Act Commission in a critical way about how the purchaser/provider split 'impeded getting services to clients.' Conforming, or appearing to conform, seemed to be part of the price of getting resources for your clients

> I do see our role as being there to get the most we can for our clients in their interests, and if you don't conform, play the game, you won't get anything at all. I do use some of the new jargon some of the time and I do it purposefully to try and make people think I'm one of them and get what I want.

But fighting back in this way has not offset the deep sense of demoralization for the TL who characterized the effect of the changes in terms of the team's work for LD:

> Everything in our particular bit of the service that we have spent the last ten years building up is bit by bit being dismantled under our very eyes and that is very painful.

For the future

In the TL's view planning is essential in the provision of LD services but is currently virtually impossible with the purchaser/provider split.

> Providers are not supposed to do it and purchasers are totally taken up with the 'here and now'. Planning and preparing for the future is the absolute core of what most LD social work is about and is the central dilemma for most families with an LD member. Individual personal plans have virtually been abandoned as 'useless' to purchasers and the multi-agency approach is also largely seen as irrelevant.

The team leader would like to see the return to a *whole-hearted* service for people with learning disabilities. A crucial element in this would be the development of close collaboration in joint planning with health. But even more important, in his view, is to make it possible for professionals to get on and do what they know how to do. 'It could be done *now* if they *trusted* us.'

Case Study 11

'We're being pushed into competing against each other': change in a voluntary organization for adults with learning disabilities. The director of a voluntary organization

Background

The subject of this study is director of a well-established voluntary organization which runs a supported housing programme for people with learning disabilities. Work of organizations of this kind grew as a result of the policy to close down the long-term 'mental handicap' hospitals and to resettle their patients in the community. Their aims are also entirely consistent with those of the community care reforms in that they are concerned with maximizing the independence of those they are helping and their ability to live in their own homes.

The organization has depended since its inception on its ability to obtain funding from a range of other agencies and so the emphasis on contractual relations between statutory and independent sectors in the 1990 Act did not in itself pose any special problems. However, the special significance of this case study is that it provides a vivid example of how the *nature* of contractual relationships began to be radically altered in the implementation of the Act and how aspects of the reforms may threaten the ability of the independent sector to provide a service for people with learning disabilities which combines high quality with financial viability. The promotion of competition within the sector emerges as a particularly contentious consequence of the reforms with worrying implications for the future.

The case study is based on the views of the director of the organization. She is an experienced and highly qualified social worker and manager, who, before appointment to her present post had held a variety of jobs in social services departments and had extensive experience in working with people with learning disabilities.

Before the changes

Establishing a new organization and a new way of working

The origins of the organization go back to the 1970s when a group of parents, relatives and individual professionals who were critical of the contemporary services for people with learning disabilities got together. In their view what was on offer simply wasn't good enough. It consisted mainly of hostels and training centres, which at that time were themselves regimented places. There were people stuck in hospital who should never have been there and, indeed, the group questioned whether *anybody* at all with learning disabilities should be in hospitals.

The group was very committed to the model of normalization and it was this commitment which provided the impetus for setting up a new organization:

> It was the model that drove the idea. There was a really strong belief amongst a number of people that there's no reason why people couldn't be in ordinary housing. So it was the idea which was very, very strong with the kind of principles that drove the organization. And of course a number of things followed from that, including the fact that people should be able to use the ordinary facilities that other people do. They were all very committed to normalization.

The director sees the value base as central to understanding subsequent developments in the organization.

The organization was registered as a charity, a management group was chosen and members set about finding the financial support they needed to employ staff. Eventually, by the early 1980s, it succeeded in obtaining funding for a project to resettle people with learning disabilities leaving hospital in supported housing. The director was recruited and, operating with a small team of seven others, began working with individual patients and bringing them into the community.

The organization had houses for the people to live in but no other facilities or support. The challenge for the director was, 'How were we going to get them into real life? How are they going to get integrated?' They could not look for expertise or much support from social services for, as she says,

> at that time we were in some kind of practice limbo with some social services staff thinking quite strongly that this was all a bit mad. 'It can't possibly work. How could people [with learning disabilities] possibly live in houses?' Unconscious as well as perhaps more conscious blocks were being set up and there was a belief that 'It's all going to go horribly wrong'.

The lack of appropriate specialist facilities in the local community turned out to be a blessing in disguise, for it encouraged the organization from the very beginning to implement practice which supported normalization. Maximum use was made of ordinary community facilities and the organization set up its own employment scheme instead of sending people to segregated adult training centres.

The established organization

In the last twelve years the organization has grown steadily. It now has a staff of over a hundred and provides support for many more people with learning disabilities living in houses for which it is responsible. Its overall structure and style of working have remained unaffected by the community care changes. The range of funding sources also remains broadly similar but, as is shown later, was affected in terms of the relative importance of different funders.

Funding

The organization gets its funds from two main sources: first, money received from the people who live in the houses, coming from housing benefit; second, grants from health authorities, social services departments and housing associations. It has also gained support for some of its employment developments from European Social Funding, 'on the basis of taking unemployed people with learning disabilities and training them as job supporters'. Some staff have been recruited from the people who were trained as supporters.

An important aim for the organization has been to establish and maintain as wide a range of sources for its funding as possible. The director commented, 'We don't want to find ourselves driven to compromise or change our values because of funding so we feel it's important not to be dependent on one source or organization'.

The nature of the funding – whether it was per individual or in block, whether for a person or a number of hours of service, whether at an average level per person or specific to assessed requirements for an individual – has been significant from the start and continues to be so.

The style of the organization and the service

Central to the character of the organization as it has grown and developed has been its success in holding on to its value base and the freedom which being an independent agency has given it to develop progressive practice.

The director believes that its values pervade the whole organization 'from the committee right the way through'. 'Every time we've looked at ourselves or been looked at there's no doubt that the philosophy does permeate the organization so people understand what it is we're trying to do'. This did not mean, however, that the interpretation of the philosophy had always been agreed or that there had been no dilemmas in translating it into action 'on the ground floor'.

Indeed, such issues are likely to be more common in an independent organization where there is potentially less emphasis on bureaucratic procedures than in statutory services. The director thought that the fact of being an independent organization left them 'with a degree of freedom that might not be there in health and social services'. They could 'take risks that maybe health and social services wouldn't have been able to do'. For example about how people handle their money which 'you can imagine in health and social services would have been subject to some kind of bureaucratic response and might take a long time'.

Ordinary Life

Normalization, which is at the heart of the values of the organization, is about making it possible for people to lead an 'ordinary life'. What that should be is another matter. The director thinks that relationships 'are the biggest gap in people's lives', adding that she means 'relationships that aren't with paid people'. This poses a substantial problem for the organization.

> I think people generally have quite full lives. They've developed a sense of themselves. But I know that for most people, their external relationships are very few. And that's an enormous challenge for all of us. It's a bit like being here isn't enough. Going places isn't enough. A lot of people are totally dependent on the personal support to link and to help them make arrangements. They have lots of difficulties with time and ability to use phones or whatever. And we struggle, basically. At the same time we're aware that often we're in the work because we like working with the people. So, we've got some very good project workers who make excellent relationships and are really very good with the people but may present barriers to other people getting involved. How do you manage to step back, because people have needed the experience of the relationship with the project worker to grow in themselves ?

She gave the example of neighbours who sometimes might want to develop relationships with the people the organization was supporting but who could feel that staff were getting in the way by being too protective.

A supportive environment for leadership

The director personally found her work environment highly supportive and one in which the organization could develop a reputation for integrity and outspokenness in advocating and defending its principles. Underpinning this is the management committee to whom she reports. The chair of the management committee sits on the user services committee, a sub-committee of the main group. So the management hears about what is going on. 'Provided we're doing things that reflect our philosophy, I've always felt the support right the way through.'

Against this background she feels secure in her job and has felt free to speak her mind in dealing with other organizations, contrasting her situation favourably with that of colleagues in statutory organizations:

> I think I've always felt personally freer through not being at social services. Sometimes we've said things that some of the people in a meeting in health and social services wanted to say but weren't able to because of their particular positions.

She regards this freedom as one of their strengths both in dealing with other agencies and in building up the reputation of the organization.

> We're at the receiving end of powerful organizations telling us how much money they're going to give us and what they're going to do. It's perhaps only right that there should be a countervailing force.

Changes

With the implementation of the new funding arrangements under the 1990 Act and the division of the county social services department into purchaser and provider organizations there have been major changes both in the general climate in which the organization works and in the detail of relationships with the organization's funders. These changes have not only had the cumulative effect of making the life of the organization more complicated and uncertain but have raised wider concerns about their negative impact on services for people with learning disabilities in the area as a whole.

The underlying changes described by the director concerned the tendency for a growing monopoly in funding, the loss of trust between purchaser and provider, and the advent of competition. But the impact of the changes was also reflected in issues in assessment and in a battle to defend standards.

A growing monopoly

As the health authority hands funds and responsibility to the social services department, the director pointed out, 'it does mean that you've got one very powerful purchaser and in today's situation we need to make sure that we're maintaining as much independence from that as we can'. The former situation was that the health authority passed across money for other organizations to use, more like a grant for the provision of certain services. This of course had the potential for reliance on particular funding bodies but the danger is magnified when there is more precision from 'the purchasing body' as to the nature of the service that is provided.

Within the organization, she says,

> we became increasingly conscious that we had to develop our own base of funding that's separate from the service because otherwise we could be in danger of being a sort of quasi local authority group, some sort of odd extended arm of the local authority.

It is significant in her view that purchasers from her local social services department do not have control over all the money that is spent on community care. In fact the purchasers only control the additional funds available, not the money that the authority spends on its own provision. This results, for example, in the authority using its own day services before it is willing to purchase from other organizations which is an obvious limitation for non-local authority organizations.

The advent of competition and erosion of trust

The official introduction of 'market' conditions came in April 1993 when local authorities started receiving the special transitional grant, transferring social security and other community care funds (Chapter 1, p.17). The impact on relationships with social services observed by the director was dramatic:

> It was almost like from April third, 1993 or whenever it was, somehow we providers became tainted and if we were going to suggest anything or say anything in relation to a person it would obviously be because we wanted to provide the service. So it would suddenly be seen in business terms; we were trying to get the market or the money. Yet on March 31st we had obviously been regarded as talking about our clients in a thoroughly professional, responsible way.

The director's fears about competition were not about the future of her own organization which had decided it didn't want to grow and get into the business of being 'a kind of county council' but that it would concentrate on piloting new approaches and trying to develop more creative ways of service delivery. What worried her was that its general impact on services as a whole would be to undermine rather than improve their quality by weakening or destroying cooperative relationships that had existed before, by emphasizing presentation rather than performance and by eroding the basis of trust on which past work had depended.

Competition rather than quality

The director is particularly concerned about the adverse effects of competition:

> The fear I've got is the very real thing about the competitive bit. There was a very co-operative provider base, or service base, where everybody worked together and there wasn't any sense in which you were worried about who was doing what, because you were working together. We are now in the situation to help ourselves, where we're being pushed into competing against each other, if it's only on price. And once upon a time, people could have anything, any information or anything that we'd developed here, I wouldn't even think about it really. Now, I'm actually thinking about quite a lot and being more thoughtful about what I hand out.

Presentation rather than performance

They want to go on sharing the results of their innovative work but are

> worried about people taking the top of it and using it without the underneath of it, which I think the competition pushes you into. We could be developing stuff for irresponsible providers to pick up and run with who won't look after the clients and their interests in the long run.

She was worried, too, at the problems that might be created by 'hard marketing'. Another organization in their field had recently produced a glossy brochure about what it had to offer. Not only does that make it more difficult for the individual client to make an informed choice, but it also encourages people to present their service 'as if everything's OK or as if we're delivering a perfect service and we're marketing a perfect service when we know it isn't perfect'.

The erosion of trust

It can be argued that all contracts, however precisely defined, ultimately rely on trust, a reality caught in the saying, 'My word is my bond.' In the example of contracting for social services the degree of trust that purchasers have in providers' abilities and intentions to fulfil their requirements is likely to be reflected in the detail of costings and service specifications. The director's experience indicates that before the community care reforms a high degree of trust tended to characterize their contractual relationships with statutory services. This was based on the good record of the organization and mutual confidence in the people concerned. The result was a flexible and, it would appear, cost effective system of funding. In a sense what is at issue is the nature of *contract*.

An example highlighted by the director was the practice of *average* funding. An average price is agreed for a service for a person, on the understanding of both parties (purchasers and providers) that this will be more than is needed for some clients and less than required for others. 'If somebody's needs go up, we may be able to meet those because somebody else's have gone down. So we do a lot of shuffling around.' The system has the advantage that it is easy to administer, and allows the provider to respond quickly and effectively to changes in users' needs without frequent reference back to the purchaser.

In the new regime, however, the purchasers prefer *individual* funding. They are questioning the organization's prices on some of its existing users and pushing for individual costings. The director has warned the purchasers that if 'you squeeze the price right down, I'm going to be coming back to you every five minutes' because she will have lost the flexibility average pricing left her to cope with the ups and downs in individual needs. Individual costing also opens the door to the unscrupulous provider who saves money on a contract, as when a client becomes unexpectedly easier and so less expensive to care for, simply to retain the savings. Providers will be tempted to over-emphasize people's disabilities.

She knows some purchasers who think that 'They're in the market place and they can just bash down the price'. She's worried about 'the different competence levels of the purchasers we're dealing with'. If providers do not trust the information they get from purchasers, there will be even more pressure for them to look for the worst scenario. 'We will end up with everybody getting into this thing where providers are describing people as things they're not'.

> Purchasers, of course, quite rightly by then would be suspecting people. They will
> be into the scenario we've always been into (in relation to block contracts). And so
> they'll offer you slightly less because they think that's the game you're in.

There is a relationship here between specialist knowledge, understanding of the needs of the client and resource level. Previous health authority people were specialists and, in the director's eyes, knew what they were talking about even though she didn't always agree with them. 'Health authority purchasers now don't know the product.'

Assessment

The case for a much higher standard of assessment of people needing help was a central plank in the proposals leading to the 1990 Act. In the learning disabilities field, at least, these improvements have yet to be demonstrated. The director identified three problems in particular in her organization's experience of assessment since the changes were introduced: the ambiguities of the assessment process, the pressures on assessors to be over prescriptive in their assessments and the uneven quality of the assessors themselves.

Ambiguity

The 1990 Act leaves the role of the assessment unclear. How far is it meant to provide a full account of the 'needs' of the client? How far must it take account of the resources of the organization to meet need ? In the director's view the assessing social workers are getting into a very difficult position:

> They're being told in no uncertain terms that they mustn't tell people what they
> need, or that they must be very careful because they'll be raising expectations
> beyond what can be met. But at the same time social work is a process of doing
> things *with* clients. Together you have to explore and determine things.

Specificity

There is an increasing risk that where resources are very tight and when social workers are under pressure to be very careful about committing their department's budgets, or where they do not have the appropriate knowledge, their assessments may be too specific and may not allow sufficient recognition of changes in the needs of the user.

In the director's view good assessments should be much less specific. They ought to be saying,

> This person needs some day activity or some development in relation to personal
> relationships or they need some service because they are at risk if, for example, they
> don't get meals properly. It shouldn't be, 'They need to go to a particular service'
> or, 'They need a dispersed housing scheme', even. I think people have to be very

> careful about the way they discuss where people might go or what might happen to them.

Thus a report should not even specify residential care, let alone a particular hostel.

> What people may need is supervised support and accommodation and there may be a number of different ways to provide that. There are further risks to specifying 'residential care.' There is a risk that people might need a full service in the short term but in the longer term won't.

In her own organization there are people who, after ten years, have very little oversight from staff. She doubts whether that would happen with a residential home.

The assessors

The director was concerned about the somewhat confused position in health and social services over general and specialist assessment for care. She did not back the use of specialists for all assessments of people with learning disabilities 'because we don't want to put clients into specialist services when they don't need them'. There was a case for a gatekeeper to prevent this happening. But specialist assessment needed to be available at a second stage in the process, if required. Current services fall short of this: in the local social services department the people carrying out the assessments are specialist social workers and in the health authority there are specialists in learning difficulties but they are all in provider services, not purchasing.

Defending standards

The organization's fight to defend the standards of services for people with learning disabilities does not mean a refusal to acknowledge the reality of the resource problems confronting the purchasers. The director approaches these problems on the basis of the organization's long experience of having to cope with strictly limited resources. Her response has been to be as creative as possible with what they have got.

> So we'll enter into that dialogue with people and are quite happy to do it, but we're not about dumping our principles and saying, 'Because it's too expensive, we'll now have a block of twenty and herd them all in', or something. I know it sounds ridiculous but there's been an item to social services committee in some detail stating that they are no longer to resettle in groups of less than four and maybe five people. And they're actually talking about reviewing their services to increase the numbers which are in their current service to see if they can get a fourth in tenancies which have only two or three people.

Faced with such dilemmas she and others have wanted a place to examine some of the issues and to work out a strategy for dealing with changed demands.

The question becomes one of searching for alliances. The director has found support in a voluntary sector forum, 'a legitimate place for consultation and feeding back and I'm very active in that'. The group liaises with health authorities and social services departments; it has produced a statement of principles and practices, some of which had been printed by the local authority as part of the policy in relation to contracting with voluntary organizations. There is also a local group of learning disability providers which has come together to achieve some solidarity over values and services for clients. They feel under substantial pressure to compromise their values and worsen services for clients. It is said that people in the social services department talk of 'no longer being able to afford the Rolls Royce model'.

> We're calling it 'To defend the model'. But it's actually about saying, 'How can we?' Are there ways that we can do things more cheaply? What are our creative ideas? How could we be doing things better? Is doing things bigger going to be cheaper? Let's look at some of the research.

The wider question is to consider the systems which will allow, indeed promote, such searching for improvements.

And the future?

The director urges that there should be better information on the real costs of services so that there could be an informed debate on what are the best ways of providing services. Social services departments tend to be interested only in the cost to them not in the real overall cost and exactly what is the service provided. 'It would make it more possible to make some decisions about what they were doing, really to move things on a bit'.

She is confident that there are ways of improving services:

> In order to be creative we've actually got to engage in that together and there are ways, I am absolutely sure that there are ways, that can save money, or bring more money in from other places. Sometimes you need pressure to make that happen.

Case Study 12

'A merciful release': the life and death of a gentle man.
A guardian and a care assistant

Background

The central figure in this case study is a man with learning disabilities, or what in earlier times would have been described as a mental handicap. For many years he lived in a large mental handicap hospital. When a resettlement programme was started there he was keen to move out with his friend, another patient.

The final destination of patients settled in the community depends ideally on the degree of support they are judged to need. A common structure is a core and cluster system. More dependent people may be housed in a hostel where they have quite close support from staff. Less dependent patients are settled, typically in small groups of two or three or more, in houses and flats within easy reach of the core hostel. Their support systems are organized and managed from this base. It was in such a system that Thomas, the subject of this case study, was resettled from a long stay hospital about five years ago and in which he lived until his death.

This account focuses mainly on his last five years. It describes some of the real gains in his quality of life achieved by the resettlement, but it also identifies major shortcomings in training, funding and managing the community services for people with learning disabilities in the area concerned, and in particular the risks that institutionalization in long term hospitals may be replaced by a new form of institutionalization in the community (Morris, 1993). Finally it shows, in the example of Thomas's last illness, how a pressured health service can fail to provide adequate care for a patient with disabilities such as his. Indeed, the people with learning disabilities in this study are far from having achieved normalized lives or full status as citizens. The reforms resulting from the 1990 Act seem to have done nothing to change that.

The case is seen through the eyes of people who came to know Thomas very well – a friend who later became his guardian and one of his carers. His guardian had met him over 20 years ago when she was working as a volunteer in the hospital where he lived, and became a close friend. When a few years ago his mother became too ill and frail to keep in close touch, she agreed to represent her at meetings about Thomas and became his guardian. The carer was employed by social services as one of a team of four people who looked after him during that part of the day he was in his own home, and who slept in overnight.

Thomas's early life and his years in the learning disabilities hospital

Thomas was born soon after the end of the Second World War. His family lived in a small village where his father had a job in a local business. Thomas incurred brain damage during his birth although the extent of the damage was not realized until he was a toddler. Initially, he attended the village school but mainstream education at that time couldn't cope with him and there were few of the educational provisions for children with special needs which exist today.

At the age of nine he was sent to an assessment centre and it was decided that he needed to live in a 'mental handicap' hospital which was some 20 miles away from his village. The decision was based not simply on the lack of suitable educational provision in the community for him but also the view that he would not be safe living at home since he had no real understanding of danger. Thomas's mother was 'heartbroken that he had to go away' for Thomas 'was very much a mother's boy' but she and her husband visited him every week without fail.

Thomas was put into a dormitory with other boys of his age and grew up in the hospital. His guardian, who met Thomas in the mid-1970s when he had been in the hospital about twenty years, judged that he was generally happy there. Like the other patients he had come to accept the routine in a fairly fatalistic way. He had made a good friend of an older patient, Robert, and had plenty of opportunity to do work (such as making rugs) which he enjoyed, and to use his artistic talents. There was a downside to the place. He had been vulnerable to sexual attacks from other male patients, although later Robert protected him from them. The hygiene of the place was poor and infections common. He went through periods of depression, but overall he seemed quite content.

His guardian felt very attached to Thomas.

> He needed me but I needed him. Thomas was like a brother to me because he was always there, he was always happy and he cheered me up. And he was quite positive and things in life which got other people down didn't get him down.

Both his guardian and his carer remarked on Thomas's kindness and generosity: 'He was very caring and generous. Thomas would give you his last sweet, his last penny, his last biscuit'.

Resettlement: Thomas's life in the community

When resettlement in the community became a possibility, Thomas was very keen on the idea.

> He wanted his own front door, he wanted his own key, he wanted his own kitchen, he wanted his own settee and his own bed, his own bedroom and his own bedside lamp. Then he would be, as he put it, like everybody else.

The plan was that he should be found a flat or house with his friend Robert, who was also keen on leaving the hospital. The resettlement process was handled with great care over a two year period ending in 1990 when they were found a semi-detached house in a core and cluster scheme in a town near their family homes.

Thomas was assessed as needing care 24 hours a day while Robert required much less physical care but needed emotional support. The routine established for them was that during the day, Monday to Friday, they were at the nearby Adult Training Centre (ATC).

> The staff would pick them up from the ATC and bring them home, sleep over, and drop them off back at the ATC in the morning. That's how it worked. At the week-ends they were there right through from Friday till Monday morning, with two or three different staff.

Life at home

Thomas and Robert each had a dowry of £4000 to enable them and their helpers to furnish their house and buy the personal belongings which they needed for everyday living and which had previously been provided by the hospital. They loved their new home and the experience of having their own place. In his guardian's view rather than going to the ATC, 'they would have been quite happy to sit at home all day in this house that they had never had before'. Thomas depended more on his helpers but would often go out with his guardian and his carer and would visit their homes. He enjoyed long walks, horse-riding, going for drives in the countryside.

Not all the team of helpers who were with Thomas and Robert in the hours they were not at the ATC befriended the two as the carer did. In her view they felt that they had done their bit by keeping them clean and fed. They were sympathetic and kind but could not see Thomas and Robert as whole human beings. Their perception, she felt, was 'that it's much nicer for them in their own homes, they've got a really good life, and it's good enough for them to sit in front of the TV'.

An untrained workforce

His carer, who is in her twenties, put these attitudes down in part to age – her fellow carers were women in their late fifties and sixties. But she also noted that none of the carers had had any relevant training for the job. Her own experience was typical:

> I've been there for three years and I've had one aromatherapy course which was a

day. That's the only training I've ever had. I had a job interview for the hostel and when I got the job I had no idea what I'd be doing, who I'd be working with. I didn't know what learning difficulties were then and, as far as they know, I still don't. If I had had some training I might have learnt to cope more quickly.

The care of Thomas and Robert was supervised by a residential social worker, based in the nearby hostel who in turn was responsible to the manager of the hostel. Neither was professionally trained in social work and there was no specialist input in planning their care from professionals in the learning disability field. In practice the life plan, which is meant to guide the overall care of people with learning disabilities, was in the carer's words, 'not taken seriously'. The plans were prepared by the untrained care workers themselves and didn't involve anybody else.

The Adult Training Centre

From 9.0 a.m. until 4.0 p.m., Monday to Friday, Thomas and Robert were at the local ATC. ATCs are intended to provide a stimulating environment for adults whose learning disabilities are too severe to allow them to hold down jobs in the outside world. They are meant to include educational and training activities, and often an element of sheltered employment. In the opinion of both his carer and his guardian the ATC attended by Thomas and Robert was a disaster area, providing almost no stimulation at all.

His carer commented:

> You read historical accounts of institutionalization and you think, isn't that awful! Anybody could walk into this ATC today and it would be there, in front of them. It's totally cut off from the community. There are large groups, there's no organization, no structure. Robert literally sits in his own armchair and goes to sleep from 9 o'clock till 4 o'clock. That's Robert's day care. He has no group worker because the group worker was seconded and not covered.

Things were not much better for Thomas. He did do cooking once a week and went out to a local art college once a week, which he really enjoyed. But most of the time there was little to do. According to his guardian, 'Thomas just learned to sit in a chair and just accept it and think "Oh hell! I can't fight. It's not worth fighting this".'

Both his guardian and his carer were struck by the lack of personal concern for their charges shown by the ATC staff and their failure to understand them. This often led in their view to unnecessary rows with Thomas when their only interest seemed to be to get him off the premises as quickly as they could. 'There is no warmth as you come through the door, nothing, not a thing'. The staff seemed to be driven by nothing more than the aim of containment. 'They literally contain these people in the building.'

Arguing for reassessment

Thomas' guardian was pressing hard to get him out of the ATC and to find a better day placement. A fundamental difficulty was that the 'endowment' or weekly allowance for day care with which he left the hospital was very low and quite insufficient to pay for any independent sector alternative.

> The social services said there was no need for a reassessment. So I said, 'Well, there is a need now because I want Thomas reassessed and I want to look at alternative provision in the area'. Well, you'd have thought literally that I had dropped a bomb in there.

She also insisted that the reassessment should be undertaken by a social worker not employed by the ATC. She was told 'nobody asks for that' to which she replied 'Well, I'm asking for it. I don't think Thomas would get a fair assessment otherwise'. The focus then switched to the lack of resources and the whole issue was still being argued backwards and forwards a year later when Thomas died.

Inspection

The 1990 Act gave prominence to the creation of 'arms length' inspection which was to play a crucial role in checking on the quality of services. The inspection of the core and cluster scheme in which Thomas lived was, in his carer's view, cursory and failed to identify any of the major weaknesses in provision of which she was so acutely aware.

> The inspector comes once a year, usually in the Christmas holidays. There's a great big kerfuffle for a week beforehand. Last year he looked at documents like life plans, including the life plan of Thomas that was never ever finalized; he looked at the fire alarm test book to make sure the fire alarm testing is up to date. I was there both of the last two years when he came. He talked to me about my car a bit because he has the same make of car. He talked to Thomas a bit.

Thomas' last days: the accident, hospital and death

The accident and initial period in hospital

Some years after moving into his own home Thomas had a severe fall and badly damaged his back. Both his guardian and his carer visited him frequently while he was in hospital. They became increasingly concerned both at the problems that were being encountered in finding recuperative treatment for him and by the poor standard of care provided in the ward, once the initial period of diagnosis and treatment was complete. They were convinced that what happened to him was substantially affected by his learning disabilities and the perception of them.

The initial treatment appeared to be very good. The scan showed that his spine was fractured. Thomas had lost feeling in his hands, although he could still move his arms. His guardian found Thomas very cheerful in spite of everything. To begin with, she said, his neck was in a brace 'while they were still assessing the damage and the swelling which they thought could have been the reason why there was a lack of feeling and paralysis'. The care was very good at this stage:

> There's a lot of input then, isn't there? The consultants are visiting every day and a doctor comes every day while they're on this assessment. While it's all being sorted through, it's very, very dramatic. But then you soon realize that once the assessment's gone over and they realize that there's not an awful lot that's going to be done, the standard of care of the nursing kind went down hill from then on.

The problem facing the consultant responsible for Thomas was that the treatment he would normally have chosen for such cases, provided by another hospital in the region specializing in the rehabilitation of patients with spinal injuries, could not be made available to him. The hospital would only accept patients where they could expect that rehabilitation would reach a level at which the patient could look after him or herself. Apparently this did not mean that they had to recover full use of their limbs but that they would be able to manage well enough with the help of their own carers whom they could instruct in their day-to-day needs. A person without learning disabilities with the same injury as Thomas could have been expected to achieve that level but, given his communication problems, the spinal injuries hospital did not believe Thomas could do the same.

The consultant therefore had to look for somewhere else that could accept Thomas for rehabilitation. In the meantime, he lay flat on his back in a bed on the orthopaedic ward, his neck in a collar, and heavily drugged to prevent the risk of a fit that might further damage his neck.

Declining standards of care

On their visits, his guardian and carer became increasingly concerned and angry about what they felt was a poor and declining standard of care by the nursing staff. At the root of the problem seemed to be nurses' lack of training in working with patients with learning disabilities and their fear and lack of understanding of Thomas. But most of them, it seemed, made little attempt to overcome these barriers.

There were many instances of poor care seen by his guardian and carer which exhibited a lack of empathy with his physical and mental condition, and suggested a view of him as a member of a different species, a second class citizen. To begin with, Thomas was given no named nurse to whom he and his visitors could relate, in spite of the fact, as his guardian pointed out, that there is a charter pinned up on the wall of the ward telling patients that they would have one.

> I sat and read it one day while I was waiting to speak to the nurse. I brought this up

every time I saw the sister. She said it wasn't necessary in Thomas's case because everybody knew the case history. And I kept saying but it's necessary for me. Who the hell do I talk to? She said it's not necessary. We all can tell you the same. But they didn't. They all told us different.

When on one occasion Thomas shouted for his guardian and wanted to know where she was, the nurses 'really told him off and they moved him into a corner and put a curtain across'. Drinks were placed by his bed. However, he had lost the use of his hands and could not drink unaided but was seldom given any help by the nurses. Similarly, he could not turn over or replace the tape in his personal stereo, but only one of the nurses ever thought of doing this for him. He arrived in hospital with his own pyjamas but these were soon replaced by hospital issue and the nurses denied that he had any of his own. His pyjamas and sheets were dirty much of the time and little effort was made to change them. Normally he never drank tea, much preferring coffee. In the hospital they always gave him tea and claimed that was his preference.

Most of the nurses struck his guardian and his carer as brusque and cold. They appeared to resent any criticism of the care being provided for Thomas and to dismiss any concern they expressed about his deteriorating health. On a number of visits, the guardian began to notice a curious smell round Thomas' bed. When, on one occasion, she put her arm behind his head collar to ease his neck which he said was hurting, her hand came away wet and smelling terribly and she noticed his pillow was stained. She showed it to a trained nurse who said it was only sweat. But the next day he had a new collar and she saw that a massive bed sore had been revealed where the old collar had been rubbing. 'That was negligence. That was real negligence, that sore.'

Far more upsetting, in retrospect, was the nurse's refusal to listen to either the guardian or the carer when they reported that he seemed to have a throat infection and that his voice was going. They told the nurses two days in succession, only to get the response that 'there's nothing wrong'. The third day they arrived to find him with drips everywhere, an oxygen mask, and to be told that he had pneumonia.

Five days later Thomas died. The post-mortem recorded the main cause of death as bronchial pneumonia.

Coda: after Thomas's death

At times in the last weeks, as the problem of finding a hospital to take on the rehabilitation of Thomas dragged on, it appeared to both his guardian and his carer that the staff were waiting for him to die. Certainly, it seemed to his guardian that they were not interested in him and when he did die the predominant attitude both in the hospital and the social services seemed to be that it was a 'merciful release'. His carer commented:

This is what everybody said. Everybody said 'Oh! it was the best for Thomas, he would have had no life afterwards.' I think they knew he was going to die because the week just before his death the wheels started to turn in the social services department: they shortlisted people for the house, even before Thomas died.'

Changes the guardian and carer would like to see

Both the guardian and the carer were clear about the kind of changes that should be given priority to improve the quality of life of people with learning disabilties moving into the community. Raising the standard of the carers who work with people with learning disabilities was the first item on their agenda. The guardian felt that the staff that are going to care for these people need to be up to date on everything that is available and have a very positive approach to their work.

The carer stressed the same point and emphasized the importance of improving staff conditions so that the high rate of turnover could be reduced and staff training could be undertaken. A central aim must be improving day care provision. It is pointless working hard to create the conditions for independent living in the users' homes and then to tolerate the conditions in the ATC between 9.00 am and 4.0 pm every week day in which they were exposed to a form of 'institutionalisation in the community'. For the carer it was also essential that management realize it could not achieve these improvements without 'maintaining the goodwill of staff, which they don't do any more'.

Where the hospital treatment of learning disabled patients was concerned, both wanted discriminatory blocks, of the kind encountered by Thomas, removed and both felt that nursing and medical staff needed to learn how to work with such patients as a part of their basic training.

5

Working with people with mental illness

Definitions of the term 'mental illness' are contested in our society. Some argue, for example, that it is a largely socially constructed condition, with meanings related to the interests of different groups. Medical models, however, which predominate in the health service and are widely accepted in other public agencies, tend to seek 'objective' definitions and explanations in individual pathology. These include a range of conditions from mild neuroses, such as some forms of depression, to disabling psychoses. In these terms, some estimates suggest that about two per cent of the adult population may have a serious mental illness at any one time.

Mental health services in the community are provided by both the NHS and social services departments. The GP and community psychiatric nurse are central in health provision. Local authority services may include hostels, day centres and respite care. Approved social workers (ASWs) have a key role in managing the process of compulsory admission of people to psychiatric hospitals. In 1993–4 local authorities in England and Wales devoted 4.2 per cent of their gross expenditure to mental health services (CIPFA,1 1994). Over the last two decades the need for collaboration between the different professionals providing mental health services has increasingly been recognized and led to the widespread adoption of multi-disciplinary mental health teams involving hospital, community health and social services staff.

The two case studies of mental health services in this chapter consist of one based in the health service, in a multi-disciplinary team, and one based in the social services in a conventional social work team. The health service team provided a model of excellence before it was destroyed by the effects of the 1990 Act. The social work team case study illustrates the frustrations of professionals in a traditional bureaucracy edging forward slowly in improving their service before the Act, and the difficulty of merely surviving, in an organization perceived to be in chaos, after the implementation of the Act.

Case Study 13

Change without leadership: a mental health team in a failing organization.
A senior social worker

Background

This case study describes the experience of a senior social worker who joined the social services department in the late 1980s when it was moving from generic to specialist field services. With substantial previous experience in mental health social work, she was attracted to the job by the challenge of helping to develop the new services. Throughout the last seven years she has led one of the department's mental health field teams.

Her initial experience of the department was disappointing for it seemed to her to be hierarchical, sexist and resistant to change. Nevertheless, she remained hopeful that she could make progress in improving mental health services and was heartened by the promise of the 1990 Act which seemed to support the improvements she felt essential. The reality of the two years since the legislation was supposed to be fully implemented has, however, replaced hope with disillusionment and alienation. The department, in her eyes, has comprehensively failed to respond to the changes demanded of it and is floundering, essentially leaderless and without a strategy.

The department and team before the changes

Context

The case study social services department served a large, predominantly rural county. In the late 1980s it had replaced generic social work teams with specialist teams covering children and families, elderly people, people with learning disabilities, people with physical disabilities and mental health. The mental health team led by the senior social worker (SSW) consisted of five social workers and, together with another team covering the adjoining area, was overseen by a manager. The manager also was responsible for a hostel and local day centres for mental health clients to which the teams had direct access.

The mental health team and its work

The team covered a large rural area. Referrals were followed either by assessment interviews at the divisional headquarters where the team had its base, or in people's homes. Clients tended to fall into three main categories: those in acute crisis where immediate intervention was needed; those with chronic mental illness problems; and those with anxiety and mild depression who are sometimes labelled as the 'worried well'. The clients in crisis might need immediate admission to hospital. If that could be avoided, the team might put them in touch with a local day centre that could offer continuing support. These were the only resources the team had for such cases. Long term cases received continuing social work support. The 'worried well', who were often trying to keep their jobs going, would receive more short term counselling, timed to fit in with their work.

Problems facing the team

The SSW found a substantial task facing her when she inherited the team. Most of the social workers had little experience of mental health work; there were no systematic files on cases; resources available to the team were very limited; and relations with other agencies were often poor. She began to tackle the problem of the inexperience of the team by instituting a lot of informal supervision and she worked collaboratively with her team to set up their own recording systems. There was little she could do about the poor resources of the department for mental health clients but she worked hard to establish the credibility of the team with other agencies operating in the same field.

The independent sector in mental health consisted mainly of two struggling branches of Mind which had had only minimal support from social services in the past. Local GPs and consultant psychiatrists seemed to have little faith in the team. 'I think that GPs had a great suspicion that we didn't know what we were doing. So we didn't get a lot from GPs.' Some psychiatrists would refer cases but there were reservations on the lines that social workers are 'trendy lefties who know nowt'. The SSW saw it as part of her job to change these attitudes but was faced with the difficulty that it was hard to prove the effectiveness of the team 'because there wasn't any evaluation or monitoring being done'.

Dilemmas in relationships with management

The SSW had taken her job in the department confident that the organization wanted her expertise and welcomed her eagerness to help in raising standards and developing the mental health services. 'I walked the interview,' she said, 'because I'd got such a lot of experience and I thought they really wanted people like me. They said all the right things.' But it gradually became clear to her that the department didn't want anyone who might rock the boat or challenge their seniors.

The case of an acutely ill client offered the steepest learning curve about these attitudes in her new organization and its relationship with other agencies. The SSW quickly realized that the client urgently needed assessment and should be in a secure setting. She referred the case to a consultant psychiatrist who refused to take her or the case seriously. Turning to her own management for support she found they were quite unwilling to back her up. The view seemed to be 'What on earth is she thinking of this line of action for and why does she think she's qualified to propose it?' When the SSW pointed out that she had considerable experience in working with people who demonstrate challenging and potentially dangerous behaviours, the attitude was that that didn't count for anything. She felt there was also a sexist element not far below the surface, with people ready to say she was being 'hysterical' about the case. Only her persistence in finding another consultant to look at the case put an end to this risk. The second consultant described the client as one of the most dangerous people he'd ever met and the man was committed to hospital for assessment.

However, the SSW now realized that she had offended against a key canon of the department by rocking the boat. Colleagues warned her to 'just watch it'. She learned that the model team leader, in management's view, was someone

> who doesn't make waves and doesn't criticize the system and doesn't raise her head above the parapet. Someone, I suppose, who goes along with the drift of things. If they bring out a policy that is just unworkable, never say it is unworkable. Just accept it and work with it as you can.

The SSW was not ready to give up trying to change things but realized if she was to get anywhere at all she would need to adopt very different tactics.

> Whenever I approached a manager after that I had to go through my case with a fine tooth comb. I had to dress in a particular way. I had to use certain language and even if I got annoyed I had not to show it. And I had to go in looking as dizzy and charming as could be, but not too intelligent because that could be threatening. Then I'd get somewhere.

The senior social worker's evaluation of her work experience

Despite such disillusioning experiences the SSW enjoyed her work very much 'because I thought that there was hope. Even if I got the door slammed in my face, I thought, one day they'll come round to this'. Meanwhile there was enough flexibility in her day-to-day work to get real satisfaction and bring advantages to both clients and members of her team. 'For clients, through a variety of creative means, we could attempt to meet their needs as well as we could.' The team had the advantage of her unequivocal support and together they could change at least some aspects of their working routine as, for example, the paperwork. 'So for both workers and users we could interpret the system and bring about the maximum benefit.'

Yet frustration with the management of the organization remained.

> What really got on my nerves were these grand statements that they put out with nothing to back them up. No policies, no procedures, no infrastructure, no way of evaluating them. There was the cold dawning of reality that what they were saying and what they were doing were two totally different things.

Change

The SSW was enthused by the proposals to reform community care and their implications for mental health services: 'I read the Act, and read Griffiths and everything else and thought: Gosh! This is it! This is really going to get everyone working well and efficiently'.

When she shared her hopes with her team for the ways in which they would be able to improve the quality of services for clients, however, she found them less impressed.

> They were looking at me as if I was a nut case and leaving little notes on my desk suggesting various forms of medication and pointing to the fact that they had been here longer than me and that I shouldn't get too excited about anything.

Subsequently the SSW was to find that her team's warnings were only too well founded: 'What the changes meant was just absolute total confusion from the moment of the first cop out about it until today'. To the internal confusions of the social services department were added the additional problems of working with other agencies, notably the health service, which were then undergoing similar changes. Here, increasing competition and conflict seemed to be the order of the day.

The organization and work of the team after the changes

The difficulties experienced by the team in the reorganization of the department in response to the community care legislation included confusion about the purchaser/provider divide; the drying up of resources; the failure to provide assessment procedures relevant to mental health; and the pressure to drop preventive work. 'We were supposed to split ourselves into purchaser and providers but no one told us how to do it.' At first, it seemed that the team would be a purchaser of services for the hostel; day centres were taken away from their section and put under another manager as provider services. The team would in future purchase places in the facilities for their clients. However, it also appeared that they were expected to continue to provide direct social work support for their clients so that they would at one and the same time be purchasers and providers.

In practice, the purchaser role has scarcely developed beyond a bureaucratic ritual. The special transitional grant money ran out very early in the financial year

> so we were left in the position of not having any money to spend creatively. We had only ourselves and we then went about being providers as well as assessors ... and we have very interesting looking forms in which we look like we're purchasing but we're not.

The same situation applies in the 'purchase' of places for clients in the now separately managed hostel and day centres:

> It's really sort of slipped back to what it was before in that no money exchanges hands. We just fill in these forms that makes it look as if we are purchasing the system but there's no actual shifting of funds from one budget to the next. The only impact of all this on clients is that it may take longer to get them assessed and to find a place.

The new system spawned its own bureaucratic procedures. The department developed a basic assessment form which was meant to be used for all categories of clients although it was evolved from a model used in work with other clients whose needs were dissimilar to those with mental health problems. The form was a bone of contention with the SSW's team:

> If you say form X to my team, they all hide under the table. The department commissioned somebody to draft it and two and a half years later it's still in its draft stage. It doesn't fit our model at all.

The team caseload is now

> going much more towards the chronically ill and people in acute mental health crisis that need admission. People who are just suffering because of the stress and strains of life, we're not really offering a service to them. And that's the preventive bit because if you don't go in on those people, they are the people who eventually do get more and more difficulties and we get them at the stage where their relationships have broken down, they have lost their jobs and it's much more difficult to help them.

The main reason why the move away from preventive work has happened, in the view of the SSW, is that the community psychiatric nurses (CPNs) have concentrated much of their work on the 'worried well' who constitute this category of client. But she is critical of this development feeling that the CPNs' work is guided by a medical model which is often inappropriate in such cases and is often restricted to very short term intervention.

Inter-agency relationships

The SSW was encouraged at the time of the community care changes because her team was moved into a purpose-built centre together with CPNs and psychologists employed by the health authority and had great hopes that they would start working together. But the reality has been very different and, in her view, 'it's a warehouse of professional people, basically, who just hardly ever communicate'.

> Because we now have no joint funding we argue about such trivia as whose stationery we are using and who is doing more on the various office rotas, etcetera. We do very little co-working; there is no central computer index of users and there is no way of knowing which users the centre is serving because the agencies argue with each other about 'confidentiality'. We have no way of knowing which users are on the supervision register or care programme approach because we have no way of communicating about this.

The obstacles to working together she puts down to issues of power and competition. The senior managers were defending their power and their positions. They were very aware, she felt, that the logic of integration would mean 'that there would be an over-arching manager for both health and social services and that would mean that several managers would lose their jobs'. Anyhow, the new imperatives of the market do not favour cooperation: 'the Act says we should collaborate; actually we are in competition for the provision of services'. A prime example is in home care and other support work with clients in the community which both social services and the health service provide:

> They don't want to share any of their work with us because of the GP contracts. They've got to keep our providers out of that, otherwise jobs go. There's a terrific amount of suspicion about what we're doing and they don't want to consult us.

Local health service managers have made attempts to extend their territory into that of social services, in one instance trying to take over the after-care of mental health clients which is defined in the legislation as the responsibility of the social services department. 'Fortunately, the Mental Health Commission came round recently and realized what was happening' and that move was headed off, but the conflict continues in other activities.

Departmental culture under attack: disarray in social services management

The SSW's experience of the social services department before the impact of the community care changes was of a stable, cosy, low-achieving organization in which the pressures to conformity were overwhelming.

> There was a general feeling before the Community Care Act came out that we were all jogging along fairly well together, all muddling along until retirement, but not a lot was going to be demanded of us.

Her own desire for 'far tougher and more professional standards' was not welcomed by her superiors who preferred to stress that 'we're all mates together, so let's keep it that way'.

The passage of the 1990 Act did not at first disturb this comfortable culture.

The implications of the Act, the SSW said,

> didn't hit us until 1993 and I think that it didn't hit us until then because they thought
> the County could ignore it because it would go away like everything else that meant
> that they had to change.

She did not think there was anything political in this position, such as the hope that the 1992 general election might return a government which would reverse the legislation. The local authority itself was 'hung', with no one party in control. Besides, she commented,

> I don't think we've got the brains to be political. I just wish I could say 'yes', it
> was that, that there was some sort of great strategy behind it. But I don't think we
> have.

However, by 1993 some kind of change had become imperative. A reorganization was devised to take account of the requirement to separate purchasing and provision. But this was done in such a way, as already discussed in the case of the mental health team, that lacked clarity, and presented the impression of a 'total lack of direction'.

> There's no leadership. There's no one saying 'Look, this is what we can do, this is what
> we can't do'. There's no planning. It's like a body detached from a brain, our organiza-
> tion. There's no strategic thinking. There's no attempt to look at evaluating and
> monitoring. There's not a point in time when someone says: 'OK. Enough is enough!
> Let's have time out and plan'. Nothing like that goes on. It's all react, react, react.

Even when attempts were made at planning the SSW felt that they seemed to come to nothing. She gave as an example an evaluation of the mental health services commissioned by the department some eighteen months earlier which involved extensive consultation.

> The report was widely acclaimed as an excellent piece of work because it clearly
> identified what needed doing and when. To date, however, the department has failed
> to implement *any* of it.

The SSW feels that senior management has simply been overwhelmed by the task facing them and are now only concerned with the survival of the organization. The result is the loss of any remaining integrity when the price of survival means abandoning basic social work values and keeping information from clients about their rights and at any cost preserving the pretence that everything is fine.

Impact on the mental health team

The team, says the SSW, has become tired, stressed and resentful. Sickness rates have spiralled, a worker in her forties has taken early retirement from stress-related illness. One worker now will not help out by doing extra duty when others are off sick, another refuses to do his paperwork adequately. When the SSW says she will have to discipline him, he replies: 'Fine, you discipline me and I'll say why should I be clear about what I'm doing when managers aren't being clear to me?' Workers take days off sick when they are not actually ill 'as revenge'. It has become almost the overriding task of the SSW to do all she can to hold the team together and protect it from the impact of the confusions and incoherent demands of the wider organization.

The senior social worker's evaluation

The impact of the changes on clients of the team, in the SSW's view, had been to make the service less accessible and to reduce the capacity of the social workers to provide them with effective help.

> They're being serviced by people who are burnt out and stressed up to the eyeballs, who don't want to make waves, who are frightened to death of complaints, who are just not comfortable any more.

An audit of clients' views confirmed their awareness of their workers' problems. Clients were saying things like:

> Oh, yes, they really tried hard but it was obvious that once the crisis was gone that they wanted out. They'd got other people to see, they're frequently late, they looked stressed. I don't want to put too much on them because they've got problems of their own.

The impact on the SSW herself had been profoundly alienating. She finds herself becoming increasingly tired and puts that down to the completely irrational and illogical behaviour of the organization as much as to the sheer volume of work:

> I say to myself, 'I do what I can'. I stick with that mentality for three or four weeks and I start to get tired because it is so illogical. I mean, I can't stop being who I am in myself and I can't stop my brain from functioning though I have tried. Every time I'm very tired I take a day off and I stay in bed because I'm looking after me now.

Today she gets 'very little enjoyment' out of the job, finding the lack of direction and loss of integrity and any concern for social work values in the department particularly frustrating. But perhaps the loss of hope that things will get better is the most depressing element in her work now. When she first joined the department, her work had been very demanding as it is now in the sense that 'it feels like trying to keep a lot of balls in the air and being terrified that one of them is going to come down'. But *then*

> there was this overall feeling that it was going to get better; once I'd got a system in place in this team we'd go gloriously ahead. I also felt from my point of view that they really wanted me here so I'm going to move up this organization and it's going to be good.

Now her feeling is 'Oh for God's sake why did I come? There's no hope about the future and it can only get worse'. And she finds that even she, a self-confessed optimist and idealist, is thinking 'For God's sake, get out!' On her birthdays she calculates how many years there are to go until retirement, and she thinks of leaving now on grounds of ill-health: 'More and more people are going off with stress. Get out and enjoy your quality of life before a stroke gets you'.

Her feeling of lack of job security now is

> dreadful, terrible, you don't know where they are going to react next. I have got this view of all the senior managers wanting to cut jobs further down before *they*'re cut.

In this context she finds that there is even less freedom to speak out than there was before. 'There is no freedom whatsoever.' When she does try to raise serious issues and gets nowhere with management, even the union will no longer be guaranteed to provide support, 'partly because they're too busy and partly because they are too close to higher management'.

Occupational survival

The SSW has, in spite of everything, found her own ways of maintaining her sanity and self respect, and of working for clients and her team. At an emotional level she does her best to bottle up her frustration during the day and then 'I go home and do an hour of aerobics to get the anger out of my system'. She plans her work strategically and concentrates on the bits 'that I think will have the maximum benefit for users'. She also tries to protect her clients by maintaining unofficial contacts with colleagues in other agencies including health and voluntary organisations.

She has disengaged from her own organization in the sense of no longer thinking about promotion:

> I don't want to be there. I don't want to be with these people. I don't want to be tarred with their brush. I don't want to have to be the sort of people they are.

The one remaining reward of any significance in her job comes from protecting her team.

> The only way I get satisfaction now is because I try to protect my team from as much of this as possible and I try and give them as much autonomy as possible. At least I've been open and honest about what we can do and what we can't do.

All of this has required her to become tougher and sometimes even devious in her work with other parts of the organization. She has developed her own way of living with that, too:

> I have to go home at night and I sit in front of the mirror and I think: you're still a nice, kind and loving person. You love your friends and your dogs. You're still a pushover!

For the future

The SSW held out little hope for improving services in the County without radical shifts in organization and the distribution of power. The present situation is 'so chaotic' that she has little confidence that senior managers are in touch with what needs to be done. This, combined with a general fear about rocking the boat, means that influential members of the organization do nothing in order to safeguard their sanity and their jobs. What they need to do is to face the realities of the limited budget and what can be achieved with it and to

> confront the politicians with that reality saying to them 'Look, we're either going to do this properly or we are not going to do it at all'. But they don't. It's absolutely crazy. There's all sorts of bowing and kowtowing to the politicians which I don't understand.

In her view improvements within the existing framework would not succeed:

> Things have gone too far. I can't see how the staff now are going to have the necessary umph to go to do anything different, unless power is devolved right down to my level.

In the meantime she keeps a dream of improvement alive:

> I do the lottery every week simply because if I win I'm going to set up a mental health service on my own, non-profit making, that will replace social services and will be set up on all these models I want – evaluation, quality assurance, that sort of thing.

Case Study 14

The death of excellence: the demise of a multi-disciplinary mental health team. An occupational therapist

Introduction

The quality of services before the changes described in this book was perceived by most of our contributors as varying widely from the very good to the mediocre and the downright poor. The particular significance of this case study is that it provides an example of team practice in the 1980s and early 1990s that was experienced as unequivocally excellent but which was swept away by the implementation of the 1990 Act. It was replaced by a system which, in the view of the practitioner recounting this story, would almost inevitably result in an inferior service to clients.

This account of the impact of change on practice was given by an occupational therapist who was a member of the multi-disciplinary team. In her mid-forties, she had about ten years' experience as a qualified practitioner.

The team and its work before the changes

The multi-disciplinary mental health team (MDMHT) was established in the mid-1980s, one of a number of teams in Britain pioneering the MDT approach. As such it attracted wide interest in its work, receiving visitors from all round the UK and abroad.

The team was one of several in the health district and was concerned primarily with acute cases. The members of the team were drawn from two different services – the NHS and social services – and four separate organizational hierarchies. The team consisted of five community psychiatric nurses (CPNs), an occupational therapist (OT), one or two approved social workers (ASWs) and a psychologist. While each of the workers was supervised by a senior worker or manager in his or her parent organization, no formal leader was appointed to manage the team.

To begin with the members of the team were unhappy with this situation.

> When I first went there we were constantly asking if we could have somebody to actually manage the team because it was so difficult. But we were told to get on with it and to decide for ourselves how to do it.

Responding to this challenge, the team developed a democratic decision-making process which in turn was backed by very close interaction and mutual support in working with clients. Methods of recording their work fully were worked out and introduced and, apart from the separate supervisions with their line managers, they were left to get on with running themselves. Only if a waiting list built up was their performance as a team likely to come under close scrutiny from the general manager of the unit. The core of this system was the regular weekly team meeting at which all decisions affecting the operation of the team were discussed and decided collectively and through which the team ethos was shaped and shared.

Ethos

Key elements of the emerging ethos were attitudes to referrals, discrimination and the concept of mental illness. As well as the normal methods of referrals from other professionals such as GPs, consultants and nurses, self-referrals were encouraged.

> The ethos of it was that it was a mental health centre. It would be open to people to come and we would accept referrals from people who self-referred without their GP's knowledge, if they wanted that.

The team had very strong feelings about gender being important:

> If women did not want to see men workers then you would try very hard to accommodate that, and vice versa. There was a very strong view that part of people being mentally healthy is feeling that they are able to have some say. A lot of people don't feel they have control of their lives and so it's quite important for us to help them feel more in control.

Part of this approach to clients and their illnesses was to insist on being non-judgemental about them, to encourage a psycho-therapeutic approach to treatment rather than medically dominated responses, and to respect their rights as citizens.

The operation of the team

In contrast to the typical case work model of intervention in which individual workers work with individual clients, the team developed a system of sharing crucial activities to enable members to pool their knowledge, strengthen skills and support each other through stressful episodes. A duty roster was devised so that there were always two workers on together at any one time.

> Working on duty you'd often be quite vulnerable. If you get someone who's in a complete crisis and you just don't know what to do, the fact that all of us felt able to go and ask someone else their opinion was hugely important.

If visits were to be made to assess clients for the first time, these would often involve two workers to provide the advantage of different perspectives. All new cases were reviewed after their initial assessment by the team as a whole. Although there would typically be some specialization in the initial allocation of cases, according to the profession of team members, everyone had a caseload and everyone was the key worker for her or his cases. If cases developed in ways that went beyond the skills and knowledge of the worker allocated, he or she could call on the help and advice of colleagues and in this way all members of the team were continually expanding their competencies.

Quarterly team reviews and provision for workers to bring up cases as emergencies at any time at team meetings ensured that there were regular occasions when colleagues' support was available. The OT experienced these team reviews very positively. After the initial referral it was possible to pass the case on to a colleague

> if someone else had more skills than you, or the problem was different from what you thought. It might be that you were totally bewildered and might want to check it out with everybody in the team. People might challenge you and say 'Why did you decide this or why did you not do that?' It was a very open session.

Similarly, the regular team reviews were helpful in strengthening individual practice. 'We'd review everybody on our caseloads and by doing that would find out a lot. We would be revealing a lot about ourselves and about our work and it was tremendously supportive.'

The OT's role

Apart from her time on duty, when she was based in the office, the OT's daily pattern of work was varied, depending on the make-up of her case load at any one time. She might start the day in the office to pick up and act on any messages, or might begin the day with a visit to a client.

> We had various meetings or ward rounds. If they were admitted to a psychiatric hospital, then we would keep in touch; go on the ward round; talk about their care in the hospital and have a lot to say about that. We would also be around for when they were discharged to actually work out a plan for them being discharged. We would see people individually, typically between four and six a day, sometimes talking with them, sometimes going to see them at home or sometimes going with them to another facility, or to actually take them to some work placement or some day centre or to introduce them or to see if they liked it. We were also involved in group work, stress management, confidence building and the development of social skills. Then there was admin. A lot of that. We would squeeze that in somewhere.

The special focus of the OT's work was

> looking at function and trying to help clients to think about change. I did quite a lot of counselling about past events because of the way they linked with how people are in the present. I would be much more concerned than some of the other team members about how they were living their lives now and looking more at skills than

some other people do: communication skills, assertion skills, relaxation skills. Those sort of coping mechanisms. But not only that: also looking at other things which were making it very difficult for them to live their lives in the way they wanted.

When I was talking to people and they would be telling me how terrible it was, I would then feel I was reflecting it back on to them to say 'Well, what are you going to do about this? What is the problem to you? What do you want to change? How can you change it?'

Outcome for clients and workers

The OT felt that the team's method of working was highly beneficial to both clients and workers. Clients gained in the first instance from very thorough initial assessment made of their needs. Sometimes people were referred who were suffering from natural reactions to life-events such as bereavement or separation but who were not mentally ill. After initial counselling they could be speedily channelled to more appropriate help from voluntary bodies such as Cruse and Relate. Sometimes the team tried to get GPs to refer such clients directly to these bodies but GPs tended to feel that the team's knowledge of the range of alternatives was better than theirs.

The clients accepted by the team were a mix of people with problems covering depression, anxiety, self-harm and suicidal tendencies. Although the team was supposed to restrict its work to short-term intervention, in reality cases were kept open for many months and even years if it was felt beneficial to clients to do so.

The OT singled out openness, choice and expertise as particular advantages of the team for the client. The openness of the team meant that the clients could refer themselves. It also meant that 'they could change worker very easily if they didn't like a certain style or whatever'. The multidisciplinary character of the team was

> hugely beneficial to clients because it would mean that if they saw me they wouldn't just have to have my OT bit. They could have all the rest of the team as well because of the good relationships within the team and the lack of defensiveness. If I was stuck with somebody and didn't know what to do, I could find out and I think they benefited hugely from the system.

She was equally positive about the benefits to the workers.

> We gained enormously in confidence and skills and felt really supported. The work is very, very stressful. We have huge responsibilities. If, for example, clients start getting suicidal it is very very stressful. Having other people in the building who are carrying some of the stress made you feel hugely supported. People understood. People would support you. People would do their utmost to help you.

She also described a more general synergy from the positive effect team members had on each other:

> There were huge amounts of energy. At the meetings we had everybody was interested; everybody was heard; we all had equal control; we all had equal say.

> Everything was done democratically. I think it was wonderful, an absolutely wonderful environment to work in.

Evidence cited to support the OT's view of high morale and commitment in the team included very low staff turnover, low sickness and absence rates, and a readiness to work overtime without pay whenever necessary in the interests of the client.

The changes

The changes which were ultimately to lead to the disbandment of the MDMHT began to bite in 1992, two years after the passage of the 1990 Act. The creation of a community hospital trust and the introduction of the purchaser/provider split were to destroy the integrated structure of the team by redefining the roles of its members.

There was no formal consultation about the changes, only rumours and then the changes themselves, piecemeal, unexplained. The main change followed the arrival of GP fundholding. It was decided that the GPs, as purchasers of services, must have direct access to their own CPNs. The referral process in future for mental health was to be through the GPs to the CPNs. The CPNs were, it appeared, to be both providers of services themselves (as before) and purchasers of the services of others, including the OTs and psychologists. The ASWs, within the same purchaser/provider split in the social services, were also to be service purchasers. As news of these changes seeped down to the team members it became clear to them that the finely crafted multidisciplinary method of working they had built up over nearly ten years was to be abandoned.

Initially, the only formal change introduced was that of attaching the CPNs to the general practices in the area and channelling all new referrals through these. The team members all remained in the same offices. Everyone kept their existing cases. The routine of team meetings continued as before but there was less and less to discuss and decide. No one told the OTs, the psychologists, or the ASWs how they were to fit into the new order of things. They were simply left in limbo.

Rationale for the changes

The OT identified the source of the changes in the policies of central government and, in particular, those bringing in the split between purchasers and providers.

> It was responding to what the government said had to happen. So it was never discussed as to whether it was a good idea or not. This was an ultimatum. This is how it happens.

However, she felt that management in her own trust had singled out her team as an early target for its changes and had deliberately 'smashed' it.

I use the word 'smash' because it feels like that's what has happened. We were a very powerful team and because of being told to do things on our own, we developed systems that were very strong. It feels as if we were chosen to be changed because of that power. The government was saying about professionals having too much power. It feels like this was part of this too: things have been taken from us deliberately. It feels like we had too much power.

Work patterns after the changes

Plans for a new organization of the community mental health services following the changes had still not been finalized three years after the implementation of the 1990 Act. It had been decided by the health trust that the two acute teams which had existed before would be replaced by four teams, each with its own consultant and two or three CPNs. These teams had been established but the possibilities of linking OTs and psychologists to them had still not been worked through and they had yet to be allocated to particular teams. It was planned that the ASWs should join another team being set up for people with long term problems. However, the social services department refused to agree to this since the ASWs' skills were specifically related to acute illnesses and would be inappropriately deployed in this team. As a result the role of the ASWs remained unresolved.

In the new system the large majority of referrals for community mental health now come through the GPs to the CPNs. The result, in the OT's view, is that the CPNs have become 'overwhelmed'.

They're getting ten or twelve referrals a week. One person had ninety-nine cases. One CPN will have to take a whole week out to write up all his assessments because he has so many.

In the new context, working directly with GPs in the role of providers, the CPNs find it more difficult to screen out the kind of referrals the team would in the past have regarded as inappropriate because the GP expects them to cope with cases directly. 'It's like they have less chance of saying no'.

The CPNs are still supposed to be able to ask for input on cases from other members of the team and sometimes do. But 'because they are so completely overwhelmed it's more difficult for them to do. It's easier sometimes to see somebody' than go through the process of referring to colleagues. As a result, the work of the other members of the team is now a mixture of the cases which they have retained from the period before the changes, for which they remain key workers, and secondary work on those cases which the CPNs choose to refer to them.

The OT's role after the changes

Three years into the changes the OT has still had no official notification of how her work fits into the new organization and has no way of knowing what the future holds for her.

I still have the key worker role for about twenty clients and I also take on secondary work from CPNs. This is mostly about people wanting more structure to their day, more activity in their week, and it's very much about linking people to different groups and day services. So it tends to be a very limited and very brief involvement. I am only simply doing some aspect and very often I do an assessment and actually they are not wanting anything I provide.

The OT has not been linked officially to any of the new sectors but on the advice of her line manager has chosen to attend meetings in one of them where staff are attempting to form a new team. 'I go to these meetings because it feels like the only way I've got of being part of a team.'

Uncertainty and frustration

The OT frequently reiterates her sense of uncertainty about her role and her future and describes the sense of frustration and loneliness which results. In contrast with the CPNs who are swamped with work,

all the rest of us are floating about in the middle not knowing what we're doing. I'm totally unclear about my role. I am totally unclear about my future. I have felt over the last year undervalued and I keep dreaming about being made redundant. Half the time I don't feel as if I exist.

I don't know what I'm supposed to be doing so I'm just doing what I'm doing until someone tells me not to because I don't know what else to do. I'm trying to develop new systems as far as I can work it out. I feel I'm having to cope on my own now. Instead of it being a collective decision I get a referral and I have to make a decision about it on my own, which I can do, but I'm not certain how much to do. I'm used to being part of a team and being part of a whole. So it feels very lonely.

Ethos

The OT felt that the ethos of her work environment had altered since the period before the 1990 Act.

There's a lot about splitting things up into small boxes. And it feels different. Although it's supposed to be needs led, I don't think it is now. I don't think it's so open. I think it is becoming more medical.

She explained what the 'splitting up' meant to her in terms of the purchaser/ provider division, the use of contracts, the sharper distinction between different teams and categories, and 'trying to box people, put clients in boxes. People are in box so-and-so and score this. It feels as if business ethics have definitely come in.'

Medicalization meant to her a greater emphasis in physical rather than psychological intervention in treatment.

People going into hospital now are not encouraged to talk about their problems. There's definitely a change towards silencing people. Whereas before there was a definite move, if for example people had been abused in childhood, to giving them a chance to talk about that and find a way of expressing some of that and moving on, now it's much more medical. 'It's much better if you just put it all behind you and shut up and take these pills.'

Outcome for clients and workers

In the view of the OT the outcome of the changes had been largely negative for both clients and workers. Some of the ways that clients lost out have already been described. In particular, the range of expertise readily available to them as clients of the team was no longer so likely to be brought to bear on their cases now that CPNs were the main point of referral and the key workers for most new cases. Further, the latitude previously allowed in how long they remained on the books of the acute team had been removed and a maximum of three months was supposed to apply, a period the OT regarded as too short for effective work with many clients. She saw a move towards the 'short term, quick patching people up' approach which was 'about saving money, saving resources, whereas before the system was more about people'. The medicalization of treatment was also defined as a step backwards. It was true that it was now easier than before to get referred to a CPN, as a result of the direct access available to GPs, but she did not see this as necessarily being an advantage since for some it was inappropriate and the CPNs themselves were so overstretched that they had difficulty in responding effectively.

From the point of view of those who had been members of the MDMHT the change was, she felt, little short of disastrous. Talking of her own feelings she said that the reduction in her responsibilities for clients meant that in one sense she was less stressed than before but her 'personal stress is far greater because I feel undervalued, underused, and unsatisfied'. She attributed the increase in sickness in the unit to the prevalence of such feelings:

> In the old system people were hardly ever sick. We were all under stress, we were all overworked, we all worked far longer than our hours. We hardly ever took lunch breaks but because we were the ones that decided what we did and how we did it, and had a lot of control about our diaries and our time, and a huge feeling of responsibility, even when we were sick we would come in and we would work. But there was hardly any sickness. In the last couple of years we've had several people on long-term sick leave and at one time there were four people out of twenty off sick for quite a long period.
>
> A lot of people have talked about leaving. People haven't left because they don't know what else they would do. Because their jobs are permanent at the moment it's very difficult to think about leaving and getting another job where your pay and conditions might be altered because you'd be on a trust contract.
>
> I've wanted to leave several times. I haven't been off sick but I had a holiday last year and I spent the whole holiday worrying about going back to work. The whole holiday. And I felt so angry and I felt so upset. I cried lots of times. You know, I've really cried at work in meetings. Which is terrible, very difficult.
>
> Other people also broke down, people got angry. But not now. Everybody is now

either completely apathetic or a few people are feeling a bit more optimistic because their roles are slightly clearer.

My feeling is that the majority of what I've been feeling personally, and a lot of other people have been feeling too, is grief for what has been lost. Grief that we have lost something that was so good and so effective and it has gone on over a long period of time. I felt as if my team was terminally ill. And it was terminally ill for quite a long time and it wasn't until it actually died that I started to feel a bit better.

The future

The OT felt that, although she could not see just how it might be achieved, the only way to restore a quality mental health service for the clients of the service would be to reconstitute a multidisciplinary team which could draw on the strengths of collaboration and mutual support that had been the hallmark of the original team.

Part 3

Analysis and discussion

The case studies in Part 2 stand in their own right as examples of the experience of the changes taking place in organizations providing community care. In Part 3 we explore wider issues which we believe they raise.

While we have emphasized that the studies are not in any statistical sense representative of others who work in the community care field or their organizations, we have suggested in the Introduction that there are good reasons for arguing that they have a wider relevance than as merely the stories of fifteen men and women in health and social services organizations. Systematic evidence emerging mainly from a number of more quantitative studies, much of it published in the period during which we have been preparing this book, adds weight to that view. These data, which are briefly reviewed in Chapter 8, report common findings on a number of areas dealt with in the case studies.

Our first aim in Part 3 is to bring together the accounts of the fourteen case studies, to tease out the patterns of experience before and after the community care reforms and the underlying factors which may explain these patterns.

Chapter 6 focuses on the views of the sample of their world of work in the years immediately preceding the changes. It provides a sketch of the strengths and weaknesses of the system which was turned upside down by the reforms and provides a yardstick against which sample members have judged the subsequent reforms. Chapter 7 moves on to consider the implementation and effect of the reforms, as seen by our interviewees. It reviews experience of the change process itself and its impact on their working lives, their evaluation of the gains and losses that have resulted for service users and for themselves, and the effect it has had on their careers.

We then turn in Chapter 8 to make a broader evaluation of the effects of the changes identified by sample members and to compare their experiences with other relevant studies. In Chapter 9, seeking to understand the confused and troubled state of the community care reforms, we examine the nature of the change strategy adopted by the government and the difficulties inherent in it. Our final chapter takes up the Thatcherite challenge that there is no alternative and briefly considers a radically different approach, guided by a broader conception of human nature.

6

The worlds they have lost: providing community care before the changes

Change in the organization of the health and personal social services providing community care in the last few years has been dramatic and far-reaching. It is important, however, before focusing on experience and evaluation of these changes, first to summarize the perceptions of the members of our sample of their world of work *before* the changes. This is both because in part it was criticism of the services provided in that world which led to the pressures to reform, and because, for the professionals themselves, it is likely that their memories of their work at the time will have coloured their evaluation of the world that has replaced it.

We begin, however, by seeking to identify the views of interviewees on the conditions required to provide effective professional work in community care. We then examine their actual working environments in terms of these criteria and show how far they felt appropriate conditions actually existed.

Conditions for effective professional practice

Our analysis of the case studies indicated that there was a largely implicit but widely shared view of the framework of conditions which were required to achieve effective professional practice in community care. We constructed this account in the main not from direct discussion of the topic with interviewees but from their identification of the conditions which they valued, or missed if they were not present, or which prevented them from working well; we have drawn also on an analysis of the changes they wanted to bring about. In this sense the account was about *ideal* conditions, which probably nobody expected to see achieved in their entirety, but which captured the direction they felt organizations should move in if services were to be improved.

It seems that this largely inexplicit but nevertheless coherent set of ideas was quite strongly internalized by the sample. Its origins are probably a mixture of influences in which conventional notions of professionalism and the socialization process of training have played a part. Beyond these, however, was the influence of the sheer practicalities of operating in the complex world of community care, where success called for close collaboration between formal and informal systems, where flexibility and ingenuity were required, and where neither traditional bureaucratic nor traditional professional methods of operating were adequate. Finally, it is likely that the very features of the work may have attracted those who enjoyed the potential that the field of community care could offer for creative and innovative practice.

Table 6.1 below brings together these views on the effective working environment in the form of a framework.

Table 6.1 A framework of conditions for effective professional work in community care

---

1   Relationships with the user are:
       needs-led
       open and honest

2   Relationships with the organization encourage:
       discretion and autonomy
       multiple accountability
       continuity and security
       an understanding of the organizational world
       participation and the freedom to speak out

3   Relationships with colleagues are based on:
       shared values
       trust and integrity
       collaborative working

4   Relationships with the wider social and political system recognize:
       possibility of improvement
       potential to influence

5   personal development is encouraged by:
       use of skills
       opportunities for development

We can most usefully explore the meaning of each element in this framework by using examples from the case studies.

Relationships with the user

The interviewees all emphasized that their users were their first concern and that their work with them should be *needs-led*. In some cases, such as the child care organization, this was judged to be the view of everybody: 'kids were central'. But even where few others seemed to see users' needs as the first priority, as in the nursing home, the carer was sure that they were *her* first duty. It was also taken for granted that openness and honesty in all dealings with users were first principles in building an effective relationship.

Relationships with the organization

Discretion and autonomy

These were important to workers who were dealing with complex cases, negotiating with other agencies, developing projects and so on. They were taken for granted in some occupations, such as those of the geriatrician and general practitioner. They were regarded as an attraction of the job in the case of others such as the community nurse. When they were unduly restricted or denied, as in the example of the senior social worker it was deeply resented.

Multiple accountability

Most members of the sample, while employed by a particular organization and answerable to its management, also regarded themselves as accountable to their users and, where they worked in teams, to their colleagues. While formal organizations often have great difficulty in accepting this kind of complex reality, the people in our sample needed at least a *de facto* acceptance by their bosses to do their jobs well. This was clearly the case, for instance, with the occupational therapist in the multi-disciplinary mental health team and the nurse manager. In the traditional bureaucracies, in contrast, management showed much less sympathy to the worker's dilemma and expected complete control.

Continuity and security

To build enduring relationships and to raise awkward questions when necessary the workers needed to be able to take their continued employment for granted and to assume that their jobs were reasonably secure. By and large this was the case with most of those we interviewed in the period before the reforms.

Understanding of the organizational world

To operate effectively on behalf of their users, the workers had to understand how their own organization functioned. This required an attitude of openness throughout the organization and a readiness to inform people fully when changes were being made.

Participation and the freedom to speak out

It was also important for people, operating with considerable discretion in their daily work, to have a regular voice in the wider decision-making processes of the organization and to feel that they could speak their minds freely with their managers and other colleagues. This was most formally recognized in the constitution of the multidisciplinary teams in mental health. However, even in the case of the learning disabilities team leader in a bureaucratic organization, management was willing to be regularly involved in informal consultation.

3 Relationships with colleagues

The conditions defined under this heading – shared values, trust and integrity, mutual support, and collaborative working – were all important elements of working effectively in the complex world of community care before it became transformed into a business transacted through formal contracts. Sharing values with colleagues in one's own and other agencies, being able to trust them and work collaboratively with them, amounted to the conditions for open-ended informal contracts in working together. It was in this way, for instance, that much of the work of the community nurse with the local social services department was handled.

4 Relationships with the wider social and political system

It seemed important for most of our interviewees to feel that if necessary they could engage with the wider world and that as a result some kind of improvements might be achieved. If they saw changes that were necessary but which could not be brought about within the current constraints of their organizations, they felt that they should be able to advocate alternatives. In this way, for example, the geriatrician was active in promoting more community-based health services for older people in the world beyond his hospital.

5 Personal development

A key condition for all interviewees was being given the opportunity to use their professional skills to the full. The high level of satisfaction of the occupational therapist in the mental health team was closely linked to the challenge to do just that; the frustration of the senior social worker was caused to a considerable degree by her organization's refusal to recognize her expertise and give her the chance to use it fully. In the same way further personal development and the opportunity for promotion were valued by most of the interviewees.

Ideal and reality: varieties of organization

It will be clear from the examples given, and will become more so in the second part of this chapter, that the extent to which the working conditions set out in the model were seen to exist varied very substantially within the sample. Our analysis of the case studies taken as a whole suggested that this variation was far from random but related quite closely to the *type* of organization in which the interviewees had worked.

A popular view of the pre-reform health and social services is that they were dominated by a single type of agency, the bureaucratic or bureau-professional organization. A bureaucratic organization in this sense was hierarchical, with highly sub-divided work tasks, tightly governed by rules, recruiting and promoting people on the basis of formal qualifications and tests, and offering job security and the prospects of a career. In the bureau-professional variant, the front-line professional workers had acquired a substantial degree of influence.

The analysis of our sample, however, suggested that this characterization of public services could be a gross over-simplification. Our interviewees between them experienced a much wider range of work settings, some referring to teams and others to the organization as a whole. While in one sense almost all of them were employed in organizations with strong bureaucratic elements, in less than a quarter were bureaucratic, or bureau-professional versions of them, dominant in determining the day-to-day environment in which they worked.

Taking as our starting point perceptions of the ethos of the agency (or the part of it to which the interviewee was referring) and the main influences within it, we found evidence of three further types of organization in addition to the bureaucracy: professional, proprietorial and political. These distinctions, which are to some extent paralleled in Mintzberg's organisational configurations (Mintzberg, 1989), held up well when other areas of people's experience were analysed and in particular were associated with varying degrees of work satisfaction and perceptions of the effectiveness of organizations concerned in providing a good service.

In the following pages we seek to show the significance of these different patterns of experience of organizations within our sample.

Four organizational worlds

The commonest of the four types of organization which we identified in the sample was the *professional*; there were eight of these. There were four *bureaucratic* or *bureau-professional* organizations, one *proprietorial* and one *political*. The main distinguishing features of the different types, derived from the interviews, can be briefly summarized:

The *professional organization* is one in which the day-to-day work of the front-line professionals is of central importance. They have considerable discretion in decisions concerning users; the principles guiding their profession have a widespread influence; and they are likely to be represented in policy-making, at least in so far as it directly affects their work. All the health service, and both the voluntary sector organizations fell into this category.

The *bureaucratic organization* is primarily controlled by its formal structure, the division of labour within it, the rules governing roles and relationships, expectations of disinterested behaviour, and rewards in terms of a career and pension.

The *bureau-professional* variety of this type is one in which professional workers are given (or have won for themselves) significant discretion in their day-to-day work but have little influence in management or policy. Four of the five case studies set in the local authority social services departments described organizations which were classified in these categories.

The *proprietorial organization* both in terms of its ethos and management is strongly influenced by those owning it. It is represented in our sample before the reforms by the nursing home.

The *political organization* is one where the elected representatives take the leading role in determining both policy and the organization and management of services. The Labour-controlled metropolitan authority is the example in our study.

Table 6.2 shows the distribution of the 14 case study organizations by these types.

Table 6.2 A typology of social and health service organizations before the community care reforms

1. *Professional organizations*
    Multi-disciplinary mental health team
    Community nursing
    Geriatric department (acute hospital)
    Learning disabilities hospital resettlement programme
    General practice
    Community psychiatric nursing
    Learning disabilities agency
    Child care agency

2   *Bureaucratic organizations*
    Local authority mental health team
    Local authority learning disabilities core and cluster
    *Local authority learning disabilities team
    *Local authority disabilities and mental health team
    * Bureau-professional

3. *Proprietorial organizations*
    Nursing home

4. *Political organizations*
    Labour-controlled metropolitan authority

Professional organizations: a supportive environment

These were the organizations where the workers were most wholeheartedly engaged, most likely to report that they enjoyed their work very much, could be creative and where, in their judgements, users received a good service. In them a majority of the conditions specified as necessary for effective professional work in community care were satisfied (Table 6.1). The main features of this supportive environment, beyond the pervading professional ethos and influence, were the degree of control the workers had over their jobs, the close collaborative relationships most of them enjoyed within their team, and with others and the opportunities this provided for personal development and achievement through service improvement. Freedom to speak one's mind and feelings of security in the job were both taken for granted.

All the health service teams involved are described as operating in a predominantly collegial style. The two voluntary sector organizations, though operating through well-defined hierarchical systems, gave both the managers concerned wide discretion to use their professional judgement in the development of services.

The main obstacles to improving practice in these organizations were identified first, as the clash of different professional conceptions of what good practice involved and, second, the under-resourcing of services. The clearest examples of the first are found in the case studies of the geriatrician and the hospital resettlement manager. Under-resourcing was a general problem but was particularly evident in the case of the community nurse. The lack of sufficient ancillaries meant that patients sometimes simply had to go without the basic care that they needed.

Overall, however, workers who were in professional settings believed that they and their colleagues were able to provide good services characterized by accessibility, relevance, responsiveness and high quality based on expertise.

We are in no position to analyse the detailed circumstances creating these 'professional organizations' and we are certainly not suggesting that all health service teams and all voluntary organizations shared these features. Indeed, it is worth noting that all the health service case studies were either based in the community or had strong links with it, factors which may have been influential in shaping their practice and in attracting staff who liked their open and flexible ways of working. The two voluntary sector case studies describe the experiences of managers engaged in pioneering work, both with considerable autonomy. More routine provision of services in the voluntary sector is not represented in the study.

Bureaucratic organizations: degrees of frustration

The bureaucratic organization, as described in the case studies, was a very different world from the professional organization, and one in which committed professionals clearly found it much more difficult to work. Far fewer of the conditions defined as necessary for effective practice were satisfied. Although the personal motivation of workers in the bureaucratic organizations appeared very similar, they described lower levels of enjoyment and achievement than those working in what we have called 'professional' settings. Their scope for action was much more restricted and pressures to conform more evident.

However, bureaucracies also vary. Even in our small sample it was clear that two of the four organizations concerned were much more rigid than the other two, more difficult to work in and, from the interviewees' accounts, produced lower quality services. Both case studies of these more *typical bureaucracies* described social services departments in which the main aim of politicians and managers seemed to be a quiet life. This was to be achieved by strictly observing rules and procedures, covering up mistakes and above all avoiding any kind of behaviour that might be called 'rocking the boat' by drawing attention to failings of the system or proposing improvements in current practice.

This environment encouraged the preservation of mediocre or poor services as in the case of the adult training centre that was described as 'straight out of an historical account of institutionalization'. In such a context, committed workers have to scale down their ambitions, as had happened in the cases in this study. But this did not mean that *nothing* could be done to improve services. Once you had learned the rules and how to appear to be obeying them, small scale, very local changes could be quietly introduced. So the job had its satisfactions, even if they were low key ones.

The other two examples of bureaucracy both described organizations (or parts of organizations) which were more open to professional influence. In these cases of *bureau-professionalism*, the management was described as both more competent and more sympathetic to the professional goals of the interviewees than in the examples of more traditional bureaucracies. Managers were sometimes willing to try to help achieve these goals by bending the rules. This might create other problems if managers allowed people to bend the rules but leave the junior worker to take the rap if this backfired. There was agreement on the long term goals of improving services; open discussion within the organization was tolerated; and administrative lapses could be excused where there was evidence of professional commitment and achievement. Progress was slow but visible and there was a degree of unofficial local autonomy. There was frustration and disappointment, but also room for considerable satisfaction.

Proprietorial organization: where the boss's word is law

Where the owners (or their managers) are in charge, yet another organizational world is created, one largely dependent on their personal ethos and will. While economic and social criteria set boundaries to minimum acceptable standards, such organizations can still encompass a wide range from the most creative and life enhancing, in which the conditions for effective professional work are encouraged, to the narrow and unimaginative where they are largely absent.

In our single example of a *proprietorial organization* before the reforms, the nursing home management practised a benevolent but authoritative form of leadership and the managers were defined quite simply as 'dictators' by the qualified carer in the case study. The caring but over-protective regime produced good physical conditions but paid little attention to the psychological or social needs of patients. Yet the carer did have enough scope, in her view, to enhance patients' quality of life and as long as this continued to be the case, she drew great enjoyment from the job.

Political organization: where the party rules

All the social services departments in our study were formally subject to political control through the local council. However, only in one of the four (prior to the reforms) was this political control seen as a dominant influence by an interviewee. The Labour-controlled metropolitan authority exercised a strong paternalistic influence over the department. It had established high levels of provision for disadvantaged groups and introduced excellent terms of service for its staff. It opposed the policies of the Conservative government and did all it could to delay their implementaton while continuing to enact its own agenda.

This environment was a curious, sometimes frustrating but often exciting one in which to work as a senior manager, since it met many of the conditions for effective professional work. Free speech was encouraged, full consultation throughout the organization on any major changes planned was the norm and officers working on new policies had to be ready to defend them before politicians and workers alike.

An overview

These assessments by members of the sample of the world of health and social services organizations before the reforms suggest a very mixed picture both of the quality of services produced and the subjective experience of providing them.

The range of experiences of the members of the sample extend from excellent working conditions which, in their view, produced generally high quality services, to organizations in which it was a struggle to bring to life even a glimmer of good practice and users were provided with mediocre or poor services. The most productive working environments were mainly those in the professional organizations. In the bureau-professional organizations the constraints on good practice were greater, but there was scope for the determined worker to achieve satisfactory and sometimes excellent results. In the conventional bureaucracies the workers were driven to work within narrower boundaries and to accept more restricted goals. The poorest examples of service were found there and in the proprietorial organization.

The experience of the sample in no way challenges the powerful case made by critics of the old system in terms of the failures of different elements of that system, especially health, social services and social security, to relate effectively to each other (Audit Commission, 1986; Griffiths, 1988). Nor does it contradict the evidence produced on the unevenness of service provision. The quality of services would depend very much on which of the fourteen organizations she or he happened to be dealing with.

But the study challenges the growing myth that before the changes there was only mediocre practice or worse and supports the view of the Audit Commission that examples of excellence also could be found (Audit Commission, 1986, pp.65–72). Further, the case studies indicate an impressive level of commitment among these practitioners to make the most of the organizational context they inherited, even at its least promising. For all the shortcomings of some of the work settings, most of the providers were strongly committed to public service and to making the best of the system. Wistow and colleagues (1994, p.59) comment on responses in their study that a 'striking feature was the extent to which local authority members and officers expressed a pride in public sector provision'. Most could find satisfaction both in working to improve the service they were involved with and in seeing the gradual evolution of better services, even in the most rigid bureaucratic environments. In their accounts, there was little evidence of alienation, much of engagement and goodwill.

Nevertheless, few of those we interviewed would have resisted the idea that services needed to be improved further and several welcomed the prospect of the changes promised in the legislation for a more needs-led, less bureaucratic service, whatever misgivings they may have had about the means proposed to achieve this.

If the attitudes and commitment of these workers were in any sense typical of a significant proportion of those working in community health and social services as a whole, then they provide some indication of the quality of the human resources which were available to any reformer who was successful in enlisting their support. It would appear to be an act of folly to ignore or squander such rich assets in the process of planning and introducing change but as our next chapter shows, that is just what seems to have happened.

7

Brave new world? Providing community care after the changes

The 1990 Act heralded the most far-reaching changes in British health and social services since their establishment in the post-war settlement. As we have shown in Chapter 1 these changes were not introduced into a previously calm and stable environment, but into one in which public services were already under intense pressure trying to cope with the effects of rising demand and tightening budget constraints. In addition, the NHS was still absorbing the effects of the introduction of general management, while local authorities were trying to deal with the consequences of the continued attrition of their powers, responsibilities and funding. Both health and social services were also carrying through other demanding programmes, notably the closure of the long-stay hospitals and the resettlement of their patients in the community.

When the accounts of the interviewees are brought together the massive scale of the impact of these changes on their worlds of work becomes starkly clear. They describe a new organizational landscape in which the ethos, sources of influence, freedom to speak out, experience of the job and outcomes have all been profoundly changed. Sometimes they identify real gains for service users from these changes. More often they express deep concern that standards of care have declined and provision has become more rather than less arbitrary. And throughout nearly all the interviews there is a common feeling of loss and alienation, sometimes amounting to hopelessness and despair.

In this chapter we analyse this experience as our interviewees have recorded it, summarizing their views and opinions of the strategies adopted by their agencies to deal with the changes, the implementation of the reforms and their impact.

Strategies for change

Health and social services organizations were required by the new legislation and guidance to become *managed* organizations, to revolutionize their structures, adopt a business and market oriented philosophy, and somehow enthuse their workforces with the new ethos. It was scarcely surprising that the prospect was not viewed with universal enthusiasm, that some should hold back as long as they could and that many should be perceived by their staff as making a mess of it all.

In the accounts of our sample, three distinct responses by the organizations concerned can be identified: defence and delay, pre-emption and compliance. Some people also described what might be called sub-strategies for change when interest groups and individuals opportunistically used the period of upheaval to bring about local changes that suited them.

Defence and delay

Two organizations deliberately delayed the changes because the local council, anticipating a change in government at the general election following its passage, hoped the 1990 Act would not be implemented. The metropolitan authority with a Labour council went ahead with its own preferred reorganization. The shire county failed to respond because of poor political and managerial leadership. In another case study, delaying tactics were used to defend specialist services for people with disabilities and mentally ill people because the senior manager concerned saw the changes as potentially disastrous for them.

A defensive strategy was adopted also in the independent sector learning disabilities organization. The manager did all she could to resist the loss of control of standards and values which seemed to be threatened by the growing monopoly power of the local authority and an increasing emphasis on market criteria.

Pre-emption

Getting the changes installed before events forced the organization's hand appeared to be the motive in a further two cases. One was a Labour-controlled shire county which, in spite of ideological objections to the market element of the reforms, decided that adopting them rapidly and thoroughly would give it a much better chance to defend its staff and key resources. The other was the independent child care organization, whose managers were convinced that a more business oriented and managerial emphasis was essential for survival and growth.

Compliance

'Compliance' includes elements of enthusiasm and of reluctance. Hospital and community health services were seen as being swept into change as the movement to adopt trust status gathered momentum. The extent and nature of the cultural and organizational shift involved, however, seems to have varied. The CPN, for example, found the trust management increasingly intrusive and directive. The occupational therapist, while her team was broken up by the community trust management, was left in a vacuum with no clear indication of what work she was supposed to do. The community nursing service found itself *less* closely managed after the formation of the trust than before because its new manager was too over-whelmed with work to find time to come out from headquarters to exercise hands on leadership.

Opportunism

As is often the case with periods of wide-ranging reform, the changes can in some circumstances provide a smokescreen behind which opportunistic people can advance their interests. The dilution and then the effective disbandment of the geriatric department in the acute hospital provides an example of this. Other, more personal instances of opportunism described included attempts to outmanoeuvre and replace one's manager as services are reorganized, and to get promotion ahead of more qualified colleagues by exhibiting unbounded enthu-siasm for the new order and a suitable potential for ruthlessness.

Implementation of change

Consultation

Most texts on the management of change emphasize the obvious importance of consulting those affected, whether to obtain their views and possibly modify the changes accordingly, or simply to try to elicit staff support. In our study some organizations consulted thoroughly, some consulted half-heartedly, some seem to have skipped the process altogether. Further, there were organizations which consulted thoroughly at the introduction of the 1990 Act but did not do so at a later stage.

   At one extreme, the child care agency engaged in an exhaustive year-long period of debate, inviting the opinions of everyone working for the agency, before any plans were drawn up. The metropolitan authority also mounted a lengthy consultation exercise with its staff. At the other extreme, some of the trusts seem to have simply imposed their decision to change, as in the case of the occupational therapist's organization, saying to staff 'this is how it will happen'. Other organizations occupied an intermediate position, allowing for a limited period of discussion. However, no matter what system was used, in the end the process of consultation, in the eyes of sample members, made little if any differ-ence to the actual changes adopted.

The new organizations: coherent and incoherent

In the large majority of cases our sample described major changes in their organization. These have dissolved most of the differences in ethos, influence and power on which the pre-reform categories of professional, bureaucratic, proprietorial and political organizations were based. Now, in virtually all cases the main influence in the organizations is seen as managerial or managerial and political. However, a striking difference did emerge in terms of interviewees' perceptions of the coherence of the emergent new organizations. The majority, at least as viewed from their particular positions in the agencies, appeared to be in a disarray verging on chaos. Only a handful gave the impression that those in charge had a grip on the challenges confronting them and a viable programme for meeting them.

There are four *coherent* organizations: the local health authority through which the general practitioner now feels much more answerable for his work; the metropolitan social services department in which the assistant director has established a tightly defined structure on purchaser–provider lines; the child care organization, which has adopted a system of devolved management with a detailed system of monitoring and control; and the learning disabilities agency which continues to fight to control its distinctive character. The remaining organizations are classified as *incoherent*, in the main having in common that management is seen as having lost control and as imposing or condoning changes which are more about a desperate search for survival than the development of rationally organized services.

Their principal problem is solving resource and funding issues. These issues account for the confusions and defensiveness of the social services departments in which the leaders of the mental health and learning disabilities teams work, the appointment and dismissal of new managers in the CPN's health trust, and the difficulties of the overworked community nursing team.

Competition between previously cooperating agencies is another factor in creating incoherence. This is illustrated by the case of the acute hospital in which the geriatrician works. The formation of the trust, its separation from the community trust and the weakness of the local health authority have combined to create a situation in which managerial and professional politics have ensured that provider rather than patient interests have become the predominant influence.

The impact of change on the job of the professional worker

For almost all the people we interviewed the experience of change has been one of loss: the loss of being valued, the loss of having a clear purpose and hope in the future, the loss of enjoyment and, for some, the loss of a career. Changes were of three main kinds: the loss of the previous role; the acquisition of managerial responsibility for the implementation of the new order or responding to it; and the transition from a comprehensive professional role in which the worker was responsible for assessment and service provision into a narrower role of only one of these functions.

Role loss

The reforms, or internal politics linked to them, led to the disappearance of the core part of the roles of two people in the sample. The occupational therapist, as we have noted, was left in limbo with no clear task; the geriatrician was redesignated as a general physician.

Managerial responsibilities

Those who were managers in the sample had to face the new responsibility of implementing the reforms or coping with their impact. The assistant director chose to take on this task. Two other managers, the middle manager in a child care organization and the senior manager for learning disabilities and mental health, resisted some elements but had no choice but to comply. The manager of the independent sector learning disabilities organization was under no pressure to inflict the new managerialism on her own organization but rapidly had to learn how to cope with its practitioners in the statutory sector.

Becoming providers

The majority of people in the sample found themselves redefined as providers. The impact of this was most marked for those working in the social services. The leader of the learning disabilities team, for example, found his team deprived of part of the crucial assessment element of its work and was soon plunged into a kind of guerrilla warfare with purchasers to try to secure resources for his clients.

For workers in front line health care, apart from the occupational therapist, the effect of the changes has been less dramatic since the split between purchaser and provider has taken place higher up in the organization at the level of the trust or health authority. The CPN has experienced increased managerial control and interference; the community nurse has a substantially increased work load and poorer liaison with hospital and social services.

Subjective experiences of services after the changes

The subjective experience of services changed for our interviewees as a result of the reforms carried out in almost every aspect of their work that we explored with them.

Ethos

Some find it difficult to talk of an organizational ethos at all other than in terms of their own alienation, while others simply define it in a managerialist vocabulary. The community nurse, for example, answers the question on ethos by saying that 'everyone is fed-up' while the qualified carer in the nursing home describes an atmosphere of fear and anxiety amongst the patients. For others, such as the mental health team leader, there is a lack of any sense of hope or direction, a view shared by the geriatrician who talks of the predominance of 'irrational forces' and 'chaos'.

A managerialist ethos is described by several people. For some, like the occupational therapist, it means a world in which managers are taking control and splitting everything into 'small boxes' or, as in the case of the learning disabilities team leader, the dominance of financial criteria backed by 'macho management'. The managers themselves expressed comparable views on the pre-eminence of the role of finance; they identify value for money and the mixed economy as defining the ethos.

Pressures to conform and freedom to speak out

Almost all the interviewees identified new pressures to conform; there was a sharp decline in the proportion of the sample who thought that there was freedom to speak out in their agency. Only the assistant director, carrying the responsibilities for introducing the reforms in her organization, and the head of the learning disabilities agency, backed by a supportive management committee, felt no constraints in either sense. Conformity, as the senior social worker noted, is now not a matter of maintaining professional standards but of doing nothing that might adversely affect the survival of the organization.

Some people commented on the development of a feeling, unsupported by explicit evidence, that if they did not conform and especially if they spoke out critically, something awful would happen to them. But others received explicit directions to keep quiet and toe the line. One example was the geriatrician who had been forbidden by the medical director of the trust to give a paper critical of the disintegration of geriatric services at a professional conference. In other cases people were told to shut up or were accused of disloyalty if they raised objections to management plans and decisions.

In spite of such warnings, several people emphasized that they continued to speak out because they were so upset at what was happening. In addition, a few also took what might be called subversive action outside the organization to escape these constraints. Examples included writing anonymous articles for the social work press, liaising with colleagues in other organizations to by-pass or manipulate their systems in order to protect users, enlisting the help of professional associations and protesting privately to MPs about planned cuts in services to vulnerable groups.

Freedom to do the job to one's own satisfaction

For the majority this freedom had diminished significantly because they have less ability to provide a good service to clients or because the changes have resulted in a loss of the aspects of the job that meant most to them. Additionally, the head of the learning disabilities agency was concerned at the growing monopoly power of the local authority and the risk that it would lead to increasingly tighter control of independent sector organizations. Only the GP, previously uneasy about the lack of accountability of general practice, did not resent what he saw as greater control of his work. Of course, in their new roles the two people who had started private agencies valued highly the ability to work as they thought best.

Security

Security of employment had become an issue for everyone except the GP and the head of the learning disabilities agency. The main source of insecurity is the evidence of redundancy, by removal of a level of management and by job cutting. The occupational therapist even finds her sleep plagued with nightmares about redundancy and the geriatrician has been directly threatened with it if he does not bring his work into line with that required by the trust. Other sources of insecurity include the risk of take-over by another trust with the likely consequence of a decline in working conditions, the introduction of short term employment contracts and ill health.

Enjoyment of the job

Nearly every one reported a marked deterioration in their level of enjoyment of their jobs. Only the assistant director, planning and managing through the reforms herself, felt unambivalent about the satisfaction the work gave her with the intense interest of getting a large organization to change.

Before the changes nearly all those interviewed had enjoyed their jobs 'very much' or between 'very much' and 'somewhat'. After the changes only one interviewee remains in this category and most define themselves as enjoying the job 'very little' or between 'very little' and 'somewhat'. The major frustrations now are not having the power to do the job adequately, seeing standards of service decline and not knowing where they and their organizations are going. The remaining sources of enjoyment, such as they are, are mainly to do with continuing contacts with users and projects, and protecting one's team from the worst effects of the changes.

Evaluating outcomes for service users and for staff after the changes

Advantages to users

Although several of those interviewed had believed that the reforms would improve services to users, very few think that any clear-cut advantages have yet resulted.   About half can see no advantages at all in the way services are provided. A minority, however, identified the emphasis on assessment in the community care reforms as an advantage or a potential advantage. Assessment is likely to be carried out more expeditiously than before and, if a user is assessed as needing help, he or she will get it more quickly. In two local areas it was noted that such assessment also carries some degree of choice as to who should provide the service. However, others were sceptical that faster assessment meant anything more than that. The GP, for example, stresses that there is no guarantee that assessment will lead to a service.

Disadvantages for users

The large majority of interviewees describe substantial disadvantages to users. First there is less access to skilled staff, illustrated by the disbandment of the multi-disciplinary mental health team, the replacement of specialist assessment by the learning disabilities team with generalist assessors, the removal of qualified social workers from most front line provider teams in the metropolitan authority, and the loss of a dedicated geriatric department in the acute hospital, with the holistic approach it offered. Secondly, shortage of resources is highlighted in the problems described by the community nurse, the qualified carer in the nursing home and three of the learning disabilities staff, and is further compounded in these and other examples by over-stressed or 'burned out' staff.

Other aspects cited as having an adverse effect on services to users include the fragmentation of previously integrated services, the return of a medical model of treatment in inappropriate contexts, the reduction of preventive work and the failure to generate an effective inspectorate in the residential sector.

Advantages for workers

Very few people in the sample can see any advantages to themselves or their colleagues from the changes. In the child care organization middle management now has less paperwork. The senior manager for learning disabilities and mental health feels that he gained an element of control over cash budgets but qualified this by pointing out that all that had been promised had not been delivered and that such responsibilities should be more than just saying 'no'. The two interviewees who have lost their core roles say that they experience less stress in terms of the numbers of clients they must deal with but both regard this as a poor exchange for no longer being able to do the work they loved.

Disadvantages for workers

The worsening service for users directly affects workers. Having gained much satisfaction in the past from providing a good service, the deterioration in standards is taken personally. For instance, the qualified carer in the nursing home is frustrated and upset by the worsening conditions for patients and her own powerlessness to do anything about them. Similarly, the assistant director is unhappy at seeing the conditions of staff driven down and the role of social work in the organization marginalized. Those moving from the statutory sector to start their own private care agencies are distressed to find that they too are now forced to offer their care staff poor wages if their businesses are to survive.

Again, the loss of access for users to specialist workers, such as the geriatrician and the occupational therapist, directly affects staff who can no longer deploy their specialist skills.

The manager of the learning disabilities agency defines several disadvantages for workers which have resulted from the changes including, most notably, being over-monitored by social services, competition between provider agencies, and the lack of trust and goodwill between the agency and social services.

The most frequently mentioned disadvantages of the new order, however, are increased stress and lack of time to do the job properly. These are attributed to three main factors, singly or in combination: rising demands, resources which fail to keep pace and the dysfunctions of the new system of management. For the GP, increasing demand is fuelled by deteriorating conditions in the inner city and fanned by rising expectations of what the health service should be able to provide. The community nurse is run off her feet as the result of the 'quicker and sicker' policy which increases throughput of hospitals but does not augment community services sufficiently to cope.

Some interviewees comment on the wasteful costs of the new system dividing staff into 'opposing' teams of purchasers and providers. For instance, the learning disabilities team leader attributes much of the stress in his job to the fact that he now has to contend with internal conflicts with purchasing managers in addition to the struggle to provide adequate services to users in the face of severe funding cuts. The ultimate irony is when stress itself becomes a prime cause of increased stress, as in the example of the mental health team.

Changed lives: personal responses and careers

Perhaps the most telling commentary on interviewees' evaluation of the impact of the reforms is the effect they have had on the way this once highly committed group of people have come to view their own jobs and to see their future careers. Only a small minority of the sample are holding course and continuing to see a clear future for themselves in their existing posts. Most have quite simply become disillusioned and have adopted one of three alternative strategies of disengagement: exit, role change, or survival.

Holding course

Two of the managers and the GP remained fully engaged in their work and, although none was an uncritical supporter of the reforms, they could still see worthwhile futures for themselves in it. The managers (the assistant director and the manager of the learning disabilities agency) were actively engaged in trying to limit the damage done by the changes to their organizations and, where possible, in using any opportunities for positive improvements. The GP too saw real possibilities for the future in the development of locality purchasing.

Exit

Three people felt so negatively about the impact of the changes on their work and their clients that they had decided to resign their jobs. Two had subsequently established their own small companies providing community care services, hoping that at least in this way they could again become involved in professional practice of a high standard.

Role change

A third strategy was to retreat into, or accept, a role change involving a move to a job out of the firing line. The nurse manager deliberately chose to leave his increasingly stressful post and switch to a training post. Similarly, the geriatrician accepted his transformation to a general physician when he acknowledged that he had lost his battle to retain an integrated geriatric service.

Survival

Others who once saw promising futures for themselves in their jobs, including the possibility of promotion, are now preoccupied with short term survival for themselves, their clients and their colleagues. They are too harassed and stressed to get much satisfaction from their present work, beyond perhaps out-manoeuvring purchasers to get better services for a client, or protecting team members. The future looks bleak and promotion to become part of the management of the discredited new system is rejected. In the longer run, for the younger workers at least, there is the possibility of finding work elsewhere. And then there are the dreams of the mental health team leader who keeps playing the lottery and planning the independent sector agency she will set up with the winnings to provide decent services to her clients.

Comment

The majority of workers in our sample describe situations in which they think the system of services has deteriorated rather than improved, with both users and workers losing out. In spite of the claims of overall progress issued from time to time by the government and its agents, their reality is more often defined in terms of disappointment, confusion and frustration, than as the emergence of a new, more just, efficient and effective order.

8

Emergent issues

While we have insisted on the caution required in interpreting the possible wider relevance of small-scale qualitative studies such as ours, we have also emphasized their potential value for identifying central issues which can escape other approaches. Such issues, once exposed, can then themselves be the subject of more systematic and large-scale exploration.

In this chapter we summarize the key issues which emerge from the analysis in the preceding two chapters. We use for this purpose the main headings of the framework developed in Chapter 6 to describe the conditions our interviewees regarded as necessary for the practice of effective professional work in community care. The framework is based not on professionals being able to do what they want but on key factors which they regard as preconditions for the performance of their work. Significantly, these are in accord with much in the contemporary industrial literature focusing on the conditions for the effective involvement of people in organizations (e.g. Peters and Waterman, 1982; Quinn, 1988; Brady, 1989; Flynn, 1994). However, the framework does not attempt to define wider aspects of organizational systems and does not attempt to address the issue of the management of the community care programmes taken as a whole.

The framework, of course, is based on the perspective of the front-line professional and does not claim to incorporate wider managerial or policy questions. As such it would be quite insufficient as a tool for the evaluation of the overall operation of the community care system.

Nevertheless, in the context of this study of the impact of the changes seen through the eyes of practitioners, it is entirely appropriate to employ it as representing the criteria which they are likely to use, and thus to gain a better understanding of their reactions to them. Even our current policy makers, often sceptical of the motives of providers, should be able to see that their perceptions of their work, and their motivation and commitment to it, remain critical factors in the successful implementation of the reforms.

In the second part of the chapter we turn to consider the possible wider relevance of these issues. As a first step we briefly review evidence from other recent studies and reports which bears on some of the issues we have identified. The work involved allows no definitive conclusions but indicates some important common ground with our research and shared concerns for the operation of the reforms, as well as providing further evidence that the whole community care initiative is riddled with inherent contradictions.

Relationships with the user

New barriers to needs-led services

Our interviewees saw needs-led services as the essence of what their jobs should be about. Several of them thought that they were able to achieve such standards in their own work before the reforms although others were prevented from doing so by inappropriate organization and practice.

The reforms, as we have seen, give a central place to the aim of turning what were said to be 'service-led' systems into 'needs-led' systems. Leaving aside for the moment the tricky problem of exactly *how* a person's needs were to be defined, this meant that instead of users being fitted into existing services, services would be designed which were specifically appropriate to their needs. The key instruments in achieving this end were to be the process of assessment, the separation of assessment from the provision of service, the encouragement of user choice and a market to provide alternatives from which to choose.

The new system, as it has been described in several of the organizations covered by the sample, would appear to contains basic defects. To most of our interviewees this means that in spite of improvements in getting cases assessed and achieving a higher quality of service for *some* users, in many respects services are *less* rather than more likely to be needs-led than before the reforms.

- Assessors often do not have the knowledge, time or specialist back-up to make accurate assessments of need.
- The separation of assessment from provision creates an artificial distinction in a process that, to be effective, should be continuous and interactive. This is particularly important in on-going, long-term cases.
- The purchaser/provider split has spawned a new bureaucracy, more greedy by far in its appetite for paperwork than its predecessor, and experienced as more time-consuming, controlling and restrictive by those who work in it.
- The requirement of the reforms to focus services on those in greatest need undermines the basic professional tenet that prevention is better than cure. It is as though dentists had been told they had to restrict their work entirely to teeth in the last stages of decay. Early intervention, including carefully planned support of existing caring systems, can delay or prevent deterioration to the point where a heavy commitment of services is necessary to avert admission to an institution. Preventive work is now difficult or impossible to justify and sustain.
- Most important of all, the reforms have not altered the basic fact that the

resources available for services are finite and fall far short of potential demand. This inevitably means that in the end only *some needs* of *some users* or would-be users can be met. Since the decision as to who gets help and how much remains with the health and social services, all state provided services remain, in this sense, service-led or, as it might now be more appropriately described, budget-led.

- As a direct consequence of this, there is a conflict between the duty to be as efficient as possible in helping as many users as they can, and providing choice and quality for a smaller number. It is not surprising, in a country which still supports notions of fairness and equality of opportunity, to find that in many cases services favour the first option and that those responsible for assessing and providing services are being directed to maximize the use of existing facilities in their own organizations and to go for the lowest cost independent sector options.

Learning to be economical with the truth

Most of the organizations in our sample have not been prepared to acknowledge openly the deficit between needs and available services in dealings with their users. Workers are not able to give straightforward assessments but must hedge what they record in terms of what the organization may be able to provide and by considerations of legal liability. This is as if a doctor had to take account of resources before completing a diagnosis.

Relationships with the organization

Effective professional work in community care, as defined in the interviews of our sample, required having a substantial measure of discretion and autonomy in the way the professionals carried out their day-to-day work; an acceptance that they had accountability to their users, to their colleagues, and to professional standards as well as to their employers; continuity and security of employment; and an understanding of the organizational world in which they operated.

Before the reforms, some felt their work organizations met most of these conditions and some did not. The changes, however, are seen by nearly everyone as representing a sharp deterioration in each of these aspects of relations between the workers and their organizations.

Surrendering discretion and autonomy

In the social services the split between purchasing and providing imposed an immediate reduction in both discretion and autonomy by splitting the role of the social worker. But in all agencies there was evidence of the proliferation of managerial controls. Part of the logic lies in the devolution of budgets, the commitment to set standards of performance, the growing influence of the contract culture and the close monitoring of the reforms by central government. But our interviewees are also aware of the influence of the development of a new form of scientific management that sees detailed information on workers' activities as an essential prerequisite for controlling the organization.

The growing managerial monopoly of accountability

Workers are confused and resentful that they feel under pressure to put the organization before everything else, a challenge to *their* ultimate test of their work which is the well-being of the client.

A pervasive insecurity

Our interviewees thought that a degree of continuity and job security were essential if they were to provide a good service for long-term users. Redundancies, job cuts, the replacement of professionals by semi-skilled and unskilled workers all worked to undermine or destroy such conditions.

Confusion and secrecy in the new organizational world

In the views of our interviewees an adequate understanding of the world in which the worker operates is essential for professionals in the complex field of community care. Even before the reforms, the accelerating rate of change made this an increasingly challenging task.

The situation after the reforms has worsened dramatically for most of our sample, particularly in the organizations where management appeared to have no coherent strategy for their introduction. It seems that the problem is not simply or even mainly a difficulty in understanding the formal changes which are supposed to be taking place but a combination of management defensiveness and the problems faced by workers in trying to make the new system work. Managements under stress, coping with what may often seem impossible demands and totally inadequate means, are likely to give priority to survival strategies. The first imperative in such strategies is to present a good public image, to *appear* to be fully in command of the situation. The free flow of information and open discussion of the performance of the organization are inconsistent with this goal. Instead the demand is for selective statistics and secrecy, made respectable (with the arrival of markets) on commercial grounds. The result is that the majority of workers in our sample find the behaviour of their organization increasingly confusing and difficult to understand or predict, and become suspicious and cynical about the motives, pronouncements and actions of their managers.

Side-lining participation and free speech

Interviewees suggested that if professional workers are to work responsibly and creatively they need to be able to talk regularly and openly to management about the relationship between their work and the conduct of the organization. Before the reforms participation ranged from high to non-existent. After the reforms involvement of this kind is increasingly rare in most organizations. In some instances the new managers dismiss even the use of terms such as 'participation' and 'free speech' as 'oldspeak'. In other cases, the ability to speak out is simply lost in the stress and uncertainty that is described as overwhelming management.

Relationships with colleagues

Conflicting values.

The shared values which provided the taken-for-granted basis for much cooperation within and between agencies before the reforms have, in many cases, become more and more difficult to sustain. The emphasis on the divisions between purchaser and provider, managers and managed, and the growing competition between different agencies, encourage conflicting rather than common values and priorities.

Mistrust and expediency

These tend to replace trust and integrity, partly through the same processes. Our interviewees in the main do not feel trusted to get on with their work and are themselves increasingly mistrustful of their managers and their motives.

New barriers to collaborative working

Because of the increasingly controlled nature of the managerial organization, including the detailed specification of budgets, priorities and responsibilities, front-line flexibilty (on which much collaboration with other agencies has depended) becomes harder and harder to defend. For all the rhetoric in favour of close cooperation between agencies accompanying the introduction of the new system, its managerial and competitive structures and dynamics favour defensive and cautious, rather than welcoming and open, attitudes to such partnerships.

Relationships with the wider social and political system

Possibilities for achieving improvements in the policies affecting services and for exercising some influence in the process now seem remote to most people in our sample. The persistence of the same political regime over four Parliaments, the perceived antipathy of that regime to public services and the determination to persist with the reforms come what may, make the prospects for achieving any kind of change not clearly in line with existing policies seem remote. Further, for the reasons already discussed, personal involvement in such political processes would be likely to be unpopular with managements and incur their hostility. Action through professional associations and unions to try to influence policy has, of course, continued but there seems little hope that this will be effective. For most a feeling of alienation from the political process would seem more typical.

Personal fulfilment

The professional workers' ambitions to work where they can fully apply their skills, and continue to develop them and their careers in a creative environment, are increasingly difficult to realize in the new order. In the social services departments the very role of the social worker has been called into question by the purchaser/provider split and its consequences. The strengths of community nursing are threatened by dilution through the substitution of ancillaries with limited training. More widely, almost all workers now report levels of stress from workloads that have increased to the point that they have little time, energy or enthusiasm to plan to advance their training and their careers.

Taken together, these are the issues which have worried, frustrated and alienated members of our sample and to which most see no likely resolution in the years ahead. We turn now to consider whether there is evidence that their experience and perceptions are shared more widely.

The study sample in context: some other evidence on experience of the reforms

Evaluating the reforms

The central thrust of government-sponsored evaluation of the community care reforms has so far been in terms of process rather than outcomes (e.g. Audit Commission, 1994; Henwood, 1994; Henwood and Wistow, 1995). In other words the main concern has been to establish whether the new structures and procedures are in place rather than whether or not they are producing better services. This may be an understandable priority in the first years of the implementation of the changes but there is little evidence of interest in any objective evaluation of their general impact on users for there appears to be no sponsorship of baseline population studies against which improvement or deterioration can be measured. Even a major current evaluation of care management by the Personal Social Services Research Unit (PSSRU) at the University of Kent, *Evaluating Community Care for Old People,* funded by the Department of

Health, which monitors user allocated services, includes no control of would-be users whose applications for help were turned down.

However, other research funded by the Department of Health at the Centre for Social Policy Research and Development (CSPRD) in the University of Wales has given scope for evaluation by care managers of the implementation of the reforms. The first results from this work have recently been published (Grant, 1995). Other surveys of providers' experiences of aspects of the reforms carried out recently include a survey of care managers sponsored by the journal *Community Care* (Marchant, 1995); a survey of community nurses by the Industrial Relations Service and the Royal College of Nursing (IRS/RCN) (Ballard, 1994); a survey of social workers and other staff undertaken by the National Institute for Social Work (NISW, 1995); and a survey of local government workers for the Commission on Local Democracy (Pratchett and Wingfield, 1994). We have also drawn on a report by the NHS Consultants Association reviewing the NHS market reforms (NHSCA, 1995); a report on progress in implementation of the community care reforms based on discussions with panels of users, workers, and managers (Henwood, 1994); a study of the implementation of the changes in five local authorities (Lewis *et al.*, 1995); and a number of other reports or articles on specific topics.

The overlap between the issues which were the focus in these surveys and reports, and the issues raised in our study, is only partial. Nevertheless, they serve to allow us to establish if in these areas, at least, the issues identified by our sample have a wider resonance. The main topics are reviewed under four of the five headings used in the first part of the chapter: relationships with the user, with the organization and with colleagues, and personal fulfilment.

Users

Resources

Some real improvements in services to individual users noted by a few of our interviewees were also reported in some of the studies. However, there is no indication of how commonly such improvements are taking place. The problems of rising demand and fixed or diminishing resources, and by implication the limitations posed for providing needs-led services, were widely described and it was evident that care managers were aware of much unmet need.

Both the care management and community nursing surveys found that the reforms have been accompanied by a steep rise in demand for services, that workloads have increased and that resources available have diminished. In the IRS/RCN survey 79 per cent of the community nurses responding said their workloads had increased as a result of the Community Care Act; the CSPRD study reported that 84 per cent of the care managers surveyed said that the demand for services had risen over the last year while 75 per cent considered that resources available to them had either decreased or remained at the same level. As one manager in the latter study commented:

> The gulf between what is actually needed and what we are able to provide is getting bigger and bigger. We tend to become more and more alarmed about what we can actually deliver and that is going to become worse and worse (Grant, 1995, p.8).

The *Community Care* survey reported that 43 per cent of the care managers responding had found themselves forced, because of budget restraints, to choose between two clients they believed were equally deserving of a service.

Bureaucracy

The problem of burgeoning paperwork and administration, described by our sample, was stressed in the two care manager surveys and reported as having increased by over 90 per cent of respondents in both. The NHS consultants claimed that the administrative and managerial overheads of the NHS had doubled since the introduction of the market, not including the additional costs to GPs, doctors and nurses of managing market transactions (NHSCA, 1995, p.10).

Prevention

Preventive work of the kind which some of our interviewees could do before the changes, was identified as a likely casualty by Lewis and her colleagues.

> It seems inevitable that in the main only need defined as high risk/dependency will receive service. This must beg the question about the treasured, albeit notoriously hard to define and measure, concept of prevention and poses the risk of the less dependent people having to enter institutions if their relatively more simple, but nevertheless vital, needs for service are not met. (Lewis *et al.*, 1995, p.91)

In the community nursing field, other commenators drew attention to the point made by one of our interviewees, that the 'dilution' of professional nurses by less skilled staff meant that the early diagnosis of health problems would be less likely (NHSCA, 1995, p.16; Luntley and Luntley, 1995).

Organizations

Confusion and complexity

A majority of those in our sample described their organizations as in a state of confusion or incoherence after the reforms. In a penetrating analysis of the reforms and the experience of social services departments in their implementation, Lewis and her colleagues help explain why such problems are likely to be common. They identify clearly the inherent tensions and contradictions of the community care policy and the enormous difficulties for the social services departments in following the logical steps for their implementation. The picture of smooth transition in the official guidelines she calls

> unrealistic given both the difficulty in reconciling the government's objectives and the huge range of tasks that social services are being asked to think about at the same time: assessment, care management, purchaser/ provider splits, contracting for services, construction of community care plans, quality assurance, complaints procedures and inspection, and new forms of joint planning (Lewis *et al.*, 1995, p.81).

The CSPRD survey of care managers gives an example of what such overload can mean in practice. It reported that 'less than half of the care managers surveyed had access to the relevant data about unit costs of services, the status of the local community care budget, or the prevailing charges for services', information essential for informed decision-making about the matching of resources to individual needs (Grant, 1995, pp.5–6).

Managerialism

The rapid growth of a neo-Taylorist managerialism in the public services, which we have described in Chapter 1, has been explored in a number of recent studies (e.g. Pollitt, 1993; Allsop and May, 1993; Clarke *et al.*, 1994). The potentially divisive effect of such managerialism in the NHS has been discussed recently by the NHS director of human resources who found managers inhabiting a different world from other staff:

> Everywhere I go, the senior people tell me of progress, of better working methods and value for money, of objectives achieved, of changes delivered. Everywhere I go, I also glimpse another world, a world inhabited by everyone else – a world of daily crisis, and concern, of staff under pressure and services struggling to deliver. Both worlds are real in the minds of those who inhabit them. Both worlds are supported by objective evidence. Both views are held sincerely (Jarrold, 1995).

Secrecy

Pressures for conformity and secrecy, similar to those in our cases, have been widely reported in the NHS (e.g. RCN, 1992; Craft, 1994; Sheard, 1994; Smith, 1994). *Community Care* (Simmons, 1995) has drawn attention to the same kind of pressures in the social services and the British Association of Social Workers reports a sharp increase in the work of its legal panel advising social workers in whistleblowing cases. Gagging clauses in job contracts have become increasingly common and workers who do speak out risk becoming the subjects of disciplinary action. In the view of the NHS Consultants' Association,

> Restriction of the freedom to speak on behalf of the welfare of patients, whether for political or financial reasons, is totally alien to the NHS which has always prided itself on open relationships as part of its accountability to the public. It is an almost inevitable consequence of a commercial system which demands a duty of fidelity to

the employer 'before the professional duty to the patient' (Roy Lilley) (NHSCA, 1995).

The growth of secretiveness in the context of splitting services into different businesses, was also a concern in a survey of local government staff. As one respondent said:

> Secretiveness – 'behind closed doors' – is increasing. Insecurity – and not just about jobs – is rife. But what does all this achieve? the construction of barriers that prevent service to the community (Pratchett and Wingfield, 1994, p.29).

Colleagues

Collaboration within and between organizations

Some of our interviewees observed that one of the significant costs of the new world of markets, of the purchaser/provider split and of competition between agencies for contracts and clients, was the diminution of open collaboration within and between organizations. Both the local government survey and NHSCA report endorsed this view. The authors of the former reported that 'In a competitive environment individual officers are encouraged to be partial and to favour the interests of their own part of the organization against those of others' (Pratchett and Wingfield, 1994, p.16) although 'For most respondents (95 per cent) inter- and intra-organizational competition was perceived as a negative factor' (p.23). The NHSCA saw losses in cooperation and accountability as part of the price that was being paid by the creation of competition and confidentiality, and the 'duty of institutional fidelity' (NHSCA, 1995, p.12).

Personal fulfilment

Morale and job satisfaction

The decline in enjoyment of the job described by nearly everyone in our sample is reflected in all the surveys of professional staff working in the community care field which we have seen. In the CSPRD study,

> Fifty per cent or more of respondents considered that there had been decreases in the time for contact with users and families, the morale of colleagues, personal confidence in the future of community care policy, feeling valued as an employee, and overall satisfaction with working conditions (Grant, 1995, p.10).

In the *Community Care* survey of care managers 54 per cent said that job satisfaction had worsened, although a similar percentage said that they found their job more challenging and interesting. The survey of community nurses recorded a decrease in job satisfaction of 54 per cent, against 15 per cent whose satisfaction increased. The NHSCA cite a study showing that 'low morale and stress were the most significant factors in a rise in sickness levels' (NHSCA, 1995, p.16). Increased levels of personal stress were reported by 77 per cent of those in the CSPRD survey of care managers and 79 per cent of those in the community nursing survey.

Conclusion

This brief review of findings from an *ad hoc* set of studies, constructed with varying degrees of rigour and carried out for a variety of different purposes, must be treated with proper caution as the basis for any generalizations. However, the degree of common ground between our interviewees and respondents in the other studies, particularly on the 'objective' factors of resources, demands, and workloads, and the 'subjective' experience of work in terms of declining job satisfaction and increasing stress, suggest that our sample represents a fairly typical cross-section.

At the very least, this conclusion supports the case for exploring urgently and comprehensively the widespread malaise which seems currently to exist in the community care services, together with its causes and consequences. This is not simply or even principally because of concern for the workforce itself but because their experiences of the reforms, and their responses to these, strongly suggest that all is far from well with their implementation.

The more analytical studies we have examined would suggest that such a review would need to be more far-reaching than an examination of the human resource questions alone. The range and nature of the issues emerging from this work, which our own limited inquiry strongly supports, point to more fundamental problems in the conception and implementation of the policy as a whole.

In particular, it seems that a number of fundamental contradictions lie at the heart of the reforms which taken together explain the confusion and alienation of many workers and their frustration at the declining standards of the service they provide.

Market versus public service values

The emphasis on managerial and market values, with the implied endorsement of self-interest and group interest as the key motivating factors (with their associated personnel policies) not only conflicts with the public service ethos that motivates many front-line staff, but is contradicted by the continued appeals of government to 'dedication and the distinctive traditions of public service' (Pollitt, 1993, p.113). Social services workers, for instance, find themselves increasingly treated like industrial workers, their activities more and more tightly monitored and controlled, and their terms of service downgraded. Yet they are still expected to show the same kind of commitment and readiness to pick up the pieces when the system breaks down.

Increased demand versus fixed supply

Demand for services has increased for several reasons. Services in people's own homes are more popular than residential care; when services get better, they become more popular; the numbers of very old people are increasing; expectations of what it is reasonable to expect are rising; hospitals are seeking to maximize the use of their 'plant' by increasing the throughput of patients; publicity and information about services has improved, partly as a result of the government's emphasis on consumer rights (the Citizens' Charters, hospital waiting list times).

However, *social* markets are not allowed to behave like real markets, for the capacity to expand and contract production in response to changes in demand does not exist. The better the service in the social market, the sooner the resources are used up and the sooner harsh rationing has to be introduced.

Needs-led versus budget-determined services

As we have already shown, the realities of budgetary constraint mean that purchasers, not users, determine which needs can be met and to what extent. Splitting purchasing and providing between different agencies does not alter that fact. The problem of rationing scarce resources remains and, in the end, how it is dealt with is a political, not a managerial, issue.

Organizational change versus organizational capacity

The organizational changes required by the reforms are extensive and fundamental. We have quoted above (p.192), for example, Lewis's summary of demands made on social services departments. Yet the organizations concerned have previously had different functions which relied on different skills and abilities. With fixed or diminishing resources, the managers have had to re-learn their jobs and to work the miracles of change within the tight timetables and declining resources decreed. The health service, with the introduction of the internal market, has had to face similar problems.

Industrialized versus responsive organizations

The logic of the purchaser/provider divide and the market has imposed a factory or industrial model of production on what can be argued to be very different transactions which require flexible and responsive structures to facilitate them. The NHSCA, for example, describe the basic incompatibility between the requirements of the market and good clinical practice which treats the whole person:

> The operation of any competitive market requires accurately defined, standardised

> commodity units of verifiable quality, so that contracts can be enforced ... Few
> people who have not been forced by circumstances to take vital decisions on inade-
> quate evidence, not once but many times a day, can understand the objective
> difficulties entailed in work within the strict guidelines customary in industrial
> production, and now flooding from well-meaning theorists who imagine they can
> make medical care more efficient by shifting it to an industrial model (NHSCA,
> 1995, p.17)

In the personal social services, the transactions between users and workers are
often equally unlike the simple exchanges of the market place. They typically
involve discursive, face-to-face relations

> often over a period of time. These are developmental relationships in which the
> establishment of trust and an appreciation by the provider of the unique circum-
> stances of the individual consumer are essential to the ultimate effectivess of the
> service being provided (Pollitt, 1993, p.128).

Treatment versus prevention

The requirement to give priority to those in greatest need in the community care
reforms diminishes or removes the capacity of social services departments to
intervene early in cases so as to delay or prevent the need for intensive support,
and to engage in more general programmes to develop and strengthen the caring
resources of local communities.

Better services versus poorer working conditions

The introduction of market forces into community care, in the absence of a
minimum wage, has led many local authority and trust employers to drive down
wages and terms of employment for staff working in residential and home care,
already a low-paid, predominantly female workforce. Yet it is these very
workers on whom the increased standards of care sought by the government most
depend.

Cooperation versus competition

Cooperation and open dealings between different agencies is urged in the
reforms and formally required in the preparation of community care plans.
However, the fragmentation of social services between purchasers and providers,
the division of the health services into separate health trusts and the pressure on
resources – taken together with the introduction of a quasi-market – encourage
competition, not cooperation, secretiveness not openness, both within and
between the organizations.

Defensiveness versus learning

The pressures within the system to demonstrate progress in the implementation of the reforms and the pressures to control the flow of information to this end and in response to the introduction of competition, stand opposed to the need for open access to the undistorted information that is crucial in the development of a learning organization which can respond effectively to its changing environment.

Whether, in the light of the growing evidence that the reforms are profoundly flawed, the government is prepared actively to support either a limited review of human resource issues or a more fundamental examination of the basic principles on which the reforms have been built is another matter. The strategy adopted by the government for introducing the changes appears to be one that has no place for such re-evaluations. In the next chapter we move beyond the immediate confines of our data and their interpretation, to explore why this is so and to consider the legacy it has left for any would-be revisionists.

9

An extravagant experiment? Change strategies in theory and practice

In potentially contested areas of social policy like health and community care, changes in the scale and speed of those which are the subject of this book carry high risks of leading to a long, disruptive and costly period of implementation or even of complete failure. The nature of the strategies used to manage them therefore becomes of critical importance.

In this chapter, then, we change gears from what has been predominantly a close examination of our case studies and their possible wider implications, to review the particular strategies employed by the government to implement the 1990 Act. This should help us to understand more fully the emergent problems of the services which have been our subject, and to inform possible future projects designed to modify or replace the reforms.

We look first at the different options open to those seeking to introduce change and contrast the gains and risks offered by alternative strategies. We then review the government's choice of an imposed model and its introduction. In the light of this analysis we argue that the whole project of reform can be regarded as an example of utopian social engineering and that its inherent contradictions can be explained in that context.

Change strategies

Those seeking to introduce change in organizations, or in whole sets of interacting organizations in a similar field, can use one of two major change strategies: change by imposition or change by consent. Of course, some blend of the two is also possible but a coherent strategy is likely to require a clear emphasis in favour of one or the other.

Change by imposition has its roots in the scientific management school, represented today by the neo-Taylorist approach which we discussed in Chapter 1 (p.13). From this perspective management is the largely technical task of establishing the best way to achieve a given end. Change is a matter for expert decision-making, not negotiation. Change by consent, in contrast, draws on the perspectives of students of organizational behaviour in which the compliance of the members of an organization is seen as problematic and the need for negotiation and consent as paramount if changes are to be successfully implemented (e.g. Kanter, 1983; Huczynski and Buchanan, 1991).

Change by consent

This strategy uses well-established methods such as education and communication, participation and involvement, facilitation and support, negotiation and agreement (Kotter and Schlesinger, 1979) to reduce the forces resisting change and increase those supporting it.

The *advantages* of the approach, if it succeeds, are that it gains the active involvement of employees in the implementation of change and in doing so is likely to increase greatly the chances of its success. If the workforce has come to 'own' the new order it can become an invaluable source of detailed feed-back on progress and difficulties, and of ideas and initiatives for overcoming problems. This strategy reinforces involvement and loyalty to the enterprise and facilitates the development of a learning organization, well adapted to the challenges of its environment. The potential *disadvantages* or *risks* of the strategy are that the price of involvement may be a significant compromise in the original intentions of the legislators, a consequent loss of focus in the changes and in the worst scenario the defeat of their very purpose.

Change by imposition

As a coherent strategy this is likely to contain at least five key elements: the identification and empowerment of the change agents; a justificatory rationale or ideology; the discrediting of the previous order; a new model of organization; and a motivational system backed by coercive sanctions.

The principal *advantage* of such strategies is that they enable the initiators to keep control over the parameters of change firmly in their own hands. No compromise is involved in their implementation unless they are fully in agreement with it. The chances that the programme will be seriously diluted and its central purposes lost are greatly diminished.

The possible *disadvantages*, however, are considerable. They include the risks of alienating significant sections of the workforce; distorting internal systems of information and evaluation (as a result of alienation, suppression of free speech, criticism, etc.); increasing bureaucratic procedures needed to assure control; losing energy and commitment of the workforce; and triggering workers' active or passive resistance.

The risks of change by imposition when the changes involved are on a grand scale and ideologically driven are, as Popper (1945) pointed out long ago, particularly great. Such large scale change, which he calls Utopian engineering, is plagued by the problem of getting accurate feedback on the progress of the project, whether because of the authoritarianism of those introducing it or because the Utopian engineer develops deafness to complaints, simply to be able to maintain the momentum of change. In small scale change ('piecemeal engineering') we can 'learn from our mistakes, without risking repercussions of a gravity that must endanger the will to future reforms' (Popper, 1945, pp. 144–5). In contrast,

> the Utopian method must lead to a dangerous dogmatic attachment to a blueprint for which countless sacrifices have been made. Powerful interests must become linked up with the success of the experiment. All this does not contribute to the rationality, or to the scientific value, of the experiment (p.144).

Government and change strategies

In the years of relative consensus which characterized the Fordist period of the 1950s and 1960s, the practice developed of widespread consultation about policy and organization. Such consultation took place not only inside state services but with national interest groups representing service providers and users, as well as with independent experts such as academics. Major organizational changes would typically be preceded by widespread consultation and debate in these forums and would often involve lengthy investigation by a committee of inquiry or Royal Commission on which many of the interests would be represented.

However, the arrival of the Thatcher administration, as we have shown in Chapter 1, saw consensual approaches dismissed. Instead the new government preferred to preface the introduction of its reforms by rapid inquiries conducted by individuals or groups selected because they shared the government's ideological position. When the government favoured the resulting proposals, it restricted consultation to the minimum and moved as rapidly as possible to legislation and implementation.

The imposed model in practice: the case of the 1990 Act

The proposals for the changes embodied in the Act were typical of a process produced by hand-picked supporters of the government. The NHS proposals, *Working for Patients* (Secretaries of State, 1989a), came from a policy group working directly under Margaret Thatcher. The community care proposals, *Community Care: Agenda for Action* (Griffiths, 1988), were produced by Sir Roy Griffiths who had also been chosen for the job by Mrs Thatcher. Neither set of proposals was first published as a Green Paper nor submitted to thorough and searching public discussion. The key components of the strategy which has been used to implement the resulting 1990 Act relate quite closely to the five central elements of our model of imposed change.

Managers as change agents

In the drive to create organizations in which professional and bureaucratic dominance was seen as part of the problem to be reformed, managers were the obvious choice as the initiators of change. In the NHS, general management had already been established after the 1983 Griffiths Report (Griffiths, 1983) although at a local level their influence had been resisted by health service professionals with some success (Walby and Greenwell, 1994). The 1990 reforms followed a 'more subtle and possibly more effective strategy for the introduction of managerialism' by encouraging senior medical professionals to become more directly involved in management (p.60).

In the social services, senior managers were more ready from the start to accept the task of introducing the community care reforms. This, it has been suggested, was not only because there was an element of agreement that the reforms could be made to work, but also because the senior managers saw significant opportunities to enhance their own status and career prospects in the process (Nixon, 1993). Further, for senior staff used to the more routine work of the old departments and to coping with the powerful influence of professionals, the challenge of asserting their authority and introducing the changes could be stimulating and exciting. Even the case study assistant director, unhappy about many of the changes she had to introduce in her authority, said she found the business of getting a large organization to accept change intensely interesting.

Ideologies: managerialism and markets

The reforms arrived supported by the complementary ideologies of managerialism and the market. Managerialism can be defined as an ideology in that it has its own set of structured values and beliefs which justify certain types of behaviour (Pollitt, 1993). At the centre of the ideology is the belief in management as a positive force which will make organizations function more efficiently and effectively. Attachment to managerialism can be seen partly as self-serving, a way of promoting one's career, (e.g. Hood, 1991). But others see it as a new version of the public service ethic, and celebrate the sense of direction and dynamism it implies. As one enthusiastic academic supporter puts it, 'The new managerialists are everywhere action men. How they describe the old style official is often unutterable in even the most liberated of gatherings' (Davies, 1995). These 'action men' do not have to confine themselves to deprecation of the old order, however, for the new managerialism sanctions their actions in sweeping it away.

The introduction of markets, or more accurately quasi-markets highly managed by the state (Legrand, 1993), into public services derived from the political values of the government rather than from managerialism itself. But whether managers felt such quasi-markets were the most effective way of promoting efficient and effective public services or not, quasi-markets further strengthened their hand within their organizations for it was they who had to oversee their implementation and functioning. Some of our case studies show how quickly old style managers were able to become new style managers when the reforms were introduced, and how their very language became altered in the process.

Business language using terms such as '*customers*', '*mapping the market*', '*quality assurance*', '*mission statements*' – what one interviewee called 'MBA-speak' – rapidly became common place. For some of our interviewees, money is at the heart of the new language. For others, the changes represent a way managers can distance themselves from the human element both inside the organization and in relationships with users. Thus in the child care organization the new language includes words such as 'stakeholders' (once known as parents, children, local authorities), 'performance review' (previously staff supervision) and 'users' (previously kids), all of which facilitate a more detached attitude towards one's fellow human beings.

However, the ideology behind the reforms had a broader target than management alone and included both the public in general as users of the services and all their other employees. Under the banner of TINA (There Is No Alternative), the 'famous acronym that became a beautiful propaganda weapon' (Young, 1989, pp.204–5), it was insisted that only through the reforms could real value for money be assured and improved services delivered.

Discrediting the past

The imposition of a new policy requires the discrediting of those who still think there is good in the old order. Highlighting the failures of the past, playing down its successes and identifying scapegoats who can be blamed are common methods used to this end. The history of occupied countries provides dramatic evidence of how successful such sustained attacks on former regimes can be. For instance, one close observer of France during the German occupation of the Second World War, recounts how the leaders of a defeated people even came to express gratitude to their conquerors for delivering them from the errors of their past ways (Vercors, 1967, p.171). This is an extreme example but the metaphor of occupation by a foreign power is one that has seemed apt to some of those working in the reorganized services. An instance is the consultant who said that since the NHS reforms he felt he was 'working in occupied country' (NHSCA, 1995, p.16). Two other examples come from our interviewees, one supporting a move to start a samizdat press reporting what was 'really' happening in her organization and the other regarding her forbidden contacts with other agencies on behalf of her clients as 'resistance work'.

Yet for every resister there are also several people who are ready to accept blame for the past and to say, even though they may not like the reforms, that 'something had to be done'. To this extent, by having done nothing to improve things when it was within their power, they are now admitting that they themselves are partly responsible for what has happened. The new emphasis on the rights of the user or consumer illustrates the focus on an aspect of the old order about which there was general agreement that change was needed. At the same time, earlier enthusiasm shown by the administration for established examples of good practice giving users more chance to be heard, as for instance the potential of community social work (Jenkin, 1983, pp.1–4), was conveniently forgotten.

The bureaucracy of control

The changes involved in the 1990 Act introduced what some of its critics, as we noted in the last chapter, have called the 'industrialization of care' (NHSCA, 1995, p.17), and provided the means for tight managerial control of the reformed sector. In the quasi-markets created, the purchasing organizations set prices and specify service standards which the providers must meet.

> This idea of the organization is likely to produce an approach to management within the provider organizations which follows the machine metaphor and the principles of 'scientific management' (Flynn, 1994, p.211).

The same process, which leads to the rationalization of production into more readily specified and controlled tasks, creates pressures to re-examine the role of relatively expensive professional workers who were trained for a system which required them to use judgement and discretion in ways now needed much less frequently. In our case studies such 'dilution' of professional skills was feared by the community nurses and was taking place in the metropolitan authority where social work had been effectively removed from the frontline teams dealing with disabilities and long-term mental illnesses.

Motivation and coercion

The ultimate sanction available to those introducing imposed systems of change is coercion. This is, of course, true for the managers of most non-imposed systems too. However, imposed change with the sense of arbitrary authority, the upheavals it entails in job changes, delayering and redundancies, and the implied threat of ruthless action, allows coercion to be seen as a normal rather than exceptional managerial tool. In the new ethos the view is encouraged that 'Real managers impose their will on their subordinates and on the trade unions' (Flynn, 1990, p.178). Even macho-management of the kind recounted in a number of our case studies, in which an individual deliberately flaunts his or her power and without discussion of an issue tells subordinates they are 'wrong', can be seen as a useful reminder of where authority now lies.

In most cases such sanctions are probably quite unnecessary for more indirect pressures such as family obligations, a mortgage and the desire for a quiet life, produce a tendency to conformity in a majority of us even when we feel uneasy about the work we are asked to do. Further, the very act of 'industrializing' the organization aids the process by substituting technical for moral responsibility (Bauman, 1989) and so helps distance us from the consequences of our actions.

Of course, not all public service managers are enamoured of the principles of new public management (as these approaches have come to be called) and contrast them unfavourably with more people-centred methods in 'progressive' private firms. With roots in neo-human relations, such methods reject the precepts of scientific management and 'stress instead the value of motivating people to produce "quality" and strive for "excellence" themselves' (Newman and Clarke, 1994, p.15). However, the widespread adoption of such alternatives, or 'new wave management' as they have come to be called, would require a very different concept of the operation of quasi-markets to that which now lies at the heart of the present strategy for public service reform (Flynn, 1994, p.224).

The reform as utopian engineering

Our study has described how negatively a cross-section of service providers has experienced this programme of imposed change. Our own analysis suggests that a kind of centralist rationality lies behind the strategy, which to most of our interviewees has seemed irrational and chaotic. But it also implies, following Popper, that the government's approach might properly be classified as a kind of Utopian social engineering. Finding it fitting that this grand-scale initiative of a Conservative government should be evaluated in terms of the theory of a celebrated conservative philosopher, we conclude this chapter by comparing the reform to Popper's own model.

Our grounds for suggesting that the reforms constitute what Popper had in mind concern both the scale and nature of the changes at issue. While the changes were confined to a sector within the social system, the sector is a large one with over a million employees and the changes were part of a much grander design to reshape the whole edifice. The proponents of the reforms have made no secret of their views that they were revolutionary in character. Thus the Audit Commission referring to the 'Community Revolution', (the title of its major paper published in 1992) and the progenitor of the case management experiments which are said to have played an influential role in shaping the changes declared that their success will depend on the government having the 'will to make this one of the world's truly great revolutions' (Davies, 1995, p.20).

The other elements in Utopian engineering to which Popper drew our attention are also present:

• There was little relevant piloting of the changes. In so far as they drew on the experience of the case management developments studied and encouraged by the PSSRU, they relied on projects that were far too narrow and specialized to test out the range of changes promoted by the legislation. As an American commentator noted:

> The experimental projects in Britain that are cited in support of care management also took place in very special circumstances with special investments of money and interest. At the heart of the problem of care management is that it cannot, like reconstituted DNA, be inserted into a chaotic structure and organize it. It needs an orderly and hospitable administrative structure; in present circumstances, few PSS (personal social services) provide this. (Schorr, 1992, p.40)

- The systems to establish the progress of the reforms tend to concentrate on evidence as to whether the formal structures and changes are in place, to emphasize any signs of gains and to minimize critical evaluation. Thus we have the establishment of a 'good news' unit in the Department of Health (NHSCA, 1995 p.13) concentrating on getting publicity for success stories, the gagging of criticism and the growth of pressures for conformity and secrecy.
- The engagement of powerful interests in backing the reforms has been assured by the commitment to their implementation of many senior managers, members of the quangos established in the NHS to oversee the new trusts, and those local government councillors and officials who have put their weight behind the changes.

If in the end, in the light of growing experience and evidence of the impact of the changes, the reforms are generally judged to have been an extravagant mistake, as we suspect may be the case, the legacy of this large-scale experiment will leave those charged with replacing it with a giant task on their hands. In the final chapter of this book we tentatively explore some of the different options that present themselves, all of which, we believe, avoid the hubris and delusions of the Utopian engineer but might offer some way out of the morass created by this apparently deeply flawed policy.

10

Alternative futures

We began this book by asking what is really happening in the implementation of the community care reforms. The common themes we have reviewed, reinforced in several respects by more widely based inquiries, suggest that the new system may be ill-conceived in theory and defective in practice. The particular strength of our evidence lies not in the number of heads counted but in its consistency in identifying the numerous contradictions which characterize the new order.

But after over sixteen years of one-party government which has a proud philosophy of 'no turning back', the reader who shares our conclusion may still feel inclined to ask 'So what? Surely, we are landed with the changes now and if they are poorly conceived, so much the worse for us'. Yet if we take that line we have, whether we intended it or not, accepted the preposterous and hubristic claim of the Thatcherites that 'There Is No Alternative'. Preposterous, because history is little else but a tangle of alternatives; hubristic, because it suggests a monopoly of the truth.

It is easy to understand how we have been led to accept it. We have been warned of the need to be cautious 'lest the capture of language by ... economic ideas and their implications subtly subverts rather than properly modifies our views and feelings' (Beedell, 1989, p.87). Gramsci's notion of hegemony, defined as the success of a class 'in projecting its own particular way of seeing the world as "common sense" and part of the natural order by those who are in fact subordinated to it', (*ibid.*) describes quite accurately the effect of the persistent propaganda of the current administration over its years in office and how far it has succeeded in limiting our ability to imagine alternatives.

So the first step in challenging the existing order must be to recharge our imaginations and, bending Fritz Schumacher's 1973 phrase about economics to our purpose, to consider social policy 'as if people mattered'. To do so we begin with ends rather than means, values rather than techniques.

Ends before means

It would be easy to construct a case that disputes over community care are about means, not ends. The widespread agreement that dependent people should be helped to live in the circumstances they most want can lead to the view that the only issues are about the methods for achieving this. Yet, increasingly, we are aware of the difficulties in describing the ordinary activities of welfare in general, and community care in particular, without using value-laden words and language that have become an everyday currency under a long-lived Conservative administration. There are immense dangers in writing about the mechanics of community care, for example of separating purchaser from provider, and ignoring the understanding on which they are premised and the ends for which they are designed.

The fundamental issues at the heart of community care are, in fact, first and foremost value issues. How do we define and respond to the vulnerability of the human condition ? The way we answer this question relates to the way we define society and relationships within it. Women, for instance, provide by far the larger part of both informal and formal community care. The weakness of statutory support for informal carers and poor financial reward of most formal carers reflects and confirms their lower status. Community care must be looked at as part of society, not as a matter of alternative technologies. The systems in which we live and work are consequent on beliefs about people and their relationships, the nature of a good society and, at a level of greater detail, the very motivation for work.

The neo-liberal project

Underlying the whole of the neo-liberal or Thatcherite project is a view of the nature of human beings and the dynamics of an effective economy. The substance and limits of this view are evident in all the major initiatives of the administration including the health and community care reforms.

At the core of this philosophy is the notion of the self-interested individual pursuing his or her own maximum good. Given the existence of a free market, the expression of individual needs and preferences will result in the greatest good for the greatest number. That greatest good is largely defined in terms of material wealth and what it can buy. More complex definitions of social bonds such as 'society' have little meaning. The role of the state is to ensure the liberty of the subject and the free operation of the market. Public services beyond such functions, where politically realistic, should be purely residual, run on scientific management lines and designed to maintain the minimum level of existence required to ensure sufficient social cohesion for the 'failures' in the system. People who devote their careers to public service for larger reasons are hard to understand in this perspective except as saints or charlatans. Inequality is an essential element in the dynamics of such a society, and relative poverty will always be with us. Money is the measure of all things.

This compressed view of the neo-liberal perspective necessarily fails to capture its subtleties and the extent to which it is subject to compromise in practice. But, in so far as it represents the underlying direction pursued by the administration, it helps to explain both the inadequate resourcing of the community care reforms and the contradictions in their structure and operation. The first is explained by the policy of residualism; the second can be attributed at least in part to mere indifference.

Alternative perspectives

We reject the neo-liberal version of human nature as impoverished and impoverishing. Its shallow vision is encapsulated in Neil Kinnock's pithy assessment of Thatcherism:

> No obligation to the community, no sense of solidarity, no neighbourhood, no number other than one, no time other than now, no such thing as society – just me! just now! (Kinnock, 1993)

In such a world even the lives of those who achieve the material affluence of the successful are tainted. As Zygmunt Bauman (1994, pp.39–40) says:

> Such lives are not an unmixed bliss. Far from it. The belief in bliss endemic to a life of consumption is anything but 'trivially true'. What about uncertainty, insecurity, loneliness and the future being a site of fear instead of hope? What of never accumulating anything securely, of being sure of nothing, of being never able to say with confidence 'I have arrived'? What about seeing in the neighbourhood only a jungle to be warily and fearfully watched, in the stranger only a beast to hide from; what about the privatised prisons of burglar-proof homes?

At best, we believe, the neo-liberal view captures only a part of the human potential. Human beings are social animals. They are defined by their relations with each other. Conflict and competition are matched by cooperation and mutuality. 'Fraternity', 'sorority', 'sisterhood', 'interdependence', 'humanity' – all represent wider elements of our loyalties and concern for others (Beedell, 1989, p.93) perhaps best captured in the term 'mutuality'. Such mutuality, meaning 'the recognition of mutual obligations to others, stemming from the acceptance of a common kinship', (Holman, 1993, p.57) is an essential ingredient in some of the most important parts of our lives.

The very basis of the informal systems of care, which provide by far the largest part of care in the community, is just such mutuality: a complex set of interrelationships founded on a multitude of motives including love, empathy and obligation (e.g. Wenger, 1990; 1993), and in which direct material reward is certainly not the major force. Important though the satisfaction of basic material needs must be, people clearly have many more ways of realizing themselves than through accumulation and consumption alone, and the central institutions of our society such as the family, education, politics and religion bear witness to that fact.

It follows that if we are to work towards a society that recognizes this richness and variety in human beings and regards it as a strength, not a liability, it will be necessary to develop institutions more sensitive to diversity and the needs of the different groups it represents than any commercial market can be. At issue is the creation of what the anthropologist Ruth Benedict (1973, p.210) called a high social synergy culture:

> I spoke of societies with high social synergy where their institutions ensure mutual advantage from their undertakings, and societies with low social synergy where the advantages of one individual becomes a victory over another, and the majority who are not victorious must shift as they can.

At a micro-level most of our case studies, in their descriptions of services before the community care reforms, exhibit elements of such social synergy in that they describe work in which the interviewees believed they were contributing *both* to the common good *and* gaining high personal satisfaction at the same time.

Social policy in a high synergy society

A market-dominated society is, however, in Benedict's terms, a low social synergy society for it is based on a world of winners and losers and creates extremes of wealth and poverty. The high synergy alternative will need as its foundation a robust social security system. The report of the Commission on Human Justice (Borrie, 1994) goes some way towards this but lacks clarity on the financing of community care. We believe that social care, as far as possible, should be financed collectively and be free at the point of use. How this might be achieved is a matter for national debate and decision.

Important as such a development would be, the problems that lead people to want and need support will not wither away. Fairer financing will mean that many people will be in a position where they will not need to call on the state for assistance. But the problems of dependency are not just those of money: they relate to the tensions and vulnerabilities that exist when, as adults, we are unable to cope. These are matters which take us back to the nature of society and the responsibility of one person for another.

Neither the market nor scientific management is compatible with a synergistic approach to collective action in the provision of community care. Public resources available for community care, in our view, should and could be significantly increased, but in the end they will always be finite. The issue of finding the most effective ways of using these resources remains. This calls for a continuing dialogue in every locality between all the contributors to such care and the ability to respond flexibly and creatively to any decisions which result, untrammelled by the rules of competition or the 'managers must manage' credo. We suggest that the following are likely to be required ingredients in developing a creative relationship between the different interests involved.

- *A national debate to determine the values and the objectives for community care*. Everyone should have the opportunity to be involved in the debate and it is essential to get as near as possible to a system based on shared values. From this *a nationally agreed framework* would define overarching objectives, financial resources, rights to services and information, and responsibilities and standards.

- *Locality control over resources and systems*, enabling their deployment in ways that reflect local priorities and maximize the development of local initiatives and creativity. Particular systems, such as the separation of purchaser and provider, should no longer be requirements. This demands an acceptance by central government, of whatever party, that the consequence of local citizen involvement will be local difference.
- *Service user and citizen involvement* to share in decisions over local strategies for community care and their implementation.
- *A new professionalism* based on the framework for effective service provision in community care of the kind discussed in Chapter 6, acknowledging a primary responsibility to users (e.g. Clough, 1990; Hugman, 1991) and aimed at making specialist help and advice available wherever it is needed.
- *A new managerialism*, drawing on the example of new wave management and giving priority to creating and supporting the conditions for a synergistic service culture.
- *Common regulations governing the support and operation of public and independent service providers*, thus dispensing with the current discrimination against the public sector.

One of the lessons to be learnt from the systems imposed on public services by the Conservatives is that collaboration and co-operation cannot be taken for granted when changes are imposed. They are by-products of wider systems in which people find that it is worthwhile and possible to work with others. Trust is an essential element in such relationships but it cannot be decreed or demanded by managers; it grows from common commitments and understandings, and from experience. Sadly, trust has been one of the greatest casualties of the 1990 Act, victim of competition, secrecy and macho-managerialism. Only a new context, of the kind we have sketched above, and the opening of a dialogue at all levels, can provide the conditions for its revival.

From here to there

Simply to describe these few elements of a possible future world of community care is to remind us how far there is to go if anything of this order is to be established. Perhaps, indeed, even in offering this outline we ourselves may be accused if not of Utopian social engineering, then at least of Utopian dreaming.

There are obviously many obstacles in the way of such changes. They imply a society in which power is far more decentralized, in which the intrusion of the market and neo-Taylorist management into the public sector have been curbed, and a general confidence re-established in the potential of public service. These in turn probably require constitutional reforms to reduce the overweaning power of central government and its executive and to establish a more pluralistic and devolved form of government throughout the country. As Hutton (1995) has pointed out, there are formidable barriers to be overcome to achieve such goals. Much post-Fordist analysis also emphasizes the growing exposure of the nation state to international forces which it cannot control (Pierson, 1995), although the combined strength of the European Union offers some prospect of moderating these. On the positive side, it has been suggested that the fragmentation and localization of organization which is taking place at the same time might open up opportunities for greater local involvement and control (Williams, 1995, p.54). However, even if this were to prove to be the case there are likely to be other problems to deal with if such devolution is to be achieved, not least of them the threat it may represent to the power bases of professional service deliverers and elected representatives (Pollitt, 1993 pp.152–3).

Nevertheless, it is through local initiatives and in accessible and user-friendly settings that the basis for synergistic policy and practice is most likely to be established (e.g. Holman, 1993). There is already a history of pioneering practice in small-scale projects and schemes in which service providers have established close links with local communities in the shaping of the local personal social services (e.g. Hadley *et al.,* 1987; Smale and Bennett, 1989; Bayley *et al.,* 1989; Hadley and Young, 1990; Darvill and Smale, 1990; Martinez-Brawley and Delevan, 1993). These were mostly extinguished by the effects of the community care reforms but their example and experience offer a starting point for the development of policies of the kind we have described and stand as a reminder that innovation does not have to wait on grand reforms.

If this alternative future is ever to become a reality it is likely that it will begin with initiatives in the frontline, where people know what the issues and problems are and have the vision and energy to tackle them in innovative ways. The synergic community care services of the future, we believe, will owe their existence and their creative energy not to the ideas of dead economists but to the imagination, commitment and partnership of the users, the new professionals and the new managers of today.

References

Allsop, J. and May, A. (1993) Between the devil and the deep blue sea: managing the NHS in the wake of the 1990 Act, *Critical Social Policy,* Autumn, 5–22

Audit Commission (1986) *Making a Reality of Community Care.* London: HMSO.

Audit Commission (1992) *The Community Revolution: Personal Social Services and Community Care.* London: HMSO.

Audit Commission (1994) *Taking Stock: Progress with Community Care.* London: HMSO.

Ballard, J. (1994) District nurses: who's looking after them? *Occupational Health Review* November/December, i–x

Bauman, Z. (1989) *Postmodernity and the Holocaust.* Cambridge: Polity.

Bauman, Z. (1994) *Alone Again: Ethics After Uncertainty.* London: Demos.

Bayley, M., Seyd, R. and Tennant, A. (1989) *Local Health and Welfare: Is Partnership Possible?* Aldershot: Gower.

Beedell, C. (1989) Investments in being looked after: an ideological commentary. In R. Clough and P. Parsloe (eds), *Squaring the Circle? Being Cared For and Caring After Firth, Griffiths, and Wagner.* Bristol: University of Bristol.

Benedict, R. (1973) Unpublished lecture cited in A. H. Maslow, *The Farther Reaches of Human Nature.* Harmondsworth: Penguin (pp.207–19).

Borrie, G. (1994) *Social Justice: Strategies for Social Renewal.* London: Vintage.

Brady, G.F. (1989) *Management by Involvement.* New York: Insight Books.

Challis, D. (1992) *Community Care of Elderly People: Bringing Together Scarcity and Choice, Needs and Costs.* Canterbury: PSSRU, University of Kent.

CIPFA (Chartered Institute of Public Finance and Accountancy) (1994) *Personal Social Services Statistics 1993–4 Actuals.* London: CIPHA.

Clarke, J., Cochrane, A., and McLaughlin, E. (eds) (1994) *Managing Social Policy.* London: Sage.

Clarke, M. and Stewart, J.D. (1988) *The Enabling Council.* Luton: Local Government Training Board.

Clough, R. (1990) *Practice, Politics and Power in Social Services Departments.* Aldershot: Gower.

Coleman, P., Bond, J. and Peace, S. (1993) Ageing in the 20th Century. In J. Bond, P. Coleman and S. Peace, *Ageing in Society.* London: Sage (pp.1–18).

Craft, N. (1994) Secrecy in the NHS, *British Medical Journal,* 5 (309), 1640–3.

Darvill, G. and Smale, G. (eds) (1990) *Partners in Empowerment: Networks of Innovation in Social Work.* London: National Institute for Social Work.

Davies, B. (1995) The reform of community and long-term care of elderly persons: an international perspective. In T. Sharf and G. C. Wenger (eds), *International Perspectives on Community Care for Older People.* Aldershot: Avebury.

Firth, J. (1987) *Public Support for Residential Care* (Joint Central and Local Government Working Party). London: DHSS.

Flynn, N. (1990) *Public Sector Management*. Hemel Hempstead: Harvester Wheatsheaf.

Flynn, N. (1994) Control, commitments and contracts. In J. Clarke, A. Cochrane and E. McLaughlin (eds), *Managing Social Policy*. London: Sage (pp.210–25).

Gilbert, B. (1970) *British Social Policy 1914–1939*. London: Batsford.

Grant, G. (1995) Assessment and care management: a service sector view. *Centre for Social Policy and Research Newsletter* Summer, 5–12, (CSPRD, University of Wales, Bangor).

Griffiths, R. (1983) *Report of the NHS Management Enquiry*. London: DHSS.

Griffiths, R. (1988) *Community Care:Agenda for Action*. London: HMSO.

Grimley Evans, J. (1983) Integration of geriatric with general medical services in Newcastle. *Lancet* 1, 1430–33.

Hadley, R. and Hatch, S. (1981) *Social Welfare and the Failure of the State: Centralised Social Services and Participatory Alternatives*. London: Allen and Unwin.

Hadley, R., Cooper, M., Dale, P. and Stacy. G. (1987) *A Community Social Worker's Handbook*. London: Tavistock.

Hadley, R. and Young, K. (1990) *Creating a Responsive Public Service*. Hemel Hempstead: Harvester Wheatsheaf.

Henwood, M. (1994) *Fit for Change? Snapshots of the Community Care Reforms One Year On*. London: King's Fund Centre.

Henwood, M. and Wistow, G. (1995) The waiting game. *Community Care,* 2 February, 26–7.

Hoggett, P. and Hambleton, R. (1987) *Decentralisation and Democracy: Localising Public Services*. Bristol: School of Advanced Urban Studies.

Holman, B. (1993) *A New Deal for Social Welfare*. Oxford: Lion.

Hood, C. (1991) A public management for all seasons. *Public Administration,* 69 (Spring), 3–19.

Huczynski, A. and Buchanan, D. (1991) *Organizational Behaviour*. Hemel Hempstead: Prentice Hall.

Hugman,R. (1991) *Power in Caring Professions*. Basingstoke: Macmillan.

Hutton, W. (1995) *The State We're In*. London: Cape.

Jarrold, K. (1995) *Guardian,* 6 June, 5.

Jenkin, P. (1983) Patch systems and social services. In I. Sinclair and D. Thomas (eds), *Perspectives on Patch (NISW Paper No 14)*. London: National Institute for Social Work (pp.1–3).

Kanter, R.M. (1983) *The Change Masters: Corporate Entrepreneurs at Work*. London: Allen and Unwin.

Kinnock, N. (1993) Thatcherism. In N. Comfort (ed.), *Brewer's Politics: A Phrase and Fable Dictionary*. London: Cassell (p.608).

Kotter, J.P. and Schlesinger, L.A. (1979) Choosing strategies for change. *Harvard Business Review,* 57(2), 106–114.

LeGrand, J. and Bartlett, W. (eds) (1993) *Quasi-Markets and Social Policy*. Basingstoke: Macmillan.

Lewis, J., Bernstock, P., and Bovell, V. (1995) The Community Care Changes: Unresolved Tensions and Policy Issues in Implementation. *Journal of Social Policy* 24 (1), 73–94.

Luntley, D. and Luntley, M. (1995) The nursing of budgets. *Guardian Society,* 17 May, 7.

Marchant, C. (1995) Care managers speak out. *Community Care,* 30 March, 16–17.

Martinez-Brawley, E. with Delevan, S. (1993) *Transferring Technology in the Personal Social Services*. Washington: National Association of Social Workers.

Meyer, J.W. and Scott, W.R. (1992) *Organizational Environments: Ritual and Rationality*. Newbury Park: Sage.

Mintzberg, H. (1989) *Mintzberg on Management*. New York: Free Press.

Morris, J. (1993) *Community Care or Independent Living?* York: Joseph Rowntree Foundation.

Newman, J. and Clarke, J. (1994) Going about our business? The managerialization of public

214   References

services. In J. Clarke, A. Cochrane and E. McLaughlin (eds), *Managing Social Policy*. London: Sage.

NHSCA (National Health Service Consultants Association) (1995) *In Practice: The NHS Market*. Great Bourton, Banbury: NHSCA/NHS Support Federation.

NISW (National Institute for Social Work) (1995) *Working in the Social Services*. London: NISW.

Nixon, J. (1993) Implementation in the hands of senior managers: community care in Britain. In M. Hill (ed.), *New Agendas in the Study of Policy Process*. London: Harvester Wheatsheaf (pp.197–216).

Perkin, H. (1989) *The Rise of Professional Society*. London: Routledge.

Peters, T. and Waterman, R. (1982) *In Search of Excellence*. New York: Harper and Row.

Pierson, C. (1995) Continuity and discontinuity in the emergence of the 'post-Fordist' welfare state. In R. Burrows and B. Loader (eds), *Towards a Post-Fordist Welfare State?* London: Routledge (pp.95–116).

Pollitt. C. (1993) *Managerialism and the Public Services* (2nd edn). Oxford: Blackwell.

Popper, K. (1945) *The Open Society and its Enemies. Vol. 1: The Spell of Plato*. London: Routledge.

Pratchett, L. and Wingfield, M. (1994) *The Public Service Ethos in Local Government*. London: Commission for Local Democracy.

Quinn, R.E. (1988) *Beyond Rational Management: Mastering the Paradoxes and Competing Demands of High Performance*. San Francisco: Jossey-Bass.

RCN (Royal College of Nursing) (1992) *Whistleblow: Nurses Speak Out*. London: RCN.

Schorr, A.L. (1992) *The Personal Social Services: An Outside View*. York: Joseph Rowntree Foundation.

Schumacher, E.F. (1973) *Small is Beautiful: A Study of Economics as if People Mattered*. London: Blond and Briggs.

Secretaries of State (1989a) *Working for Patients* (Cm 555). London: HMSO.

Secretaries of State (1989b) *Caring for People: Community Care in the Next Decade and Beyond* (Cm 849). London: HMSO.

Sheard, S. Gagging public health doctors. (1994) *British Medical Journal,* 309, 17 December, 1643–4.

Simmons, M. (1995) Breaking the silence. *Guardian Society*, 16 August, 6–7.

Smale, G. and Bennett, B. (1989) *Pictures of Practice. Vol. 1: Community Social Work in Scotland*. London: National Institute for Social Work.

Smith, R. (1994) An unfree NHS and medical press in an unfree society. *British Medical Journal,* 309 17 December, 1644–5.

Stuck, A., Siu, A., Weland, G., Adams, J. and Rubenstein, L. (1993) Comprehensive geriatric assessment: a meta-analysis of controlled trials. *Lancet,* 342 (October), 1032-1036.

Taylor, F.W. (1911) *Scientific Management*. New York: Harper and Row.

Titmuss, R.M. (1950) *Problems of Social Policy*. London: HMSO.

Vercors (1967) *La Bataille du Silence* p.171. Cited in Loiseaux, G. (1984) *La littérature de la défaite et de la collaboration*. Paris: Publications de la Sorbonne.

Walby, S. and Greenwell, J. (1994) Managing the National Health Service. In J. Clarke, A. Cochrane and E. McLaughlin (eds), *Managing Social Policy*. London: Sage.

Walker, A. (1993) Poverty and inequality in old age. In J. Bond, P. Coleman and S. Peace (eds), *Ageing in Society*. London: Sage (pp.280–303).

Wenger, G.C. (1990) Social support: the leaven in a changing world? Introduction to special issue as Guest Editor. *Journal of Aging Studies,* 4(4), 375–89.

Wenger, G.C. (1993) The formation of social networks: self-help, mutual aid and old people in contemporary Britain. *Journal of Aging Studies*, 7(1), 25–40.

Williams, F. (1995) Social relations, welfare and the post-Fordism debate. In R. Burrows and

B. Loader, (eds), *Towards a Post-Fordist Welfare State?* London: Routledge (pp.49–73).

Wistow, G., Knapp, M., Hardy, B., and Allen, C. (1994) *Social Care in a Mixed Economy*. Buckingham: Open University Press.

Young, H. (1989) *One of Us*. London: Macmillan.

Appendix 1

The questionnaire

Background of interviewee

Gender/approximate age/family circumstances. Outline of qualifications and job history.

1. The agency before the NHS/CC Act reforms were implemented

a. Agency structure and work

Structure of agency (general)
Structure of section in which interviewee works
  (more detailed)
Your job then (title, duties)
The daily work round then
Typical case or 'problem' and how it was handled, e.g. referral, assessment,
  allocation, intervention, conclusion
Freedom to do the job to your own satisfaction?
Feeling of job security
Freedom to speak out about the job? (inside and outside the organization?)
Relationships with management
Pressures to conform with old order
Main influences in the running of the system?
  (politicians, managers, professionals, trade unions)
How would you characterize the *ethos* of the system?

b. Advantages of the system (to user and worker)

c. Disadvantages of the system (ditto)

Probe: stress of working in the system, e.g. as evidenced by sickness, absence, turnover, aggression.

d. Satisfaction/dissatisfaction

How much would you say you used to enjoy your job before the changes? (show list)

(a) enjoyed very much
(b) enjoyed somewhat
(c) got very little enjoyment
(d) got no enjoyment

What did you find most satisfying about the job ?
What did you find most frustrating about your job ?

2. *The changes and their underlying rationale*

   a. What did the changes to the structure and work process involve?
   b. What was the underlying rationale for the changes ?
   c. What strategy was used by management to introduce the changes, e.g. consultation, participation, etc.
   d. Impact of changes on you
      How did you personally experience the changes ?
      Impact on personal life ?
      Stress ?
      Identity ?

3. *The new system*

a. Agency structure and work (general)

Structure of section in which interviewee works (more detailed)
Your job now (title, duties)
The daily work round now
Typical case or 'problem' and how it is handled, e.g. referral, assessment, allocation, intervention, conclusion
Freedom to do the job to your own satisfaction ?
Job security
Freedom to speak out about the job? (inside and outside the organization)
Relationships with management
Pressures to conform with new order
Main influences in the running of the system (politicians, managers, professionals, trade unions)
How would you characterize the *ethos* of the system?
Were the changes followed by any changes in the *language* used in the organization – e.g. to describe users, managers, the job?

b. Advantages of the system (to user and worker)

comparison with previous system

c. Disadvantages of the system (ditto)

comparison with previous system
probe: stress of working in the system, e.g. as evidenced by sickness, absence, turnover, aggression.

d. Satisfaction/dissatisfaction

1. How much would you say you enjoyed your job now? (show list)
    (a) enjoy very much
    (b) enjoy somewhat
    (c) get very little enjoyment
    (d) get no enjoyment
2. What do you find most satisfying about the job?
3. What was the one job you most enjoyed during the last work week?
4. What do you find most frustrating about your job?
5. What was the job you found most frustrating during the last working week?

e. How typical do you think your experiences and views are to those of your colleagues?

f. Where there is opposition to new system, how is opposition expressed?

4. Any proposals you have for improvement/alternatives

Appendix 2

The background to community care: legislation and guidance

'Community care' is a term used both about people moving from long stay hospitals to live in houses, hostels and residential homes and about the services provided to enable people to live in the community, in particular as a consequence of the National Health Service and Community Care Act, 1990. Here we track community care in relation to health services and social services.

NB

This is not a full synopsis of the the legislation, papers or guidance notes cited: it is a note of some items most relevant to community care legislation.

Any claims made in the text, for example about the intent of legislation, are those of the authors of the respective papers, not the authors of this book.

Health

1979 *Patients First* (White Paper): to simplify the management structure of the NHS.

1980 *National Health Services Act:* further reorganization of the health service.

Area Health Authorities abolished; District Health Authorities (DHAs) introduced. DHAs given powers to make grants to local authorities for expenditure on any functions which it performed through the local authority Social Services Committee and to make grants to voluntary organizations.

1983 *The National Health Service Management Inquiry (Griffiths Report)*

Its main recommendations were accepted in two circulars HC(84)13 and HC(80)20. General managers were to be appointed at Regional, District and Unit level, under short term contract and subject to performance review and performance related pay.

1989 *Working for Patients*: White Paper on the government's proposals following its review of the NHS.

A programme of action designed to secure two objectives: to give patients, wherever they live, better health care and greater choice of the services available; to produce greater satisfaction and rewards for NHS staff who successfully respond to local needs and preferences.

Key measures proposed:
* more delegation to local level
* hospitals to be given authority to apply for a new self-governing status *within* the NHS as NHS Hospital Trusts
* new funding arrangements to enable all NHS hospitals to offer their services to different health authorities and to the private sector
* GP practice budgets: large GP practices were given authority to apply for their own NHS budgets to obtain a defined range of services direct from hospitals
* reformed management bodies: to improve the effectiveness of NHS management, regional, district and family practitioner management bodies will be reduced in size and reformed on business lines.

1990 *Working for Patients: Role of District Health Authorities: Analysis of Issues*. DHAs will need to examine both their own internal organization and their relationships with other agencies. In particular, they will need to decide how to: separate their *purchasing role* from their *management role* in relation to *directly managed units*; and establish working *alliances with other local agencies*, in particular with Family Practitioner Committees and local authority social services departments.

Social Services

1986 *Making a Reality of Community Care* (Audit Commission)
A review of the progress of earlier government initiatives to develop community care resources to support growing numbers of dependent elderly people, and to facilitate the deinstitutionalization of patients in mental illness and mental handicap hospitals. Progress was uneven across the country, generally disappointingly slow and far behind the targets set. In particular, resources for the care of people in institutions were not moving across to the local authorities as required to enable them to develop the services to support them in the community, social services were struggling to maintain let alone improve services for the growing number of people over 75. There was also a perverse incentive for older people to go into residential care which attracted social security support whereas community care services in their own homes did not. The Commission was also highly critical of the fragmented organizational responsibility of the services involved and of inadequate staffing.

1987 *Public Support for Residential Care* (Firth Report)
DHSS departmental committee established 'to review the arrangements for residents in local authority, private and voluntary residential care homes'. It stated that choice of residential home is essential; local authorities should be given responsibility for financing all residential care costs which residents cannot meet themselves; it raised the possibility that local authorities might establish tendering arrangements with other agencies.

1988 *Community Care: Agenda for Action* (Griffiths report)
Sir Roy Griffiths was asked 'to review the way in which public funds are used to support community care'. He wants to see: people 'helped to stay in their own homes for as long as possible', with residential and nursing home care reserved for those whose needs cannot be met in any other way; 'the right services are provided in good time to those who need them most'; people having a greater say and a wider choice. A Minister for State for community care should be appointed. Local authority social services departments should assume full responsibility for community care. The perverse social security arrangements favouring residential care should be ended and the community care element of social security funding should be transferred to local authorities. Local authorities would be responsible for assessing an individual's needs and for ensuring the provision of care where that was agreed, in full consultation with the person concerned and any informal carers. Social services departments should restrict their role as far as possible to procuring and overseeing care and not its provision, and central government should be closely involved in determining the priorities of a costed programme each year.

1989 *Caring for People: Community Care in the Next Decade and Beyond* (White Paper)
Six key objectives of the community care legislation were identified.

- to promote the development of domiciliary, day and respite services to enable people to live in their own homes wherever feasible and sensible ... targeting home-based services on those people whose need for them is greatest.
- to ensure that service providers make practical support for carers a high priority. Assessment of care needs should always take account of the needs of caring family, friends and neighbours.
- to make proper assessment of need and good case management the cornerstone of high quality care. Packages of care should then be designed in line with individual needs and preferences.
- to promote the development of a flourishing independent sector alongside good quality public services ... social services authorities should be 'enabling' agencies. It will be their responsibility to make maximum use of private and voluntary providers and so increase the available range of options and widen consumer choice.
- to clarify the responsibilities of agencies and so make it easier to hold them to account for their performance.

- to secure better value for taxpayers' money by introducing a new funding structure for social care.

The main changes required to achieve these objectives included making local authorities responsible, in collaboration with other relevant agencies, 'for assessing individual need, designing arrangements and securing their delivery within available resources'; publishing clear plans for the development of community care services; making the maximum use of the independent sector; taking over responsibility for funding people in private and voluntary sector residential and nursing homes; establishing inspection units at arm's length from their own management to inspect residential homes in their own organization and in the independent sector. In addition there was to be a special additional grant to promote the development of social care for people with severe mental illness.

1990 *National Health Services and Community Care Act*
- Reconstitution of RHAs and DHAs.
- Reconstitution of FPCs and renaming FHSAs.
- Introduction of arrangements between health service authorities separating responsibilities between 'purchaser' and 'provider' functions by an arrangement of NHS contracts.
- Creation of autonomous institutions to provide health care and to be known as NHS 'trusts'.
- To establish GP 'fund holding practices' to manage budgets independently and also to introduce 'indicative amounts' for other practices under the control of the FHSAs.
- Role of the Audit Commission expanded to cover the NHS.
- Removal of Crown immunity from health authorities.
- Concept of community care to be widened and linked to social services provided by local authorities.
  SSD has responsibility for:
- assessment of individuals (involving health): this includes assessment of financial need as well as need for service;
- developing care packages;
- care management (development and oversight of care packages);
- purchase of services (increased proportion to be purchased from private and voluntary sectors);
- establishing an inspection unit;
- producing community care plans to set guidelines in consultation with health, voluntary, private and public/community;
- establishing a complaints procedure.

The hospital trusts would be governed by boards of directors mainly appointed by the government. The aim was to achieve more business-like organization and management; elected representatives of the population and of the professions would not be included.

Index

Where relevant, entries indicate the case studies in which they are located using the abbreviations employed in the text (listed on p.xiii) AD; GP; ARM; CN; CPN; LDTL; SSW; OT. Case studies where no abbreviations are used in the text are listed as: senior manager; geriatrician; carer (qualified carer); nurse manager; LD director (director of a voluntary organization); guardian (guardian and care assistant).

accountability (AD) 25, 29; (ARM) 48; (GP) 55; 59; (CPN) 92; multiple 165; management monopoly of 187, 192, 193
adult training centre (ATC) (LD director) 123; (guardian) 134, 135–6, 139
ageism (GP) 54, (geriatrician) 72
Allsop, J. 192, 212
anonymity of sample 2, 4, 21
approved social worker (ASW) 140; (OT) 151, 155, 156
assessment 15; (AD) 31; (GP) 54, 58; (geriatrician) 63, 65; (CN) 76; (carer) 82, 85; (CPN) 95; (LDTL) 114, 115; (LD director) 129–30; (guardian) 133, 134, 136; (SSW) 144, 145; (OT) 152–3; improvements in 180; deficiencies in 180, 185, 186
assistant director (AD) 24–33, 178, 179, 181, 182, 201
assistant regional manager (ARM) 42–51
Audit Commission 1, 14, 15, 16, 171, 172, 189, 204, 212

Ballard, J. 190, 212
Bauman, Z. 204, 208, 212
Bayley, M. 211, 212
Beedell, C. 206, 208, 212
Benedict, R. 209, 212
benefits trap (CPN) 97, 99
Borrie, G. 209, 212
Bottomley, V. 77
Brady, G.F. 184, 212
British Association of Social Workers 192
budget, management of (senior manager) 36, 41; ownership of (LDTL) 17; driven services 101; (LDTL) 118; 186; 195
bureaucracy 13, 14 increasing (AD) 30; (senior manager) 41; (ARM) 44, 45; (SSW) 145; 185, 191, 203; in voluntary organizations (ARM) 44, 45; (LD director) 124–5;
bureaucratic organization in sample 167, 168, 169–70
bureau-professional organization in sample 168, 170

Canterbury, Archbishop of (ARM) 50
care assistants (carer) 83–4, 85, 86, 88; (CPN) 94, 96; (guardian) 134–5; 139
care management 17, 205
care managers (CPN) 96; (LDTL) 119; national study 190–4

care packages 15; (CN) 76, 81; (carer) 88; (LDTL) 115
carers 15; (CPN) 91, 98
Caring for People (1989) 7, 16; (AD) 26; 221
case studies selection 2–3; characteristics of 21
Centre for Social Policy Research and Development (CSPRD) 190
Challis, D. 17, 212
change, costs of radical 2; (AD) 24, 28; (senior manager) 37–8; (ARM) 46–8, 49; in learning disability resettlement 102–3
change in organizations, alternative strategies for introducing 198–205; consent 199; imposition 199–200; in 1950s and 1960s 200; alternative responses to 174–5; loss for workers 176–7; overload 192, 195
charging 27
Chartered Institute of Public Finance and Accountancy (CIPFA) 61, 100, 140, 212
Citizen's Charters 57, 137–8
Children Act (1989) (AD) 25, 26
children's services 9, 11; (AD) 31; (senior manager) 35, 38; (ARM) 42–51;
choice 11, 15; (geriatrician) 65, 70; (CPN) 98; (OT) 154; 186, 221; improvement in 180
Choice Directive (LDTL) 118, 120
Clarke, J. 192, 212
Clough, R. 210, 212
coercion in change 203–4
coherent organizations 175–6
Coleman, P. 61, 212
Com–Care (CPN) 92
Commission on Human Justice 209
Commission on Local Democracy 190
community care, definition 7–8; development in post second world war decades 10–11; effects of 1970 reorganization 12; problems of in 1980s 15; reforms 2, 15; legislation 16; alternative proposals for 209–10
Community Care 190
Community Care: Agenda for Action (1988) *see:* Griffiths Report (1988)
community care plans 196
community hospitals (geriatrician) 62, 70; (CN) 77; trust (geriatrician) 70, 71; (CN) 73, 76; 155
community learning disabilities nurses (AD) 32
community mental health team *see*

multi–disciplinary mental health team
community nurse (CN) (GP) 53; (CN) 73–81; (LDTL) 117; 174, 177, 181, 189; national study 190
community psychiatric nurse (CPN) (AD) 32; (geriatrician) 61; (CPN) 90–99; 140; (SSW) 145; (OT) 151, 155, 156, 157, 158; 174–5, 176, 177, 177–8
community social work 203
competition 16, 18; (GP) 58; (geriatrician) 71; (CPN) 95; (nurse manager) 102; (LD director) 127; (SSW) 144, 146; incoherence and 176; 181; versus cooperation 188, 193, 196
compliance with the reforms 174–5
conflicts of interest (AD) 30, 32; (GP) 57; (geriatrician) 71; (SSW) 144
conformity, pressures of (SM) 36–7; (ARM) 42, 45, 49–50; (geriatrician) 68–9, 71–2; (CN) 80; (carer) 88–9; (CPN) 92–3; (nurse manager) 106, 109–10; (LDTL) 117–8, 120; (guardian) 136; (SSW) 143, 146, 149; 178, 203–4, 205
confusion resulting from changes 2; (SM) 40; (geriatrician) 71; (LDTL) 116; (SSW) 144–5, 147, 148, 150; (OT) 155, 157; 176, 187, 191–2
Conservative Government 14–15; (AD) 24, 27, 32; (GP) 56, 57; 171, 183, 192, 197, 198, 200–05, 207
constitutional reform 211
consultants (geriatrician) 62–72; (nurse manager) 103, 104; (SSW) 142, 143; (OT) 152; 202
consultation on change (AD) 27–8; (ARM) 45–6; (GP) 55–6; (LDTL) 115; 175
consumerism (GP) 56, 57, 195
continuity in effective professional work (geriatrician) 65; (CPN) 98; 165
contracts (LD director) 122, 129, 130; (SSW) 146
contradictions in NHSCCA reforms 191; 194–7
councillors (AD) 24, 25, 26, 27; (senior manager) 36; (nurse manager) 110; (SSW) 147, 150; 205
Craft, N. 192, 212
creativity and innovation 164; *before the reforms* (ARM) 35; (SM) 44–5; (nurse manager) 107–8; (LDTL) 113; (SSW) 143; *in the reforms*

(AD) 28; *after the reforms* (LD director) 127, 131; 211
Cruse (OT) 154

Darvill, G. 211, 212
Davies, B. 201, 204, 212
decentralization 14; (AD) 26; (ARM) 46
deinstitutionalization 11, 100; (nurse manager) 101, 102, 103, 105, 106
demand–led services (GP) 54, 55; (CN) 78
dementia 83
democracy 18; threat to local (AD) 32; in decision making (OT) 152, 154–5; 210–11
Department of Health 17; (AD) 27, 30; (LDTL) 118, 120; 190, 205
director, of a voluntary organization (LD director) 122–31, 177, 178, 179, 181, 182
disability (senior manager) 34–8; *see also* learning disabilities, physical disabilities
discrediting the past 202–3
discretion in effective professional work 165; in professional organizations 167; in bureau–professional organizations 168; reduced 186–7, 203
discriminatory practice in learning disabilities (guardian) 136, 137–8, 139
dishonesty 2; (nurse manager) 109–10; (SSW) 147; (LD director) 129; 186
District General Hospital (DGH) (geriatrician) 63, 64
District Health Authority (DHA) 18; (GP) 58; (geriatrician) 68, 69; (CN) 73, 76
district nurse 57 (*see also* community nurse)
dowry in learning disabilities resettlement (nurse manager) 105; (guardian) 134, 136

elder abuse 91
elderly mentally infirm (EMI) (CPN) 90–1
elderly people *see* older people
elderly people's homes (AD) 27–8; (SM) 35
enabling authorities, local authorities as 15, 16
ethnic minorities (AD) 25; (GP) 53
ethos *before the reforms* (AD) 25; (SM) 35; (ARM) 44; (geriatrician) 63, 65; (CN) 75; (nurse manager) 103, 106, 107–8; (LDTL) 120; (LD director) 124; (OT) 152; *after the reforms*: (ARM) 49–50; (geriatrician) 71; (CN) 80; (nurse manager) 106–7, 108–9; (LDTL) 120; (LD director) 124; (SSW) 148–9; (OT) 157–8; overview 177–8
European Union (CN) 77; 211

Family Health Services Authority (FHSA) (GP) 55, 59
Family Practitioners' Committee (FPC) (GP) 55, 59
Firth Report (1987) 15, 220–1, 212

Flynn, N. 13, 184, 203, 204, 213
Fordism 9, 200g
fragmentation 9, 12, 15; (GP) 58, 59; (geriatrician) 70; (CPN) 98; (LDTL) 116, 120, 121; (OT) 155–7; effects on users 180, 196, 211
free speech *before the reforms*: (AD) 27; (ARM) 45; (GP) 55; (geriatrician) 65; (carer) 84; (nurse manager) 104; (LDTL) 113–14; (SSW) 143; *after the reforms*: xi, 4; (ARM) 50; (GP) 59; (geriatrician) 71–2; (carer) 88–9; (nurse manager) 109–10; (LDTL) 120; (SSW) 149; and effective professional work 165; overview 178, 188, 192
fundholding in general practice 18, (GP) 52; (CN) 76; (CPN) 93; (SSW) 146; (OT) 155; resistance to; (GP) 58–9

gagging clauses 192
gender 152
general physician (geriatrician) 65, 66, 68, 69, 70
general medicine 62
general practitioner (GP) 18; (senior manager) 39; (GP) 52–60; (geriatrician) 64, 65, 69, 70; (CN) 74, 76, 80; (carer) 87; 140; (SSW) 142; (OT) 152, 154, 156, 158; 179, 180, 181, 182, 191
geriatrician (GP) 60; (geriatrician) 62–72, 166, 177, 178, 179, 181, 182; psycho–geriatrician (CPN) 91
geriatrics (geriatrician) 62, 63, 67–8
Gilbert, B. 8, 213
Good News Unit 205
government *see* Conservative Government
Gramsci 206
Grant, G. 190, 192, 193, 213
Griffiths, R. 15
Griffiths Report (1983) (nurse manager) 103, 201, 219; (1988) 15; (AD) 26; 171, 194, 200, 221
Grimley Evans, J. (geriatrician) 67, 69; 213
guardian 132–9

Hadley, R. 13, 14, 211, 213
Health Advisory Service (HAS) 68
health visitor 9; (GP) 53
Henwood, M. 189, 190, 213
Hoggett, P. 14, 213
holistic assessment and intervention (senior manager) 35; (geriatrician) 63, 64, 65, 68, 70; (CN) 75, 79; (CPN) 92–3; (LDTL) 112, 116
Holman, B. 208, 211, 213
home care (AD) 29; (senior manager) 39; (CN) 78, 81; (CPN) 93–9; (SSW) 146; 196
home carers (GP) 53, 57; (CN) 77
home help service 9; (LD director) 113
Hood, C. 201, 213
hospital discharge *see* hospitals, throughput
hospitals 18, (GP) 54, 57; (carer) 87; throughput (GP) 57; 61; (CN) 76–7, 81, 181, 195; (nurse

manager) 102–7; (guardian) 136–9; hospital trusts (geriatrician) 70–1; (CPN) 93; (nurse manager) 106–7; community trusts (geriatrician) 71; (CN) 73, 76 *see also* community hospitals; trusts
hospital social work (AD) 28
House of Commons Social Services Select Committee 15
housing benefit (CN) 97; (LD director) 124
Huczynski, A. 199, 213
Hugman, R. xi, 210
human potential 208–9
Hutton, W. 211, 213

incoherent organizations 175–6, 187, 191
Independent Living Fund (ILF) (senior manager) 37
independent sector 17 *see also* voluntary organizations; private provision
individual planning (IP) (life plan) (nurse manager) 105; (LDTL) 121; (guardian) 135
industrial model of care/treatment 19, 194, 195–6, 203, 204
Industrial Relations Service 190
inner cities (GP) 53, 56, 181
innovation *see* creativity
integration 11, 14; (AD) 33; (senior manager) 37; (geriatrician) 63, 67–70
inter-agency relations *before the reform* (GP) 54; (geriatrician) 63, 64–5; (LDTL) 112, 113; (LD director) 127; (SSW) 142, 143; (OT) 152–3; *after the reforms* (AD) 29–30, 32; (GP) 57–8; (geriatrician) 70, 72; (CN) 373, 76–8; (CPN) 96; (LDTL) 117, 121; (LD director) 127, 128; (SSW) 146; (OT) 156, 157, 158; barriers to 188, 193, 196
inspection 15, 16, 17; (AD) 26; (carer) 89; (guardian) 136; ineffectiveness 180
institutionalization in the community (guardian) 132, 139

Jarrold, K. 192, 213
Jenkin, P. 203, 213
joint commissioning (AD) 30

Kanter, R.M. 199, 213
Kinnock, N. 208, 213
Kotter, J.P. 199, 213

Labour councils (AD) 24–32; (nurse manager) 110; 168, 171, 174
Labour Party 14, 18; (AD) 24, 25, 27
language of managerialism (LDTL) 120; 202, 206, 207
learning disabilities, definition 100; case studies: (AD) 30, 31; (SM) 34–41; (ARM) 43; (nurse manager) 102–10; (LDTL) 111–21; (LD director) 122–32; (guardian) 133–40
learning disabilities team leader 111–21, 181
learning organization (ARM) 51; defensiveness versus 197

Legrand, J. 201, 213
Lewis, J. 190, 191, 192, 195, 213
local government workers national
study 190, 193
locality purchasing model (GP) 58–9,
60, 182
locally based services 14; (AD) 26,
32; (GP) 60; 210, 211 see also
decentralization; patch systems
long–stay beds 61; (geriatrician) 62;
(community nurse) 77
Luntley, D. and Luntley, M. 191, 213

macho–management (LDTL) 115,
118–19
Making a Reality of Community Care
(1986) 220
managerialism 13, 23; neo–Taylorist:
13, 21, 23; (ARM) 42, 45–50;
(LDTL) 118; as ideology 201; new
210 see also management; macho–
management; new wave
management
managers 23; (AD) 24–33; (SM)
34–41; (ARM) 42–51; (geriatrician) 71; (CPN) 92, 93; (nurse
manager) 107, 108–9; (SSW)
142–3, 144; 147; as change agents
201; and coercion 203
Marchant, C. 190, 213
markets 13, 14; (GP) 52, 55; (carer)
82; (CPN) 90, 93; (LDTL) 119;
(LD director) 127, 128; 187, 190,
195–6, 201, 207, 209, 210
medical model of care (GP) 54; (geriatrician) 70; (SSW) 145; (OT) 152,
157, 158; effect on users 180
Mental Health Act Commission
(LDTL) 120; (SSW) 146
mental illness 16; definition 140; case
studies: (AD) 30, 31; (SM) 34–9;
(GP) 57; (LDTL) 111–12; (SSW)
141–50; (OT) 151–60
Meyer, J.W. 12, 213
Mind 142
Mintzberg, H. 167
monopoly power of purchaser (CPN)
96; (LD director) 126–7
morale of staff see work satisfaction
Morris, J. 132, 213
multidisciplinary mental health team
140; (CPN) 91–2; (OT) 151–60,
165; 180
multidisciplinary team work (geriatrician) 63, 64, 65

National Health Service 9, 11–12;
1990 reform 18
National Health Service Act (1980)
219
National Health Service and
Community Care Act (NHSCCA)
(1990) 3, 7, 16, 21; summary 222;
strategies for change 173–5; implementation of change 175–9;
outcome for users and staff 180–3;
relationships with users 185–6;
relationships with the organization
186–8; relationships with
colleagues 188–9; other evidence
on the impact of the reforms
189–94; contradictions in 194–7; as
an experiment 198–205
National Health Service Consultants

Association (NHSCA) 18, 190,
191, 192, 193, 194, 195, 202,
205, 214
National Health Service Management
Inquiry (1983) see Griffiths Report,
1983
National Institute for Social Work
(NISW) 190, 214
National Vocational Qualification
(NVQ) (carer) 85, 88; (CPN) 94,
97
needs led services 15; (GP) 55–6;
(LD director) 129; (OT) 157–8;
and effective professional work
164; increased barriers to 184, 195
neo–liberalism 207–8
neo–Taylorism 13, 23, 192, 198, 210
New Human Resource Management
13
Newman, J. 14, 204, 214
New wave managerialism 23, 204
1990 Act, The see National Health
Service and Community Care Act
(1990)
Nixon, J. 201, 214
normalization 11; (nurse manager)109;
(LDTL) 113; (LD director) 123,
125; (geriatrician) 132
nurse manager 102–10, 165, 182
nurses (geriatrician) 64, 65; (CN)
73–81; (CPN) 90–99; (nurse
manager) 102–10; (guardian)
137–8; (OT) 152; 191 see also
community nurses; community
psychiatric nurses
nursing homes 15; (AD) 27; (GP) 60;
61; (geriatrician) 62; (carer) 82–9
occupational therapist (OT) (GP) 53;
(OT) 151–62, 166, 174, 177, 178,
179, 181
occupational therapy (SM) 34; (geriatrician) 64, 65; (CPN) 91; (OT)
151–62
older people 10, 11; 61–99
opportunism and the reforms 175
organizational environments 12, 19
organizational rationalization in 1970s
11–12
organizations after the reforms
coherent and incoherent 175–6

participation 13, 14; and effective
professional work (carer) 89;
(CPN) 92; 165; decline in 188; in
change 199, 210
patch systems 14; (SM) 34–5, 41;
(CPN) 73, 81; 211
Patients' Charter (GP) 59, (guardian)
137–8
Patients First (1979) 219
pay, forced down in private sector
(CPN) 90, 97–8; 187; 196
Penna, S. xi
Perkin, H. 10, 214
personal development and effective
professional work 166; strategies
for after reforms 181–3; decline in
opportunities for 189
Personal Social Services Research
Unit (PSSRU) 17, 189–90, 205
Peters, T. 184, 214
physical disabilities (AD) 30, 31;
(SM) 34–41; (ARM) 43; (geriatri-
cian) 66

physiotherapists (geriatrician) 60;
(CPN) 91
piecemeal engineering 200
Pierson, C. 9, 14, 211, 214
planning, lack of (GP) 56; (geriatrician) 71; (LDTL) 121; (SSW) 147
political organization, the 168, 171
political system, relations with in
effective professional work 166,
188–9
Pollitt, C. 10, 13, 194, 196, 201,
211, 214
Popper, K. 199–200, 204–5, 214
Post–Fordism 211
poverty 13; (AD) 25, 30
Pratchett, L. 190, 193, 214
preemption of the reforms 174
preventive work (AD) 30; (GP) 52,
61; no longer possible (SSW) 144,
145; reduction in 180, 185, 191;
treatment versus 196
primary care (GP) 55, 57
private provision 17, 61; (AD) 27–8;
(SM) 38–40; (CPN) 93–9; 179,
181, 182
privatization (AD) 28, 30
professional conservativism (nurse
manager) 102, 103; (LD director)
123
professionalism 10; new 210, 211
professional organization, the 167–9
professional practice, conditions for
effective 163–6, 184; impact of
change on 176–7
professional self–interest 13; 61;
(geriatrician) 66, 67–70, 72; (SSW)
146–7
proprietorial organization, the 168,
170–1
psychologists (CPN) 91; (SSW) 145;
(OT) 151, 155
psychotherapeutic approach 152
public service ethic 201
public service organizations 12
Public Service Orientation 14
Public Support for Residential Care
(1987) see Firth Report
purchaser–provider split 15–18; (AD)
27–32; (SM) 36–40; (GP) 55;
(CPN) 94, 96; (nurse manager)
106–7; (LDTL) 114–15, 119–20,
121; (LD director) 126, 128–30;
(SSW) 144–5; (OT) 155; becoming
providers 177; impact on workers
181, 189; creating new bureaucracy 185; conflicting values 188,
196

qualified carer 61, 82–9, 178, 181
quality assurance (ARM) 46, 48, 49
quality of service before the reforms
(GP) 55; (geriatrician) 65; (CN)
75; (carer) 83–4, 85; (nurse
manager) 104, 105, 106–7, 107–9;
(LDTL) 112, 113; (LD director)
122; (SSW) 143–4; (OT) 151,
154–5; 169, 170, 171, 171–2; after
the reforms (GP) 57, 58, 59; (geriatrician) 70–1; (CN) 80; (carer)
86–9; (CPN) 90, 93–5, 96; (nurse
manager) 106–7, 109, 110;
(LDTL) 119–20, 121; (LD
director) 127–8, 130–1; (guardian)
135, 137–8; (SSW) 148; (OT) 158,

159; effect of deteriorating on
workers 181
quasi–markets 201, 203, 204,
quangos 32, 205
questionnaire 216–18
Quinn, R.E. 184, 214

reform, definition 1
Regional Health Authority (RHA)
(geriatrician) 68; (nurse manager)
102, 103, 104–5, 107
Registered General Nurse (RGN)
(CN) 75; (CPN) 90
Registered Mental Nurse (RMN)
(CPN) 90
Relate 154
research methods of study 2–3, 4, 21
residential care 15, 17; (AD) 27;
(senior manager) 35; (GP) 60;
(carer) 82–9; (LD director) 119,
130; 191, 195, 196
resistance and opposition to the
reforms and/or their implementation (AD) 24, 26, 27–8; (senior
manager) 36–8; (GP) 58–9; (geriatrician) 68–9; (CN) 80; (LDTL)
117–18, 120; (LD director) 123,
130–1; (SSW) 148, 149; defence
and delay 174; subversive action
174; resistance work 202–3
resources 10, 14, 16, 17; (senior
manager) 41; (GP) 58; (CN) 78,
80; 102; (LD director) 130; (SSW)
144; 169, 173, 176, 180, 181,
186, 190–1, 195, 209
Royal College of Nursing 190, 192,
214

satisfaction *see* work satisfaction
Schorr, A.L. 205, 214
Schumacher, F. 206
scientific management 13, 187, 203,
204, 209
secrecy 187, 192–3, 196, 205
Secretaries of State 7, 18, 214
security of employment *before the
reforms* (senior manager) 36;
(ARM) 45; (GP) 59; (geriatrician)
63, 65; (CN) 75; (LDTL) 113;
(LD director) 125; *after the
reforms* (AD) 32; (senior manager)
38; (ARM) 50; (GP) 59; (geriatrician) 71; (CN) 80; (LDTL) 118,
120; (LD director) 125; (SSW)
149; (OT) 158; need for in effective professional work 179;
pervasive insecurity 187
self-referral 152
senior social worker (SSW) 141–50,
165, 166, 178, 183
sexism (SSW) 141, 143
Sheard, S. 192, 214
sickness, increase in rate of 2; (senior
manager) 38; (CN) 79; (SSW)
147–8; (OT) 158
Smith, R. 192, 214
social model of care (GP) 54
social security 15, 17; (AD) 30, 33;
(CPN) 97, 98; 209
social services as occupied territory
202, 202–3

social services department (SSD) 11,
15, 16; (AD) 24–33; (senior
manager) 34–41; (ARM) 44–5, 50;
(GP) 54; (CN) 78; (carer) 88;
(CPN) 94–5, 96, 98; (nurse
manager) 107–10; (LDTL) 111–22
(LD director) 126–9, 131;
(guardian) 134–6, 138–9; (SSW)
141–50; (OT) 151, 156; 169–70
Social Services Inspectorate 17
social work, deskilling and decline
(AD) 30–32; marginalizing in
learning disabilities (LDTL)
117–18
social workers (AD) 30–32; (senior
manager) 34–8, 39; (GP) 60; (geriatrician) 64, 65; (CN) 76, 78;
(CPN) 91; (LDTL) 112, 114, 117,
120; (SSW) 141–50; national study
of 190
specialism *before the reforms* (AD)
25–6; (senior manager) 34–6;
(geriatrician) 63–5; (LDTL)
111–13; (SSW) 141, 142–3;
decline after the reforms 2; (AD)
30–1; (senior manager) 36–7;
(geriatrician) 69–71; (LDTL) 117,
119, 120; (LD director) 129;
(SSW) 148; impact of loss on users
180, on workers 181
Special Transitional Grant (STG) 17;
(LDTL) 116; (SSW) 145
State Enrolled Nurse (SEN) (CN) 73,
74, 75
stress in the job (AD) 27; (senior
manager) 38, 39; (GP) 59; (CN)
78–9, 80–1; (LDTL) 120; (SSW)
147–8, 149; (OT) 154, 158–9;
disadvantages for users 180, for
workers 181; increase in 189, 194;
managers under, 187, 188
Stuck, A. (geriatrician) 63, 214
supervision, loss of (ARM) 47–8, 50
supported housing (LD director)
122–31
synergy, social 209, 210, 211

targetting (GP) 56
Taylor, F.W. 13, 214
team leader (learning disabilities)
111–21
Thatcher, M. 13, 14, 200, 208
'There is no alternative' (TINA) 161,
202, 206
Thorpe, S. xi
Titmuss, R. 8, 214
Toder, M. xi
trade unions (AD) 25, 26; (SSW) 149;
189
training, upgrading (CN) 75; lack of
in front line work (AD) 31;
untrained and poorly trained carers
(senior manager) 40; (carer) 84,
85, 88, 89; (CPN) 94, 95;
(guardian) 134–5, 139; programme
for carers (carer) 89; (CPN) 94;
189
trust, erosion of 2; (LD director)
128–9; and effective professional
work 166; loss of 181, 188, 210
trusts in NHS 18 *see also* hospitals

trusts in local authorities (AD) 28

understanding organisational world
and effective professional work
165; decline in 187
unemployment (GP) 53
user, definition 1; 10, 14; reduced
standards of service to after
reforms (senior manager) 31, 34;
(geriatrician) 62–3, 70, 71; (CN)
80; (carer) 86–9; (CPN) 92–3;
101; (nurse manager) 106–7;
(LDTL) 119–20; (SSW) 148; (OT)
158; relations with in effective
professional work 164; advantages
and disadvantages of reforms to
180; barriers to needs-led services
185; evidence from other research
190–1
user participation 14; (AD) 29;
involvement in decisions 210
utopian engineering 199–200, 204–5,
210

values, in effective professional work
166; conflict in 188; market versus
public services 194; underlying
welfare policies 206–7
Vercors 202, 214
voluntary organizations, case studies
of (ARM) 42–51; (LD director)
122–31; as advocate (LDTL) 120;
169

waiting lists (GP) 57; (CN) 78
Walby, S. 201, 214
Walker, A. 61, 214
Warren, M. 62
welfare state, origins 8; emerging
critiques 12–14; ends and means
206–7
Wenger, G.C. xi, 208, 214
Wilkinson, H. xi
Williams, F. 211, 215
Wistow, G. 15, 16, 17, 24, 172, 215
women, changing roles and attitudes
10; poorer working conditions of
196; discrimination against 207
Working for Patients (1990) 219–20
*Working for Patients: the Role of
District Health Authorities* (1990)
220
work satisfaction *before the reforms*
(senior manager) 34, 35–6; (ARM)
44–5; (GP) 55; (geriatrician) 65;
(CN) 75; (carer) 84, 85; (CPN)
91; (nurse manager) 105–6;
(LDTL) 113; (LD director) 125–6;
(SSW) 143–4; (OT) 154–5; and
organizational type 167–71; *after
the reforms*, (AD) 32; (senior
manager) 37–8; (ARM) 50; (GP)
59; (geriatrician) 71; (CN) 80–81;
(carer) 86, 88; (CPN) 98; (nurse
manager) 110; (LDTL) 120; (SSW)
147–8; (OT) 158–9; overview of
179; 181, 193–4
worried well (SSW) 142, 145

Young, H. 202, 215